PSYCHOANALYTIC STUDIES
OF ORGANIZATIONS

PSYCHOANALYTIC STUDIES OF ORGANIZATIONS

Contributions from
the International Society
for the Psychoanalytic Study
of Organizations (ISPSO)

Edited by Burkard Sievers

*Halina Brunning, Jinette de Gooijer, Laurence J. Gould
and Rose Redding Mersky*

KARNAC

First published in 2009 by
Karnac Books Ltd
118 Finchley Road
London NW3 5HT

British Library Cataloguing in Publication Data

A C.I.P. for this book is available from the British Library

ISBN-13: 978-1-85575-607-6

Typeset by Vikatan Publishing Solutions (P) Ltd., Chennai, India

Printed in Great Britain

www.karnacbooks.com

CONTENTS

v

LIST OF CONTRIBUTORS

Gilles Amado is Professor in Organisational Psychosociology, HEC School of Management, Paris, France, Co-Chief Editor of the "Nouvelle Revue de Psychosociologie" and founding member of ISPSO.

David Armstrong is Principal Consultant Tavistock Consultancy Services, London.

Harold Bridger, (1910–2005) was one of the founding members of the Tavistock Institute of Human Relations, a key contributor to the Northfield experiment and to a variety of therapeutic communities in Europe, a member and secretary of the British Psychoanalytic Society, founding member and Past President of the Institute of Transitional Dynamics. He directed Transitional Conferences around the world, and was a distinguished member of ISPSO.

Michael A. Diamond is Professor of Public Affairs, Director of the Center for the Study of Organizational Change, Associate Director for Academic Programs, at the Harry S Truman School of Public Affairs, University of Missouri, USA, Past-President and founding member of ISPSO.

Robert French is Reader in Organization Studies at Bristol Business School, the University of the West of England.

Thomas N. Gilmore is a Vice President at CFAR – Center for Applied Research, Inc., a consulting firm in Philadelphia, Adjunct Senior Fellow in the Wharton Health Care Program, and Senor Fellow of the Leonard Davis Institute of Health Economics, founding member ISPSO.

Laurence J. Gould is Professor Emeritus and former Director, The Clinical Psychology Doctoral Program, The City University of New York, founding member ISPSO.

Charles Harvey is Professor of Business History and Management at Newcastle University Business School, Newcastle upon Tyne, United Kingdom.

Larry Hirschhorn is Principal at CFAR – Center for Applied Research, Inc., a consulting firm in Philadelphia, Past President and founding member of ISPSO.

James Krantz is Principal of the Nautilus Consulting Group; New York, President ISPSO (2007–2009), founding member ISPSO.

W. Gordon Lawrence is Director, Social Dreaming Ltd, London and distinguished member ISPSO.

Susan Long is Adjunct Professor and Professorial Fellow at RMIT University in Melbourne, Australia, and Past President ISPSO.

Isabel Menzies Lyth, Psychoanalyst and Social Scientist (1927–2008) was a distinguished member of the British Psychoanalytic Society; an early staff member of the Tavistock Institute of Human Relations; and, a major contributor to the development of the Tavistock Group Relations Conferences.

Burkard Sievers is Professor emeritus for Organization Development in the Schumpeter School of Business and Economics, Bergische University Wuppertal, Germany and Past President ISPSO.

Peter Simpson is Reader in Organization Studies at Bristol Business School, the University of the West of England.

Howard F. Stein is Professor in the Department of Family and Preventive Medicine, University of Oklahoma Health Sciences Center, Oklahoma City, Oklahoma, USA.

FOREWORD

It is a great pleasure to present this volume on behalf of the International Society for the Psychoanalytic Study of Organizations (ISPSO). The satisfaction of seeing these papers in print is tempered only with regret that other equally worthy papers could not be included due to space constraints. Nonetheless, the papers contained in this volume illustrate the intellectual vitality that has characterized ISPSO during its first 25 years.

Since its founding, ISPSO's philosophy has been one of supporting efforts to apply psychoanalytic thinking to the study of organizations. This volume contains work that has been presented during our annual symposia. These chapters vividly illustrate the impact of unconscious dynamics on organizational life, at both the individual and collective levels. Together, they demonstrate the importance of extending and deepening Freud's original insights about the regressive qualities of groups and mass movements into the organizational sphere.

Our current economic crisis underscores the urgency of understanding irrationality in social and organizational life. Once again we are confronted with the devastating effects of the persistent myths of the rational manager, rational consumer and rational markets, in spite of overwhelming evidence to the contrary. Somewhere between apocalyptic, despairing fears that our institutions are imploding and hopes for profound transformation, such as the massive idealization surrounding Barack Obama, is a path to recovery and development that includes a realistic appreciation of human functioning and of the unconscious, non-rational dimension of economic and organizational life. Hopefully the kind of thinking represented here can further to our ability to find that pathway.

—James Krantz
President, ISPSO

Burkard Sievers

This book samples the groundbreaking work that has been written over the last 25 years by psychoanalysts, academics, writers and practitioners associated with the International Society for the Psychoanalytic Studies of Organizations (ISPSO) (www.ispso.org).

ISPSO has its roots with a meeting of a group of like-minded people, who organized the 'First Cornell Symposium on the Psychodynamics of Organizational Behavior and Experience' in New York in 1983. Annual symposiams have been held ever since. In the first few years, these meetings took place in the US. The first international meeting was held in Montreal in 1990; the first European symposium was held in London in 1995. Over the years, the format of these meetings was extended from a 3-day Symposium preceded by a one-day Members' Day to a one week Annual Meeting including 4 days of Professional Development Workshops. Annual Meetings have since been held in Amsterdam/Haarlem, Baltimore, Boston, Chicago, Coesfeld, Jerusalem, London, Melbourne, New York, Paris, Philadelphia, Stockholm and Toronto.

ISPSO provides a forum for academics, clinicians, consultants and others interested in working in and with organizations utilizing psychoanalytic concepts and insights. It is *the* international network for people interested in and working towards the Society's aim, i.e. to share organizational research, consultation and experiences in the context of psychoanalysis.

This collection of originally presented papers looks at organizations, groups, teams and organizational role holders using psychoanalytic, systemic and psychodynamic perspectives that collectively eschew superficial, linear, prescriptive and mechanistic views of both the system and the individual within.

As one may imagine, it has been quite difficult to choose from the hundreds of papers, which have been presented at Annual Symposia over the years; many of these have been published (http://www. ispso.org/previous.pdf). There certainly were dozens of papers and authors worthy of being included in this collection. [An extended bibliography relevant to our field of study can be found at http:// www.ispso.org/The%20Field/ISPSO%20Bibliography%202nd%20Ed ition%204-2007.pdf]. While we began the selection of papers with the idea of including one for every year and thus give an idea of the development of thinking in ISPSO, the publisher requested that we limit the number of papers to 13. As a result, many worthy papers could not be included. This is not only disappointing for the many authors who are not included but also for those of us who selected the papers. As we were looking at an existing body of work amassed over a period of a quarter of century, we were relying on the criteria by which the papers originally had been accepted for presentation, i.e. clarity, originality, links to psychoanalytic thinking, and contribution to theory, practice or both; in addition we were looking for papers that offer a psychoanalytic framework, commentary on current societal dynamics, world events and pre-occupations, contributed influential innovative ideas, concepts or new perspectives and leave an important legacy that would enrich our collective thinking and praxis. As already suggested, dozens of papers were not included in this book that met these criteria. We made our best, albeit imperfect, judgments for this volume.

These papers, published in chronological order, were delivered as presentations to the Society during the Annual Symposia of the ISPSO from its inception in 1983 to-date. Collectively they form an important commentary on the changing societal dynamics and current preoccupations facing contemporary organizations, their leaders and their workforces. As such, these papers are representative of many that have contributed to and documented the development of the thought and praxis from a psychoanalytic perspective and systems thinking over the last quarter century.

While most of these papers have been published elsewhere, the ISPSO as an organization wished to include them in this volume, recognizing their lasting influence and legacy as well as their ongoing impact upon the thinking and the practice of its membership and beyond.

The 16 authors contributing to this volume address three important themes: theoretical exploration and application of the psychoanalytic framework for organizational analysis and consultancy (Gould, Menzies Lyth, Lawrence, Hirschhorn, Armstrong, Long) the unconscious dynamics, organizational anxiety and the social character of ritualistic organizational defenses (Diamond, Krantz, Gilmore, Bridger, Stein) and finally, the exploration of the potential for creative leadership and collective creativity (French, Simpson, Harvey, Sievers and Amado).

This book is being offered as *a gift of intellectual legacy* bestowed by the ISPSO as it celebrates its 25th anniversary, both to the members of the Society, as well as to the wider community of interest. It is offered in the hope that psycho-/socio-analytic thought can find an ever wider application as a unique method of thinking and consulting, and that this will contribute to the efforts of our leaders, followers, consultants and researchers addressing the considerable challenges facing organizations.

I feel honoured and am grateful that the ISPSO Board invited me to edit this book. I would not have been able to fulfil this task without the enormous help of the committee members—Halina Brunning, Jinette de Gooijer, Laurence J. Gould and Rose Redding Mersky—whom I invited to assist me in the selection process of the papers and the editing of this book. Thanks also to Karnac Books, our publisher, and to Christelle Yeyet-Jacquot, in particular.

I very much hope that one day, on the occasion of ISPSO's next anniversary, a second volume of 'Psychoanalytic Studies of Organizations: Contributions from the International Society for the Psychoanalytic Study of Organizations' will appear.

Burkard Sievers
Editor
Past President ISPSO
Solingen, Germany
January 2009

1985 NEW YORK

The social character of bureaucracy: Anxiety and ritualistic defense

Michael A. Diamond

In the analysis of the social character of bureaucracy, one must examine the psychodynamics of obsessional neurosis in the individual and ritualistic practices in the bureaucracy. Much of organization theory either implicitly or explicitly characterizes bureaucratic activity as ritualistic. Such behavior results from obsessional thinking and compulsive action in the individual aimed at defending the self from anxiety over losing control. Ritualistic individual behavior serves to contain anxiety stemming from the uncanny experience of momentary loss in self/object boundaries and identity. This may occur in the organizational recruit at the moment of entry into the bureaucracy where one acts to deny reality by "undoing" the self-alienation that has occurred (signal anxiety) and "isolating" its affects (Freud, 1959a). Managing self/object boundaries and controlling ambivalent feelings emerges as primary motivating actions in the newcomer. Consequently, the new organizational member finds his defensive and regressive actions consistent with ritualistic tendencies and bureaucratic practices. The psychoanalysis of ritualistic behavior elucidates the human construction of and adherence to a bureaucratic form of organization as the outcome of the obsessional neurotic's actions in securing himself against anxiety about losing control over the impulses of the id.

Introduction

In analyzing the social character of bureaucracy, one must examine the psychodynamics of obsessional neurosis in the individual and ritualistic practices in the bureaucracy. Much of organization theory either implicitly or explicitly characterizes bureaucratic behavior as ritualistic. [See, for example, Weber (1947), Hummel (1977, 1982), Merton (1940, 1963), Crozier (1964), Argyris and Schon (1974, 1978), and Zaleznik and Kets de Vries (1975).] A more complete appreciation of the role of ritualistic behavior in bureaucracy recognizes its origins in the human personality. "The culture of the system reflects:... the types of people the organization attracts" (Burke, 1982, p. 76).

My purpose is to examine psychoanalytically the notion of "fit" between social character and "ideal type" bureaucracy. The social character of bureaucracy symbolizes the outcome of interpenetration between psyche and organization. Ritualistic behavior in bureaucracy arises from unconsciously motivated obsessional thinking and compulsive behavior aimed at defending one's self from anxiety about losing control (Diamond, 1984; Zaleznik and Kets de Vries, 1975; Sperling, 1950). It serves to contain anxiety, which is the unpleasant experience of a momentary loss of self/object boundaries and identity (Freud, 1959a; Klein, 1975; Erikson, 1968; Kafka, 1983). This occurs in the organizational recruit at the moment of entry into the bureaucracy where he acts to deny reality by "undoing" the self-alienation that has occurred (signal anxiety) and "isolating" its affects (Freud, 1959a).

At the point of organizational entry the recruit displays ritualistic behavior that serves as a defense against the anxiety of self-fragmentation. This anxiety arises in the entrant due to the ambivalent feelings and feared loss of individuality, which are linked to the personal meaning of assuming membership in an organization or group (Freud, 1921/1959b). Furthermore, this intrapsychic process may influence the newcomer to submit to the organizational or professional culture.

Preliminary discussion

In her case study of a nursing service, Menzies (1960) reports that the nursing staff utilized defensive techniques including obsessional rituals (ritualistic behavior) in coping with anxiety. She observes: "A necessary psychological task for the entrant into any profession that works with people is the development of adequate professional detachment. He must learn, for example, to control his feelings, refrain from excessive involvement, avoid disturbing identifications, maintain his professional independence against manipulation and demands for unprofessional behaviour" (p. 102).

Menzies is not concerned with supporting or opposing this organizationally enforced detachment and denial of feelings in the nursing profession, but in pointing out the excessive degree of preoccupation with impersonal norms and behavior patterns among the nurses. She concludes that the level of denial of feelings and detachment imposed on the newcomers by the experienced professional nurses greatly contributes to the stress and high rates of turnover among nursing trainees. Menzies' study illustrates the extent to which organizational members construct social systems characterized by obsessional rituals (ritualistic behavior) that serve as a defense against anxiety.

Another example of ritualistic behavior evoked in the entrant is found in Ritti and Funkhouser's text on organizational behavior entitled *The Ropes to Skip and the Ropes to Know*. The authors claim: "The first problem faced by the new member is that of gaining entry into the men's hut—of gaining access to the basic organizational secrets. A key episode here is the rite of passage. This is more or less an affirmation to the individual of the fact that he has been accepted into the men's hut" (1977, p. 3).

The authors describe how a new member of the organization must selectively focus his energy and attention on doing whatever is necessary to gain acceptance to the "men's hut." The "men's hut" refers to the ruling norms in a typically patriarchical and hierarchical organization, where socialization of the new member depends on his ability to assimilate the values of the organizational culture. He must prove to the organizational elites that he is deserving of membership and entrance to the "men's hut." Organizationally sanctioned performances and impressions by the new member take priority over his substantive work output. "The hut is a symbol of, and a medium for maintaining, the status quo and the good of the order" (1977, p. 3). The new member's compulsion to be accepted by, and allowed entrance, to the "men's hut" forces him to "learn the ropes" (1977). This means that a new member contains his anxiety at the point of organizational entry by exchanging his individual ego ideal for that of the organization and is motivated by the latent "hope" or "idea" that he may one day enter the "men's hut."

Other circumstances that might jeopardize the integrity of the organizational member's identity range from the anxiety of entry to changes of organizational leadership and political philosophy caused by the appearance of a new administration. Here, the member who identifies with the norms and values of his public agency, its previous mission statement and policy commitment, may perceive the change as an attack on his ego integrity and self-esteem.

He must now resolve the conflict between himself (his ego ideal) and the new organizational culture. If, on the one hand, professional opportunities are available and the degree of self-esteem and ego-strength are adequate, then he may choose to leave the agency. On the other hand, a combination of his need for security and his low self-esteem could motivate him to remain with the agency regardless of his apparent conflict with the new policy direction. In the latter case, he may repress and deny his conflicts by selectively attending to routinized bureaucratic practices and ritualistic performances that are often disconnected from practical purpose.

For example, Menzies (1960) observes nurses of a general hospital relying on "ritual task performance" as a defense against the anxiety of taking responsibility for decision-making in nurse-patient relationships. The "ritual task performance" may often be disconnected from the needs of patients, but serves the nurses' need to avoid the anxiety of personal responsibility. The "ritual task performance" characterized by its lists of prescribed actions and rigid routines, is analyzed as a "reaction formation" to the ultimate anxiety of losing control. In the stressful climate of a nursing service, assuming personal responsibility for one's actions and decisions may represent too great a risk to the individual nurse's identity and his or her membership in the profession.

The salience of ritualistic behavior for organization theory in the critical analysis of the social character of bureaucracy must be adequately explored in order to open up systems to analysis according to ritualistic content. Organizational analysts interested in understanding bureaucratic behavior should pay attention to the ritualistic (obsessive and compulsive) behavior of new members during the socialization process in order to delineate dysfunctional, meaningless, and conformist activities from functional, meaningful, and adaptive activities. The former signify symptomatic and (neurotic) obsessive-compulsive bureaucratic practices, while the latter connote non-neurotic, purposeful, organizational practices. This enables us to distinguish ritualistic behavior as symptomatic administrative action from mere repeated actions that are practical and functional. A conceptual distinction between cultural ritual and ritualistic behavior must now be established.

Cultural ritual and ritualistic behavior defined

Cultural ritual is defined as the established form; a system of rites; a ceremonial act or action; and a customarily repeated act or series of acts (Merriam-Webster, 1974, p. 604). Cultural rituals (such as religious and magical ceremonies) function to confirm and accept human emotionality (Kafka, 1983). Ritualistic behavior is defined in organizational terms as "dysfunctional and obsessive, bureaucratic practices," such as the habitual observance of an established form or process for doing things and the repetition of acts. Cultural rituals control and make the unknowable appear knowable and are meaningful to the collective (Siggins, 1983). Ritualistic behavior is experienced as meaningless routine that serves to suppress and deny genuine feelings. A major distinction therefore exists between socially useful cultural rituals and what become obsessive and compulsive features of ritualistic behavior by bureaucrats.

The rationally organized and routinized character of bureaucratic behavior is tantamount to the defensive action taken by the ego in the symptom formation of obsessional neurosis.[1] For example, when we discuss ritual in the situational and social context of bureaucracy, we are more precisely describing what psychoanalyst John Kafka (1983) called "ritualistic behavior." In his article "Challenge and Confirmation in Ritual Action," Kafka clarifies the distinction between the terms "ritual" and "ritualistic."

> Rituals can produce a feeling of completeness—a whole act, a finished sequence, the achievement (at least for a while) of satisfaction, satiation, perhaps serenity. But sometimes as in "ritualistic behavior," they may instead generate a feeling of

mechanical repetition or the absence of a meaning achieved, a sense of being enmeshed in an endless series of aborted sequences (p. 31).

Kafka's clarification distinguishes purposeful and meaningful social action from dysfunctional bureaucratic action. Cultural rituals differ from ritualistic behavior by both confirming and challenging everyday reality. Ritualistic behavior functions to deny the presence of a "reality principle" in life and death, love and hate, conflict and growth. Cultural rituals, such as the celebration of puberty rites, represent the healthy adaptive recognition and affirmation of human development and change. Ritualistic behavior symbolizes the emergence of psychological defensive tendencies, as illustrated in bureaucratic performances of symptomatic repetition, which stress rationality differentiated from feeling, and routine, stability, and control (Menzies, 1960; Jaques, 1955). Ritualistic behavior symbolizes the attempt to overcome by repression the ambivalent feelings that threaten one's self, in contrast to some cultural rituals that encourage tolerance and awareness of ambivalence (Kafka, 1983). For Kafka, the difference between ritual and ritualistic concerns the psychological function of boundaries between the individual and the group. The individual is motivated to overcome ambivalence and to establish an "unambiguous set of signals" (p. 35). Kafka interprets these ritualistic actions as "regression in the service of the ego." This distinction is crucial for identifying the prevalence of symptomatic rituals (ritualistic behavior) in modern bureaucratic organizations. It is argued that complementary human needs are served by the perpetuation of ritualistic behavior and bureaucratic practices.

In his article "Rite, Ritual and Defense," Smith (1983) writes: "The defensiveness of belief, rather than the literality of belief, is the proper object of study for distinguishing between individual pathology and culturally sanctioned ceremonials." For Smith, the distinction "could be framed within the concepts of regressive and progressive play/work," (p. 17) and defensive or non-defensive behavior (p. 18). In her article "Psychoanalysis and Ritual," Siggins defines "personal ritual" (what we distinguish here as "ritualistic behavior") as a symptom of an obsessive-compulsive disorder (1983, p. 3). "It is a personal and not a cultural construction though the form may well have cultural symbolic meaning" (p. 3). Dysfunctional (obsessive-compulsive) bureaucratic action is a "pseudo-social ritual" where instrumental human relations and impersonality promote the suppression of intersubjective meaning and mutual understanding among organizational participants. Identification of the nuances of ritualistic behavior in the self and in the bureaucracy illuminates the origins and concomitant actions of symptomatic organizational behavior.

The psychological origins of ritualistic behavior

R.D. Laing (1969) describes "primary ontological security" as the existential position of a person with a "centrally firm sense of his own and other people's reality and identity." According to Laing, it is precisely the lack of this security that distinguished the psychotic from others. In the cycle of human development, ritualistic behavior in the child integrates the self by differentiating self and other. For instance, Erik Erikson (1966) noted that the earliest ritualization (ritualistic behavior) occurs in the mother-infant greeting and recognition behavior. According to Erikson, a "sense of basic trust" or "mistrust" emerges out of the interpersonal experiences of the first year of infant development (1968, p. 96). Hence, if the mother/caretaker is emotionally healthy and the emotional bonding between mother and infant is good, then a primary sense of security and trust originates from the earliest ritualistic act. More specifically, if the necessary "trust" and sense of personal security is established during the first year to approximately 18 months of infancy, the baby comes to trust with minimal anxiety the mother's periodic absence. In the ritualistic performance one observes playful interactions between the mother and her child in coping with her mutual absence and presence. These playful interactions may take on a rather serious quality if we acknowledge their necessary ego function in challenging and confirming the child's sense of security and awareness of its separateness from the mother.

Ritualistic behavior in the form of greetings and recognition between mother and infant carries great implications for the crucial psychological foundations and genesis of self. Initially ritualistic behavior symbolizes a decisive moment in the early object relationship between mother and infant, wherein the psychodynamic process of separation and individuation, the necessary establishment of boundaries between self and other(s), makes its appearance.

Thus ritualistic behavior in its earliest manifestation is both purposeful and meaningful. It shares much in common with cultural rituals as meaningful celebrations and ceremonials with a common aim to control and make manageable that which appears life-threatening (loss of the "good" object-mother). Siggins (1983, p. 3) states that ritual acts serve common personal needs "to control, to make manageable that which is unknown, frightening, overpowering." "The more helpless one feels," she writes, "the more one calls upon outside magical aid." Surely, cultural rituals in society and ritualistic behavior in infancy share this in common. On the other hand, individuals engaged in ritualistic acts (obsessive symptomatic rituals) may also wish to satisfy these personal needs for control and manageability, but institutionalized actions may lack meaningfulness, purposefulness, and human intimacy. As Siggins writes "In the structured situation, ritual is an integral part of the organization. When a person or group revolts against the confines of the structure and wishes to be free and unfettered, he wants to be part of an individualized community based on personal intimacy, which tends to be anti-ritualistic" (p. 10). She continues: "This is one aspect of the paradoxical relationship between form and freedom that continually occurs in human life and institutions."

Bureaucratic context of ritualistic behavior

Managers' attempts at promoting integration between individuals and organizations are much more complex and emotionally loaded than (the simplistic notion of) striking a balance between individual interests and organizational goals. This apparently innocuous problem of modern organizations includes, to the contrary, a complex phenomenon known in psychoanalysis as the "return of the repressed," in which individuals experience the return of primary impulses and uncanny emotions; the reemergence of ambivalent feelings and a renewed search for the "good" lost object.

The difference between cultural ritual (a series of meaningful ceremonial acts) and ritualistic behavior (psychologically regressive, repressive, defensive and, seemingly, purposeless acts of repetition) is most notable at the point of entry for the organizational recruit. Entry is described as a transformation from social actor to bureaucratic functionary, which is a momentary but profound psychological event in which the entrant dons the cloak of an organizational role and identity by electing to participate in the institutional activities. From this moment, the organization-joiner is vulnerable to bureaucratic inducements to promote loyalty and control of subordinates. By reinforcing ritualistic behavior, bureaucracy ensures mechanisms to acculturate and indoctrinate organizational participants.

I do not contend that bureaucratization (the human construction of bureaucracy and the socialization of bureaucrats) represents an outcome of ontological insecurities arising originally from a failure of "good enough mothering (Winnicott, 1965). That conjecture is overly reductionist. But I do contend that bureaucratization is understood as emerging from defensive psychodynamic processes (Diamond, 1984) that occur as a consequence of the person's crucial need to maintain self boundaries (identity) and ego integrity just prior to, and following, entry into the formal organization. In ritualistic behavior, bureaucratic routine and repetition serve no organizational purpose. Yet that behavior plays a decisive role for the recruit in managing self boundaries and defending against anxiety felt during entry into the complex organization. At the moment of interface between the individual recruit and the organization, signal anxiety is felt in response to a fear of losing one's self boundaries and identity. At this decisive moment, any recruit must decide whether to affiliate with (by becoming a part of) the organization, or to remain separate from (and not part of) the institution.

This choice, regardless of how seemingly rational or irrational, invokes some dissonance and affects the integrity of the ego. The existential and psychological foundations of self are momentarily uprooted. Primitive human needs for attachment, merger, and dependency are reawakened. Such initial human motives encourage the nascent bureaucrat to locate his or her identity outside the self in the external quarter of bureaucracy. Along with the decision to join and accept membership in the formal organization, a renewed attachment is formulated by hierarchical arrangement. A "merger relationship" is established between superior and subordinate that contains libidinal energy and ambivalent feelings by bureaucratic practice and ritualistic behavior.

At the outset, ritualistic behavior ensures the management of self/object boundaries for the newcomer. Psychologically regressive dynamics of repetition and routine (reminiscent of primary process though essential to the child's need for object constancy and his development of focal attention) emerge in service to the vulnerable adult self. As Kafka notes "Ritualistic" action represents striving for "object constancy" and "reality-anchoring" that appears to defend one against "massive confusion and total disorganization" (1983).

Accounts from organization theorists of dysfunctional consequences in bureaucratic organizations often depict human behavior that is rigid and defensive. Viewed from a psychoanalytic perspective as an outcome of human needs (often, symptomatically expressed in human behavior), this phenomenon represents a wish to maintain the status quo, avoid anxiety-provoking conflict, and deny reality.

Ritualistic behavior and organization theory

Many organization theorists examine ritualistic behavior in modern bureaucratic organizations from different but mutually consistent perspectives. Such behavior is explicitly identified as a key factor in perpetuating dysfunctional consequences and ineffectiveness within bureaucratic institutions; at the same time, it achieves a necessary defensive equilibrium for organizational participants by managing self/object boundaries and alleviating anxiety over losing control. The following discussion outlines the arguments of prominent organization theorists and attempts to draw parallels and develop a consistent underlying pattern of thought.

Phenomenologist Ralph Hummel, for example, views the implications of Max Weber's characterization of modern bureaucracy as symbolizing a historical transition from socially organized action to rationally organized, efficient, stable, and controlled action (Weber, 1947; Hummel, 1977). He writes

> Society imposes general rules for proper social behavior, but personal discretion is allowed, providing plenty of room for actions based on mutual understanding. As society becomes more bureaucratic, however, rationally organized action finally collapses that room: in its never-ending search for control

over its functionaries, bureaucracy must destroy discretion (Hummel, 1977, pp. 33–34).

Hummel's warning is clear: as bureaucracy penetrates society it usurps individual freedom. Cultural rituals that regularly celebrate life (rites of passage) or death (funeral rites) often succumb to dysfunctional, irrational bureaucratic forms of action. In place of celebrating life and acknowledging death, ritualistic behavior facilitates individual attachment to hierarchy and conformity to impersonal rules, regulations, and procedures. Bureaucratic managers function to perpetuate hierarchy and ritualistic behavior by selectively attending to control and accountability of subordinates. Thus, managers treat subordinates as "part" human and one-dimensional for purposes of domination. Hummel illustrates this with the complaints of a functionary in the personnel department of the Cleveland, Ohio, Board of Education, who proclaims

> For a long time, I felt my role within the bureaucracy was to deal with human needs. In recent years, accountability has become so important, however, that I now must spend more and more time completing forms and compiling records. In many instances this work is duplicated by others and there is less time devoted to rendering service. My program director is caught up in this control situation and is constantly seeking new control methods and reactivating dormant rules. We had the sign-in and the sign-out procedure, the daily log, weekly, bi-weekly, monthly and yearly reports; now, we have a management information retrieval system. When similar information about all workers in the program is placed in the system, management can then analyze this (sic) data and attempt to control the daily work schedule and work distribution. Before all this paperwork there was more productivity. It seems that accountability and productivity are not compatible (Hummel, 1977, pp. 26–27).

Management's obsession with bureaucratic control, accountability, and efficiency often results in duplication and lower productivity. Bureaucratic behavior among organizational participants replaces intersubjectively meaningful, collaborative, and effective social actions (cultural ritual) with meaningless, rigidly conformist, and routine (ritualistic) actions. In Hummel's analysis the functionary is a product of bureaucratic ritualism.

Sociologist Robert Merton (1940) criticizes the dysfunctional and purposeless aspects of bureaucracy. He warns that dysfunctions arise from the bureaucrat's preoccupation with control over his subordinates and his insistence on the "reliability of response" and predictability of bureaucratic behavior. According to Merton, sentiments of loyalty and conformity in bureaucracy can be "more intense than is technically necessary." In a later work, Merton explains:

> There is a margin of safety, so to speak, in the pressure exerted by these sentiments upon the bureaucrat to conform to his patterned obligation, in much the same sense that added allowance (precautionary overestimates) are made by the engineer in designing the supports for a bridge. But his very emphasis leads to transference of the sentiments from the aims of the organization onto the particular details of behavior required by rules. Adherence to the rules, originally conceived as a means, becomes transformed into an end-in-itself; there occurs the familiar process of displacement of goals whereby 'an instrumental value becomes a terminal value' (Merton, 1963, pp. 258–259).

For Merton, the bureaucrat's reliance on impersonal rules and prescribed actions fosters ritualistic attitudes. This results in diminishing effective responses to clients, personnel, and the task environment of the agency.[2] This phenomenon is comparable to the "ritual task performance" (mentioned above) in Menzies' case of the nursing service. Merton sees bureaucratic behavior characterized by the functionary's extraordinary dependency on rules and prescriptions for action resulting in goal displacement. Originally intended to produce rationally organized and efficient practices, bureaucracy deteriorates into dysfunctional, inefficient, and irrationally organized impersonal actions. Bureaucrats emphasize means over ends; form (process) takes priority over substance. From a sociological perspective, Merton concluded that ritualistic behavior is characteristic of bureaucracy:

> Discipline, readily interpreted as conformance with relations, whatever the situation, is seen not as a measure designed for

specific purposes but becomes an immediate value in the life-organization of the bureaucrat. This emphasis, resulting from the displacement of the original goals, develops into rigidities and an inability to adjust readily. Formalism, even ritualism, ensues with an unchallenged insistence upon punctilious adherence to formalized procedures. This may be exaggerated to the point where primary concern with conformity to the rules interferes with the achievement of the purposes of the organization, in which case we have the familiar phenomenon of the technicism or red tape of the official (1963, pp. 258–259).

In a psychoanalytic framework, one might suggest that ego integrity, autonomy, and a sense of reality are unwittingly sacrificed to a collective wish for certainty and predictability in a changing environment. Managers in bureaucratic organizations tend to control and dominate their functionaries and their task environment. This is symptomatic of the ego's need in an obsessional neurosis to control "impulse activities" from the inside and distort reality from the outside. Bureaucratic managers stress conformity to impersonal rules and procedures (official behavior). This results, on the one hand, in goal displacement and, on the other hand, in destruction of individual discretion. Unlike cultural rituals that enhance a feeling of completeness and achievement, bureaucratic rituals (ritualistic acts) promote mechanical repetition and suppress feelings from thoughts and behavior. Among organizational members, compulsive routine and impersonal action symbolizes the bureaucrat's reliance on formalism, conservatism, cases, technicism, and red tape as a defense against anxiety about losing control. These defensive actions illustrate psychological repression and unconscious denial of reality among bureaucratic participants.

French sociologist Michel Crozier in *The Bureaucratic Phenomenon* further enhances our understanding of the significance of ritualistic behavior for bureaucracy. He writes:

> ... a bureaucratic organization is an organization that cannot correct its behavior by learning from its errors. Bureaucratic patterns of action, such as the impersonality of rules and the centralization of decision-making, have been so stabilized that they have become part of the organization's self-reinforcing

equilibrium. Finally, when one rule prevents adequate dealing with one case, its failure will not generate pressure to make it more complete, more precise, and more binding (1964, p. 187).

For Crozier, a typical feature of bureaucracy is its tendency to produce "vicious circles" where organizational participants repeat errors and do not learn from their mistakes because of an overwhelming propensity to defend themselves against the necessity for and the reality of change. The bureaucrat's common response to failure is reinforcement and/or expansion of his routine structural arrangements and normative assumptions—illustrated by a "more of the same" attitude.

Crozier identifies four basic components that comprise the "vicious circle" of bureaucracy: "impersonal rules, the centralization of decisions, strata isolation and concomitant group pressure on the individual, and the development of parallel power relationships around remaining areas of uncertainty" (1964, p. 187).

In his empirical analysis of dysfunctions in the French bureaucracy, Crozier views ritualistic behavior as predominantly the result of peer group pressure on individual members among the numerous strata of the hierarchical system. He expands Merton's notion of goal displacement and Hummel's assertion of limits to discretion by arguing that the displacement of goals is enforced by peer groups emerging in "the isolation of different strata" as a way of protecting group members against other groups and against the organization (1964, pp. 190–191). Furthermore, he suggests this isolation allows the unit to "control its own domain and to ignore the organization's wider goals" (1964, p. 191). Crozier explains:

> ... in order to get the best bargain for its own members, the peer group must pretend that their partial objective is an end in itself. The member's ritualism provides good means to achieve such an end. It enables the group to assert its own functions are the most crucial for the success of the whole organization. Then, finally, it helps develop and reinforce group solidarity among the group's own members. (1964, p. 191)

For Crozier, the function of ritualistic behavior in bureaucracy is both a response to and a perpetuation of bureaucratic centralization and impersonal norms. Ritualistic behavior is a dysfunctional consequence of peer group pressure intended to enhance group or unit cohesion and promote power relationships for bargaining purposes. Such behavior reinforces isolationist tendencies and defensive attitudes among the strata of bureaucracy, which in turn promote competition and divisiveness between organizational units and peer groups. This leads to intra-organizational boundaries among units (or departments) becoming increasingly rigid and protective, and with communication and coordination becoming increasingly difficult. This outcome is illustrated by the narrow-minded and parochial (often territorial) ritualistic attitudes among organizational group members.

From a psychoanalytic perspective at the organizational level, these findings suggest that meaningful reality-testing is unlikely and the organization finds itself incapable of responding to environmental demands for change. Peer groups surface as havens in an alienating and depersonalizing organizational climate. As a symbol of the organizational ego, management inadequately functions to balance internal and external systemic pressures. At the individual level, a so-called "bureaucratic personality" emerges among functionaries: someone who respects power relationships throughout the organizational strata, but who is predominantly motivated by interpersonal security needs and defense against anxiety over losing control.

In their books *Theory in Practice* (1974) and *Organizational Learning* (1978), social psychologists Chris Argyris and Donald Schon discuss (what I interpret as) ritualistic behavior and bureaucratic dysfunctions by examining "constancy-seeking" behavior and "single-loop" learning of individual and organizational "model 1 theories-in-use" and "0-1 learning systems" (1978).

According to Argyris and Schon, model 1 assumptions and governing values produce behavioral outcomes in the organization that foster limited learning, decreasing effectiveness, and the promotion of rigidity. These governing variables that effect intra-organizational behavior include the following tendencies: to achieve purposes as the individual perceives them; to maximize winning and minimize losing; to minimize eliciting negative feelings; to be rational and minimize emotionality (1976, p. 31). Action strategies of model 1 include: efforts to design and manage the environment so that the individual is in control over the factors relevant to him; acts to own and control tasks; and, unilateral protection of self and unilateral protection of others from being hurt (1976, p. 31).

The consequences of model 1 theory-in-use further portray ritualistic behavior. For example, the individual is viewed as defensive; defensive interpersonal and group relationships are commonplace; defensive norms must prevail; and "low freedom of choice, internal commitment, and risk taking" persist (1976, p. 31). Finally, Argyris and Schon (1978) point out that model 1 theory-in-use and its counterpart 0-1 learning systems result in the inability to "double-loop" learn; therefore, individual members of these systems perpetuate "self-sealing processes, single-loop learning, and, little public testing of theories" (1976, p. 31).

Hence, ritualistic behavior in modern organizations represents tacit skills of defense against the anxiety of uncertainty and predictability associated with problem-solving and change in the status quo. At the same time that cultural ritual serves to control or make manageable that which is unknown or frightening, ritualistic behavior (as symbolized by model 1 and bureaucratic organizations) serves a defensive function for bureaucrats of psychologically repressing and denying the necessity (often the inevitability) of organizational and interpersonal change. From a psychoanalytic viewpoint, change means loss at the personal (often unconscious) level of experience. Ritualistic behavior among bureaucrats functions, thereby, to avoid anxiety connected with consciously painful recognition of loss. Defensive psychological activities of denial and selective inattention operate to repress feelings and narrowly focus one's thoughts on meaningless and repetitive tasks, while functioning to meet the unconscious desire for interpersonal security in maintaining stability and the status quo. Under these circumstances, organizational and individual reality-testing surrenders to a collective fantasy of control and (what some might call) immortality (Denhardt, 1981).

Psychoanalysts Abraham Zaleznik and Manfred Kets de Vries write in *Power and the Corporate Mind:*

> Any collective experience, such as organizational planning, with its capacity for changing the atmosphere and the imagery of power conflicts, can fall victim to rigidities. The rigidities consist mainly of the formation and elaboration of structures, procedures, and other ceremonials that create the illusion of

solving problems but, in reality, only provide a basis for the discharge of valuable energies (1975, p. 135).

For Zaleznik and Kets de Vries, ordinary organizational activities like planning and decision-making inevitably produce change and influence power relationships. Consequently, "ritualistic" approaches to solving real problems arise as a common feature of modern organizations, where, for example, people come together in committees "in the naive belief that the exchange of ideas is bound to produce a solution" (1975, p. 135).

It is not the mere formation of organizational committees for the purpose of solving problems which Zaleznik and Kets de Vries view suspiciously, but, rather, "that the faith that is invested in such proposals deflects attention from where it properly belongs" (1975, p. 135). Following a proposal to form the committee to examine a particular problem, organizational participants may ritualistically perceive the simple idea of the committee itself as the solution to the problem—a "magical formula" to alleviate the anxiety of uncertainty. The idea of the committee may, for the moment, serve as the object of a collective (organizational) wish to be rid of the anxiety-provoking event.

If undetected, ritualistic behavior in modern organizations literally can act as a blinder to reality—a defensive "screen" that conceals problems and denies conflicts. Human energy (cognitions and emotions), otherwise channeled into the correction of errors and actual problem solving, is often displaced by the influence of anxiety onto substitute objects promoting the illusion of safety and security without substantive reflection and change. Under the stress of uncertainty and neurotic anxiety, bureaucratic form (procedures, regulations, impersonal rules, red tape, etc.) takes precedence over organizational mission and substantive output (problem-solving, provision of services, personal responsibility).

Ritualistic action involves obsessional thinking and compulsive behavior with which individuals defensively act to deny reality by "undoing" the self-alienation and "isolating" its affects (Freud, 1959a). As we have already seen, ritualistic action is commonplace in modern bureaucracy. Bureaucratic characteristics actually facilitate symptomatic rituals that unintentionally promote human tendencies to deny reality, and displace cognitions and emotions, in order to maintain security by momentarily avoiding anxiety. Ritualistic behavior serves a common purpose for both the individual and the organization. It functions as an instantaneous defense against personal fragmentation and organizational disequilibrium. Like rigid and "over-determined" defensive operations in the obsessive neurotic, ritualistic behavior in the organization appears to reestablish equilibrium by securing the status quo (reinforcing individual and organizational boundaries). Actually, ritualistic behavior is indicative of symptomatic administrative behavior identified by organization theorists in the occurrence of "vicious circles," "self-sealing processes," "single-loop learning," and the generalized "displacement of goals." These organization theorists have identified such ritualistic phenomena in bureaucracy as decisive to dysfunctional consequences, ineffectiveness, and organizational pathology.

Conclusion

I have attempted to illustrate not only how ritualistic behavior that is commonplace in bureaucracy contributes to dysfunctional consequences such as goal displacement and the like, but also that it is symptomatic of obsessive-compulsive neuroses in the human personality (Freud, 1963) and symptomatic of the individual's need to control ambivalence and manage boundaries between self and other(s) (Kafka, 1983; Erikson, 1968).

Further, I have located the crucial moment of recurrence of these psychological needs in the adult at the point of entry into the bureaucratic system of organization. It is at this stressful moment that one's self is most vulnerable to the anxiety challenging the recruit's ego strength and self-esteem. Here, the management of self boundaries and the control of ambivalent feelings are a most prominent motivating force influencing the entrant's actions. Consequently, the interpersonal security needs of the new organizational member, promotes conformity and over-dependency or exaggerated and psychologically regressive demands for protection and defense against anxiety. A highly structured and often rigid institution designed for control and accountability like the "ideal type" bureaucracy may unwittingly facilitate and perpetuate such action.

The ultimate organizational paradox which the analysis of ritualistic behavior helps to illuminate is that the human construction

of and adherence to a bureaucratic form of institution is the outcome of the obsessive neurotic's need to preserve and secure the self
against anxiety about losing control. In the article, "The Absurdity
of Ritual," Zuesse (1983, pp. 40–50) states: "In all ritual, it is evident
people voluntarily submit to their bodily existence and assume very
specific roles with highly patterned rules—roles and rules that end
up making the self one with an infinite series of others who have
embodied these typical' roles." The author suggests that the "free
self voluntarily submits to particular boundaries and enters servi-
tude to otherness and to an entire world of objective relationships
and moral imperatives" (1983, p. 40). Zuesse concludes that ritual
"may be self-alienating, but it is finally self-accepting in the deepest
sense. The self that is accepted is the actual Finite self of boundaries and limits, the self defined through others, and destined to die"
(1983, p. 42).

In this paper, I have attempted to point out that while both cultural ritual and ritualistic behavior are self-limiting, only cultural
ritual is truly self-accepting. In the cultural ritual, we construct a
consensually validated system of meanings, whereas, in ritualistic behavior, group and organizational participants perpetuate a
defensive social system against anxiety that fosters the suppression
of collaborative human action by depersonalization and unilateral
protectiveness.

Notes

1. Obsessional neurosis is a form of psychoneurosis in which the
   predominant symptoms are obsessive thoughts and compulsive
   behavior (obsessive rituals). Obsessional thoughts differ from
   normal thoughts in that they are experienced by the patient himself
   as unspontaneous, distracting, repetitive, ruminative, and as coming
   from elsewhere than himself; their subject-matter is typically absurd,
   bizarre, irrelevant, and obscene. Compulsive behavior is repetitive,
   stereotyped, ritualistic, and superstitious (see Rycroft, 1968).
2. 'Such ritualistic attitudes and overprecautions will not only produce
   rigidity and a lack of spontaneity necessary to organizational
   adjustment, but, at the individual level and the organizational level
   such attitudes are symptomatic of obsessive processes at work
   that promote narrow-mindedness, parochialism, and selective
   inattention—cognitive processes attending to interpersonal security

needs and avoidance of anxiety-provoking circumstances like that encountered by change and problem-solving activities.

References

Argyris, C. (1976). Leadership, learning, and changing the status quo. *Organizational Dynamics, 4,* No. 3.

Argyris, C. & Schon, D. (1974). *Theory in Practice.* Jossey-Bass, San Francisco.

Argyris, C. & Schon, D. (1978). *Organizational Learning.* Addison-Wesley, Reading, Mass.

Baum, H.S. (1983). Autonomy, shame, and doubt: Power in the bureaucratic lives of planners. *Administration & Society* 15(2):147–184.

Bowlby, J. (1969). Vol. 1. *Attachment.* Basic Books, New York.

Bowlby, J. (1973). Vol. 2. *Separation.* Basic Books, New York.

Bowlby, J. (1979). *The Making and Breaking of Affectional Bonds.* Tavistock Publications, London.

Burke, W.W. (1982). *Organization Development: Principles and Practices,* Little, Brown and Company, Boston and Toronto.

Crazier, M. (1964). *The Bureaucratic Phenomenon.* University of Chicago Press, Chicago. Denhardt, R.B. (1981). *In the Shadow of Organization.* University of Kansas Press, Lawrence. Diamond, M.A. (1984). Bureaucracy as externalized self-system: A view from the psychological interior. *Administration & Society* 16(2): 195–214.

Diamond, M.A. & Allcorn, S. (1984). Psychological barriers to personal responsibility. *Organizational Dynamics* 12(4):66–77.

Erikson, E. (1963). *Childhood and Society.* Norton, New York.

Erikson, E. (1966). Ontogeny of Ritualization. In R. Loewenstein, et al. (eds.), *Psychoanalysis—A General Psychology: Essays in Honor of Heinz Hartman.,* International Universities Press, New York.

Erikson, E. (1968). *Identity, Youth and Crisis.* Norton, New York.

Fairbairn, W.R.D. (1952). *Psychoanalytic Studies of Personality.* Tavistock Publications, London.

Freud, S. (1921/1959b). *Group Psychology and the Analysis of the Ego,* Norton, New York.

Freud, S. (1923). *The Ego and the Id.* Norton, New York.

Freud, S. (1959a). *Inhibitions, Symptoms and Anxiety.* Norton, New York.

Freud, S. (1963). *Character and Culture.* Collier Books, New York.

Freud, A. (1966). *The Ego and the Mechanisms of Defense*. International Universities Press, New York.

Greenson, R. (1978). *Explorations in Psychoanalysis*. International Universities Press, New York. Hummel, R. (1977, 1982). *The Bureaucratic Experience*. St. Martins Press, New York.

Jaques, E. (1955). Social systems as a defense against persecutory and depressive anxiety. In Klein, M., Heimann, P. & Money-Kyrle, R.E. (eds.), *New Directions in Psychoanalysis*. Basic Books, New York.

Kafka, J. (1983). Challenge and confirmation in ritual action. *Psychiatry* 46(1):31–39.

Kernberg, O. (1979). Regression in organizational leadership, *Psychiatry* 42:24–39.

Kets de Vries, M.F.R. (1980). *Organizational Paradoxes*. Tavistock Publications, London.

Klein, M. (1975). *The Psychoanalysis of Children*. Seymour Lawrence, Delacorte Press.

Kohut, H. (1971). *The Analysis of the Self*. International Universities Press, New York.

LaBier, D. (1983). Bureaucracy and psychopathology. *Political Psychology* 4(2):223–244.

Laing, R.D. (1966). *The Divided Self*. Penguin Books, Middlesex, England.

Levinson, H. (1981). *Executive*. Harvard University Press, Cambridge, Mass.

Mahler, M.S., et al. (1975). *The Psychological Birth of the Human Infant*. Basic Books, New York.

Menzies, I.E.P. (I960). A case in the functioning of social systems as a defense against anxiety: A report on a study of the nursing service of a general hospital. *Human Relations* 13:95–121.

Merriam-Webster Dictionary (1974). Pocket Books, New York, p. 604.

Merton, R. (1940). Bureaucratic structure and personality. *Social Forces* 17.

Merton, R. (1963). Bureaucratic structure and personality. In Smelser and Smelser (eds.), *Personality and Social Systems*. Wiley, New York.

Reik, T. (1946). *Ritual: Psycho-Analytic Studies*. International Universities Press, New York.

Ritti, R.R. & Funkhouser, C.R. (1977). The Ropes to Skip and the Ropes to Know. *Studies in Organizational Behavior*, Grid, Inc., Columbus, Ohio.

Rycroft, C. (1968). *A Critical Dictionary of Psychoanalysis*. Penguin Books, Middlesex, England.

Schwartz, H. (1982). Job involvement as obsession-compulsion. *Academy of Management Review 7*(3):429–432.

Siggins, L. (1983). Psychoanalysis and ritual. *Psychiatry 46*(1):2–15.

Slater, P. (1966). *Microcosm*. Wiley, New York.

Smith, J.H. (1983). Rite, ritual, and defense. *Psychiatry 46*(1):16–30.

Sperling, O. (1950). Psychoanalytic aspects of bureaucracy. *Psychoanalytic Quarterly 19*:88–100.

Sullivan, H.S. (1953). *The Interpersonal Theory of Psychiatry*. Norton, New York.

Weber, M. (1947). *The Theory of Social and Economic Organization*. The Free Press, New York.

Winnicott, D.W. (1965). *The Maturational Processes and the Facilitating Environment*. International Universities Press, New York.

Zaleznik, A. & Kets de Vries, M. (1975). *Power and the Corporate Mind*. Houghton Mifflin Co., Boston.

Zuesse, E.M. (1983). The absurdity of ritual. *Psychiatry 46*(1):40–50.

The splitting of leadership and management as a social defense

James Krantz & Thomas N. Gilmore

This article explores a maladaptive response organizations are making to the great uncertainty and turbulence they face. The authors describe the ways in which management and leadership are split apart, with one aspect idealized and the other devalued, as a "social defense" against confronting the adaptive demands of contemporary operating environments. Two variants of this social defense are examined: "managerialism" which looks to the magic of technique and "heroism" which focuses on the heroic leader. Responding effectively to current conditions requires linking what has come to be viewed as leadership, the visionary and mission setting aspects of executive action, with management, the apparatuses and tools for achieving organizational purposes.

Introduction

Contemporary organizations are undergoing an unprecedented level of change and turmoil. New technologies, fresh competitive challenges, and a changing world economic order pressure managers to adapt and innovate, resulting in the now commonplace mergers and acquisitions, cutbacks and downsizing efforts, strategic alliances, and spin-offs which, in turn, all amplify complexity dramatically.

The popular press, management specialists, and organization theorists all speak to the need for organizations to innovate deeply (Kanter, 1983; Peters & Waterman, 1982; Lawrence & Dyer, 1983; Tushman, Newman, & Romanelli, 1987) and to the requirements of leading such enterprises (Bennis & Nannus, 1985; Leavitt, 1986). Visionary, creative leadership has become essential in contemporary organizations.

In systems terms, organizations must now operate in environments which are characterized by greatly increased complexity. Dense interdependence and unpredictable connections which arise from accelerating but unpredictable social, technical, and economic changes create "turbulent" conditions (Emery & Trist, 1965). In response, organizations must learn and change continuously under these troubling conditions (Argyris & Schon, 1978; Michael, 1973; Morgan, 1988).

Yet, just as individuals experience difficulties in adapting to novel conditions and often resist or sabotage their own development, so do organizations. In this paper, we wish to highlight and explore a particular maladaptive response to these demands for change and innovation that we have observed across a variety of settings. This response consists of the splitting of leadership and management both in concept and in practice. We interpret this splitting as a social defense, drawing conceptually on the pioneering work of the Tavistock Institute. The defense arises as an effort to diminish, evade, or trivialize the profound changes required to revitalize our institutions and the difficult and painful anxieties stirred up by such a transition. We do not question the need for innovative leadership which is responsive to emerging economic conditions; rather, we are concerned with a dysfunctional reaction to these pressures.

The social defense we wish to examine has two variants: either a cult of management tools and techniques, or alternatively a cult of the charismatic leader. Idealization of one aspect of the executive process and denigration of the other prevents integration of a vision and the machinery for achieving it that is necessary for effective innovation. We view the elevating of management without leadership as allowing us not to think about substantive directions that would be disturbing (Miller & Gwynne, 1972). Conversely, the lionization of leadership and denigration of management serve to neutralize the potentially disturbing ideas of genuine leadership by keeping it separated from management, which in the best sense of the term, represents the means for realizing the new ideas.

The starting point of executive action

Effective management requires the linking together of the strategic vision and the organizational machinery, inevitably requiring an inward and outward focus simultaneously (Rice, 1963; Miller & Rice, 1967). At the boundary between any unit and its wider organizational context, or alternatively, at the boundary between the enterprise and its wider environment, a leader integrates the unit's mission or strategic orientation with the tools and means for accomplishing it. It is specifically a function of leadership to weave the two to articulate an appropriate mission which the resources of the unit can realistically achieve and to deploy its resources efficiently in the service of its primary task or tasks (Barnard, 1938; Selznick, 1957). Thus the leader or manager, and at this point the terms can be used interchangeably, must have both and external and internal view, a strategic and operational perspective, simultaneously. In other words, enterprise leadership relates means and ends.

As the complexity in both the inner and outer environments grows, we see the emergence of a widespread ideology in which this essential linking function, the integration of "leadership" and "management," is disavowed. We view this ideology as a social defense, a concept to which we turn in the next section.

The concept of social defenses

The idea of social defenses grows out of the British object relations tradition of inquiry into psychodynamic processes. Early researchers at the Tavistock Institute examined the way in which participation in task systems stimulates painful anxieties and thus leads to the establishment of equally powerful defensive systems in the organization, Jacques (1955) showed that, in addition to functional reasons for various social arrangements (efficiency, creativity, and affiliation), one of the primary cohesive elements binding individuals into institutionalized human association is that of defense against painful anxieties.

His example of the first mate on shipboard illustrates the idea nicely. The ambivalent feelings sailors feel for their captain at sea, particularly the negative side of their responses, engender great anxiety due to their extreme dependence on the captain. The first mate becomes a displaced target, or receptacle, for these unwanted feelings toward the captain, and typically comes to be regarded as far more insensitive and mean spirited than is the case. Through this, the sailors establish and maintain, unconsciously, a collective defensive system in which they are protected from painful disturbances in the relationship with the captain.

The term "social defense" was first used by Menzies (1960) in connection with her nursing study in which she describes how the "needs of members to use organizations in the struggle against anxiety leads to development of socially structured defense mechanisms." Her research illustrates how various features of the organization, such as structures, policies, operational procedures, beliefs, etc., can be used to reinforce the individual psychological defensive needs of members as well as to further task accomplishment.

The Menzies (1960) study concerns the powerful anxieties stimulated in the course of fulfilling the nursing role. There the anxiety arose from intimate contact of nurses with the difficult issues of life, death, and sickness. To prevent painful anxieties arising from identification with the patients, practices and policies arose more to help nurses evade such anxieties than to cure or care for patients. For example, rotation and charting practices diminished nurses' awareness of or responsibility for patients as whole people, and instead became "the leg in room 2" or a set of tasks unrelated to the overall care of a person. By fragmenting patients, the nurse did not have to deal with patients as whole persons which evoked painful empathies, repulsions, or erotic impulses. Similarly, excessive diffusion of delegated responsibility and authority served the same ends.

The particular modes of defense institutionalized in the nursing service led to less effective task performance, and as a result served as a secondary source of doubt and anxiety for the nurses. While effective in helping nurses relieve their anxieties, the particular collective strategies employed were done so at considerable cost to patient care, the education of student nurses, and the quality of staff nurses' work lives.

The concept of social defense links the individual and collective levels of activity. It is both psychological and social at the same time and provides a way of seeing the reciprocal interaction of the two. Disturbing intrapsychic conflicts and anxieties, which are often elicited in the course of taking up a role or joining an enterprise, are defended against as members engage in psychological splitting, denial, and projective identification. All these processes lead to an externalizing of elements of the conflictual situation. Social defenses exist when members establish or maintain situations which mirror, in the external world, their own internal psychic defenses against anxiety. While individuals alone operate defenses, they do so in ways which reify their unconscious strategies to contain anxiety and doubt (Heimann, 1952). Thus, "objective" features of organizational life symbolize, and are imbued with, psychological aspects of members. Over time, the social defense system is built up as members enter into *unconscious* agreements to diminish task-related anxiety in such a fashion.

In turn, social defenses have a great impact on individual members of organizations. The ways of managing anxiety which are institutionalized in the social defense system become part of its customary ways of thinking and doing things. Because individuals adapt to their organization, new members will adopt these ways of coping with work and with their own anxieties. Unfortunately, they often impair the functioning of organizations at the same time because they enable members to turn away from the realities they face, no matter how distressing.

In another example, Miller and Gwynne (1972) explore form of social defense on the level of primary task definition itself in *A Life Apart*, a study which examines agencies that house and care for severely handicapped people. Having the extremely painful task of "mediating between social death and physical death," the staff of these organizations came to interpret their mission in a way which would help defend themselves against this pain. The institutions adopted a protective ideology, either that all their charges can develop fully or that all require being completely cared for, which defensively simplified their complex realities. Consequently, staff members did not have to make troubling and painful judgments on an individual basis.

In this paper, we wish to consider another type of social defense which shapes the way in which leaders and managers come to understand their work. In particular, we are interested in how certain pervasive social themes and emergent trends in the wider society are imported into organizations in such a way as to serve as social defenses.

What distinguishes the social defense we discuss here is that it is an ideology which is unrelated to the specific tasks or technologies of an enterprise but instead to the cross-cutting demands arising from a rapidly changing environment. Thus, many organizations, of quite different character and purpose, share this frightening reality in common. As discussed above, we have observed an emergent pattern of social defenses appearing across many types of organizations which can be categorized into two sorts: managerialism and the cult of heroic leadership.

Before turning to these two ideologies in more detail, we wish to explicate the link among social defenses, ideologies, and culture. Following Schein (1985), culture can be defined as "a pattern of basic assumptions invented, discovered, or developed by a given group as it learns to cope with its problems of external adaptation and internal integration ..." (p. 9). Culture, in this sense, accounts for a wide range of features of organizational life including: methods of production, attitudes toward control and supervision, beliefs about organizational learning and change, the customs, habits, and ideologies of managerial practice, and even the way objectives are understood.

In his discussion of how culture forms, Schein speaks of two modes of learning: positive problem solving and pain and anxiety reduction. The latter, he argues accounts for the emergence of various features of an organization's culture, "rituals, patterns of thinking or feeling, beliefs, and tacit assumptions ... that were learned originally as ways of avoiding painful situations .... We can think of parts of a group's culture as being 'social defense mechanisms'" (p. 178). Thus, an ideology, referring to the ideas, values, and attitudes characteristic of a group or a community (Plamenatz, 1971), can serve as a social defense by providing a way of coping with painful, anxiety-provoking situations. We now turn to the roots of the managerial ideology which we argue is being used as a social defense.

The splitting of leadership and management

Early writers on organizations used the terms leader and manager interchangeably (Barnard, 1938; Selznick, 1957; Rice, 1963). Selznick's

(1957) seminal book was titled *Leadership in Administration*, clearly linking leadership with the bureaucratic machinery to accomplish purposes. In the early 1970's, Zaleznik (1974) began to differentiate among psychological types of leaders, first conceptualizing two types of leaders: calling one consensus and the other charismatic. Later (1978), he reframed the distinction as between leaders and managers, and speculated as to whether the dominant business culture was overproducing the latter. Zaleznik's (personal communication) intellectual distinction tapped a wave of pent up resentment against the rational, bureaucratic managerial class that Galbraith (1967) had discussed in *The New Industrial State*. It appeared during a resurgence of interest in entrepreneurial activity which was seen as the visionary function of bringing new business and new industries into being.

The distinction has been taken up and elaborated in many subsequent texts, both scholarly and popular, that examine types of leaders and analyze the challenges our organizations face. Burns and Stalker's (1961) distinction between "transformational" and "transactional" leaders parallels Leavitt's (1986) between the "pathfinder" and the "implementor." Bennis and Nannus (1985) pithily captured the distinction with a frequently quoted sentence: "Leaders do the right things; managers do things right" (p. 33). This distinction has been worked with, developed, and applied in numerous scholarly works (Kouzes & Posner, 1987).

In this emergent framework, leadership refers to the articulation of mission, direction setting, vision, and strategic thinking; management becomes the administrative functions of achieving the goals, administering policies and procedures, and monitoring and controlling. The distinction, which harkens back to Weber's (1947) original discussions of the differences between policy making and administrative action, is increasingly used by scholars to discuss a perceived emergent need for the visionary, mission-setting, inspiring leader in the face of contemporary conditions. Yet scholarly discussions value both sides of the coin; while the "leader-like" approaches are viewed as ascending in importance, the implementor or manager is treated in this literature with respect and seen as a vital function.

As one approaches the world of practice and more popular writing, however, a psychological splitting[1] (in contrast to conceptual differentiation in the academic literature) occurs in which one side of the equation is extolled and the other demeaned. Either the technique or the heroic leader (or the inspirational approach) becomes the savior, rather than acknowledging the critical importance of both "leadership" and "management" in tandem for robust change and development. So in comparison to Selznick's (1957) leadership *in* administration, the dominant leadership literature has come to oppose leadership and administration.

We are not suggesting that the functions represented by "leadership" or "management" in the current parlance need be fulfilled by the same individual to avoid this debilitating split. The classic differentiation between the CEO and COO may well be highly functional, and as complexity and uncertainty increase, more specialization may be called for. Yet, the specialization and differentiation must always be counterbalanced by mechanisms of integration. Among top level teams this requires the mutual respect and authorization of each other to do his or her part of the work in the context of a shared mission.

In contrast to a productive differentiation or specialization, when one aspect of the executive function is held in contempt or denigrated, then a dysfunctional split has resulted. Under these conditions, the necessary reintegration is impaired and the critical linking function of the executive is blocked.

Thus, the current distinction between leadership and management often results in a split that constitutes an attack on the critical function of leadership to link means and ends. This unconsciously produces what Kanter (1983) refers to as a debilitating "segmentalist" culture that inhibits innovation and adaptation to emerging novel circumstances. In separating leadership from management, and in idealizing one while devaluing the other, we suggest that there is an implicit attack on the essential link between ideas and the machinery necessary to realize those ideas, thus pointing to the way in which these ideologies are used as a social defense to avoid the deep changes being called for by current and emerging conditions.

The defensive ideologies

The first of the two forms of this social defense is termed managerialism. Managerialism results when the same methods and techniques that have been used to accomplish the social purposes of organizations, e.g., management, have been elevated to ends in themselves (Boguslaw, 1965). Managerialism thus refers to a stance toward management which divorces the techniques of management from any appreciation of, integration with, or accountability for the larger mission and purposes of the organization. In this form, management *per se* is lionized and the leadership function of strategic thinking and direction setting devalued.

The second manifestation of this splitting is the lionization of the heroic leader, called heroism here. In contrast to managerialism, this social defense denigrates so-called management. The maverick, charismatic heroes of business (who are being celebrated in the popular and academic press) embody this trend in a kind of contemporary mythology. Here we are presented with the hope for saviors who through force of vision and personality will overcome the inertia and bureaucratic morass of industrial organization and lead American society back to its world dominance and renew our spirit of progress (Reich, 1985). From this vantage point, the administrative work and analytic methods are regarded not as the savior, as in managerialism, but as the source of malaise and inertia.

The splitting of leadership and management in this psychological sense is dynamically conservative (Schon, 1971) in both its forms. Heroism serves to contain potentially disturbing, creative ideas by encapsulating them, and effectively keeping them uncoupled from management, which, in the best sense of the term, represents the means for realizing the new ideas. Conversely, managerialism emasculates the power of tools and techniques because they are not effectively harnessed to the purposes and ideas of leadership. Thus, in both ideologies, the essential link between new or visionary ideas and the organizational apparatus required to realize them is broken. Our premise is that the driving motivation for unconscious adoption of these neutralizing social defenses is to avoid the doubts, uncertainties, and disturbing anxieties which are stimulated in the course of confronting the adaptive requirements of the emergent organizational environments. In Bion's (1961) terms, both ideologies represent basic assumption dependency functioning in which the group evades anxieties stemming from confrontation with its tasks by creating a magical investment of hope and expectation in some omnipotent object. By pinning its hopes on persons, methods, or a text's imagined powers instead of sophisticated attention to its primary task or mission, the group relieves itself of painful awareness of its challenges and responsibilities.

Managerialism: The magic of technique

To be sure, American business organizations and schools of management have developed an impressive array of tools, ideas, and strategies that we would describe here broadly as constituting the content of management science. For example, Chandler (1962), via a careful historical analysis of the structural changes in major American industries, developed the proposition that changes in strategy drive changes in organizational structure. These ideas have driven empirical studies to test whether organizations that match structure and strategy outperform those that do not. At a different conceptual level, there are extensive writings on many aspects of organization behavior, goal setting, supervision, and performance appraisal, that have been studied in the context of their contributions to organizational effectiveness. Similarly, the vast body of sophisticated quantitive tools and methods aimed at enhancing decision making has been developed in management science. When these ideas and tools are pursued as ends in themselves and divorced from the purposes of organization they become a technocratic ideology that we term managerialism. The essence of managerialism is when a tool or technique of management is treated as a magical solution, and members invest their hope in the technique or approach as if it, by itself, will help resolve complex, conflictual situations.

Our argument centers around the emergence of a type of social defense which takes the form of a managerial ideology, cutting across all different types of settings. The explosive growth of business schools in the last two decades, and the ever-increasing emphasis on the analytic tools and techniques they teach speak to the hope invested in these methods of decision making in the private sector. The overt popularity of the MBA serves as testimony to the confidence placed in the analytic approaches of business schools.

The case material that we wish to discuss initially concerns the nonprofit and governmental sectors, and derives from our experience at an applied research center in a prestigious business school that was approached by outside groups for assistance with critical problems or for executive development programs. In reviewing a series of encounters with such varied fields as corrections, arts organizations, social service agencies, and health care institutions, recurrent themes appear in the attributions of numerous different outside groups onto the business school. In all cases involving these nonprofit institutions, we noted considerable distortion in their initial requests by imagining some magic that might lie within the business school. In each instance, this hopefulness was accompanied by an underestimating of the substantive leadership required for the revitalization or development they were seeking. Of necessity, this leadership could only be found in their own world, often requiring the working through of deep conflicts over issues of direction and purpose.

We argue that management was split off from leadership as a social defense to avoid the novel and complex challenges they were facing. Most of these organizations during the mid 1970's and early 1980's were facing transformative environmental shocks: the Reagan revolution in funding social services, the shift toward prospective payment in health care, the emergence of a get tough stance in corrections that resulted in massive overcrowding. They all were facing difficulties that called into question time-honored assumptions about mission and performance. Fleeing from deeper questions of purpose within their domains, many turned to the private sector with the belief that business can do "it" better (police, fire, social services, day care, postal service, finance the national debt, and so on). The language of business and business schools, marketing, strategic planning, "bottom line," and "product lines," came to be used by executives of non-business organizations to frame problems technically without confronting serious issues of mission and purpose that are at the heart of their contemporary difficulties.

Let us look at two cases in which representatives of the corrections and health care systems sought out a prestigious business school to help with the development of the field. In both cases, the overt request was for executive development in the respective systems. Yet, in both instances, we observed there were irrational, grandiose hopes that the joining might lead to some new resolution. There were features of the encounters that make sense only in the context of an unstated belief that the business school contains the magic tools that will cure the ills of the field. When these encounters are examined more closely, their defensive aspects become clearer.

In the area of corrections, for example, a major national organization approached the business school about running an executive development program for top leaders in corrections. A program was developed that focused almost exclusively on managerial processes, planning, organizing, controlling, and financing, with little direct attention to the substantive issues facing the field. Despite the presence of one of the top criminology departments in the country, there was no linking of the tools that were presumed to lie within the business school with the critical thinking that the criminology department might bring to the substantive and philosophical directions the field was facing.

The social defense of managerialism allowed the sponsors, the participants (senior managers in state and local correctional agencies), and the providers (faculty and staff of the business school) to be in contact with one another, yet avoid the difficult issues of purpose and mission that were and are central to the development of the field. The guiding hope of the efforts was that these fields could be transformed through the learning of managerial techniques alone. Efforts to link these discussions with the substantive questions of the field and with consideration of mission and purpose were resisted. Managerialism, then, was used to neutralize potentially divisive conflicts over deep values, such as the efficacy of rehabilitation and the death penalty. It also allowed participants to not confront differences between their espoused values and actual practices (Argyris & Schon, 1975).

Consider another example of the triumph of tools/techniques over mission and purpose. A major health care products company wished to develop an exclusive development program for top nursing officials in major teaching hospitals. Having long regarded their links to health care professionals as an integral part of corporate strategy, they believed that, in an increasingly competitive market place, improving executive capability might lead to a greater savings for hospitals than cutting costs on supplies. They approached the elite business school to develop a program for top nursing executives. The program has now been held for several years and is widely regarded as a major success. Yet, if we look closely at this program in its early years in light of the argument of this paper, a number of interesting features appear.

1. Despite the presence of a leading nursing school, the program initially did not involve the nursing school in a substantive way. This suggests that the "answers" to the dilemmas that the nursing profession are facing and that are swirling around the hospitals

were not felt to lie in the leading professional school but rather in a business school and the techniques it had to offer.

2. There was little discussion of the substantive issues facing the nursing profession. The lectures were on planning, organizing, managing people, working relationships, marketing, and finance, like a mini MBA program. On the few occasions in which there was a presenter with substantive credentials in nursing or health care, the participants often attacked the presenter and were angered and upset. Our hypothesis is that the presenters who dealt with ideas close to home shattered the fantasy that the acquisition of these magical business tools and techniques would be decisive when they return transformed by the experience. Alternatively, working with materials "too close to home" created anxiety about the intractability of the substantive challenges they face.

3. The projections from the outside were remarkable and again attested to the lionization of the business school. One participant described her surprise that her colleagues on the top management team at her hospital reacted as if 3 weeks at the prestigious business school were going to be a more powerful educational experience than her 2-year Masters in Nursing program.

4. The grandiose expectations surfaced when, in the middle of the 3 weeks, participants from prior years came back for a 3-day alumni event that mixed the groups. The reactions from the present group to the alumni were striking. The current participants experienced the alumni as invading, breaking up their group, looking tired, cynically, "very reality oriented and depressing." One participant commented on her disappointment: "I expected them to be mentors, but they were just like me." Another noted "I expected them to be bright and creative, yet they are not yet nursing leaders." In fantasy, participants hoped that acquiring the powerful tools of a business school would make them leaders, without confronting the difficult substantive issues in nursing.

These programs and others like them contain a powerful societal belief that management and the world of business contain the answers in responding to our problems. But this splitting of the substantive concerns from the managerial issues was a defense against confronting the painful dilemmas that would come from linking the two together. It operates in three ways.

1. By splitting techniques and tools from the substantive issues confronting the field in question, one neutralizes the powerful, often disturbing ideas from linking with the machinery of implementation, from provoking the group to work through difficult dilemmas and move toward authentic development. One consequence of this is to suppress some important conflicts and preserve group harmony at the expense of learning about differences and their impact on management practice.
2. By fleeing into the magical world of idealized techniques, one avoids having to confront painful, often political and conflictual issues that lie within the substantive realm.
3. The denigration and attack on leadership has elements of what Bion (1961) terms "basic assumption pairing." In these situations a prestigious business school or consultant and an organization or domain in distress join together and create a pairing dynamic in which the event is suffused with the hope that the union of these two will magically produce the new resolution, that one can somehow get to leadership programmatically, and that leadership is decomposable into a set of tools and techniques.[2]

The harmonious spirit that characterized the mood of the group of participants was achievable only be avoiding working on issues close to home that would provoke disagreements among the participants. They are unlikely to disagree over marketing concepts and even if they did, these are sufficiently removed from their daily worlds so as not to be threatening to the group's cohesiveness. Yet, we believe that in both the corrections and health care cases, the programs drew back from the anxiety-provoking, difference-confronting discussions that would have resulted from linking the managerial competencies with the issues of mission and purpose which is the *crux* of executive action and development.

Heroism: The search for heroic leadership

In contrast to the magical investment in business school techniques to free executives from the complexities inherent in their work, the alternative manifestation of the splitting of leadership and management is the search for, and creation of the heroic leader. This is the opposite of managerialism, namely the emphasis on inspirational leadership and the importance of values, purposes, culture, and the concomitant devaluing of administrative and bureaucratic processes.

Here we have the leader or executive as savior. But the current manifestation of this basic assumption dependency, in Bion's (1961) terms, has a particular flavor which is deeply contemptuous of organization itself. These charismatic heroes are distinguished for cutting red tape, overcoming turgid bureaucracies, ignoring formal processes, and relying on intuition and instinct rather than analysis or abstraction. In short, the mythology around these heroes sees the bureaucracy or organization itself as impeding success and accomplishment of the mission. And it is these independent, tough-minded men who won't let the risk-averse, business school manager keep them down. Reich (1985) has written insightfully about the pattern across many of the new texts that celebrate what he terms the "cowboy capitalists," loners, contemptuous of "bureaucracy, formal process, and intellectual abstraction" who shake up our sluggish institutions. Yet in the end, he argues, in keeping with our stance here, that the actual results of their work have been less noteworthy and that our celebration of these leaders may be distracting us "from deeper questions about the organization of our economic system."

The popular press abounds with such stories which can often be found on the best-seller list (Peters & Waterman, 1981; Iacocca & Novak, 1984; Geneen, 1984; Shoenberg, 1986; Trump, 1987; Wyder, 1987; Botero, 1987; Abodahen, 1986). Likewise, there has been a resurgence in the academic presses which are also looking to the personality traits of leaders as the crucial explanatory variable (Levinson & Rosenthal, 1986). While the personality characteristics of leaders are clearly a central factor (Kernberg, 1980), the lionization of the strong-willed leader in so much of the popular press and management literature obscures the far more complex realities of how organizations change or innovate (Reich, 1985).

One feature of heroism is to attribute to specific individuals the leadership which in reality is distributed more complexly in a system. As Reich (1985) writes "people prefer to idolize Iacocca than take in a more complex story" involving a team of highly talented people. When something like the Challenger disaster occurs, we suddenly realize with painful clarity the interdependencies and links between the persons on whom we project heroic properties and the management and administration that serves them.

Along with the celebration of the new business hero is the devaluing of the administrative apparatus, of the means of accomplishing purposes. For example, in *In Search of Excellence* (Peters & Waterman, 1982), there is implied contempt for many of the standard features of well-run organizations and denigration of staff units which, when deployed appropriately, can add significant value to an organization. The effect of idealizing the entrepreneur and creative leader has been to attribute the negative and frustrating aspects of organizational life onto the administrative and managerial realms.

The leader, as portrayed by these various accounts, is someone with a driving vision, a clear sense of purpose and mission which instills a guiding direction in the organization, mobilizes activity, and inspires commitment to that end. While the business heroes being so extolled were obviously deeply involved with the substantive issues in their respective areas, the burgeoning leadership literature pays little attention to engagement with the specific content of a field, preferring to focus on general principles of leadership and excellence.

The phenomenal popularity of *In Search of Excellence* illustrates an interesting twist on the managerial ideology of heroism. To be sure, the devaluing of the administrative apparatus was apparent in its spoofing of the MBA degree and the analytical tools and technical approach it represents while at the same time praising a new, visionary, inspirational type of leadership. Certain key phrases and code words entered business jargon (such as MBWA, "management by walking around," or using "excellence" as a strategic theme) and the notion of "excellence" became an emotional rallying point for many organizations and efforts. Paradoxically, however, these ideas were transformed into a set of techniques, tools, and recipes akin to the very things Peters and Waterman (1982) ostensibly set out to debunk.

Managerialism in heroic guise

As a tacit form of managerialism then, visionary leadership has been boiled down to a set of techniques. General statements about excellence and preeminence blur the mission definitions of one organization from another and supplant genuine leadership, direction setting, or an authentic reorientation toward new visions. By transmuting ideas of visionary leadership into a set of techniques and tools, the approach is transformed back into managerialism. One suspects that the meaning of MBWA (managing by walking around) extolled in *In Search of Excellence* is fundamentally different when used as part of a recipe for excellence from its origins in Hewlett-Packard where it was part of a real relationship between the leaders and scientists.

So while the visionary and innovative leadership may be the fashion, and for good reason, the ideology of managerialism reasserts itself in this guise. Efforts to celebrate the struggle with purpose and mission in making organizations adapt to modern conditions have been taken up in a way that does exactly the opposite, appeals to abstract qualities and obscures attention to the complex issues of mission and direction under turbulent conditions.

An aspect of this social defense is that, in efforts to emulate the heroic leaders so extolled in popular mythology, executives embrace these general techniques, shorn of content and context of a particular organization. Thus, the effort is to attain inspiration without linking direction to the bureaucracy. This is often accompanied by a fantasy that, having inspired the troops with appeals to "excellence," the managers will come alive and overcome their inertia. The image of the leader who guides the organization via direction setting and alignment, manipulating symbols alone and culture may represent all ill-founded hope that organizations can cohere without the exercise of authority. Such simplifying images can work against an appreciation by those in executive roles of the extent to which genuine leadership involves taking risks, grappling with uncertainties, containing contradictory information, and taking action under ambiguous conditions (Trist, 1976).

The "passion for excellence," as a general objective, has been taken up as an easy way to be a leader without dealing with the difficult specific issues that the particular organization is facing. So often we have seen mission statements developed around the newly popular ideas of excellence, service to customers, which then become a flight from the difficult issues that working closer to the primary task might evoke. Often these inspirational ideas are used to obfuscate understanding of difficult situations. For example, in one company "organizing for excellence" was the banner under which 20% of the employees were cut. Managers spoke of "rationalizing" certain manufacturing units, which translated into eliminating them.

Employed as a set of general, abstract inspirational principles by executives, heroism puts executives at risk. Let us look at a case of new leaders at two levels of the research and development arm of a major Fortune 500 industrial organization attempting to set a strategic direction. The president of a major technical support and research division, early in his tenure, began to discuss with his top staff a direction statement for the organization and guiding principles in the areas of people, technology, partnership, customers, and so on. He was beginning to shape these themes when budget cuts from higher up in the corporation forced him to restructure and make some deep cuts, particularly in the research group, which was halved from 200 to 100 despite his best efforts to protect this group. At this time, a new leader was also brought in to head the research division. After dealing with the downsizing during his first 3 months, he began a similar process within the research division to work on the unit's mission and guiding directions.

At a workshop attended by the top staff of the research group, they discussed their mission and developed a set of directions around which there was high consensus. As an observer of this process, one of the authors was struck by a moment when the work shifted from being developmental and clarifying, to being flight from work. The group had a shared sense of the major directions yet began to shift into an extremely focused discussion about words and phrases. The work on the mission became anti-task when people began to focus on the text and its wording in such a way that contained the magical belief that the document was self-implementing, as if getting the words perfectly would animate the requisite behavior. The flight from the appropriate next steps of thinking about concrete actions and strategies stemmed from the emotional denial of the tremendous cut. Cognitively, everyone knew that they had been halved in size, but they continued to imagine that they could do much of what was already begun as well as begin some new initiatives that were linked to the new strategic directions of the company. If they addressed specific tasks, they would inevitably come up against painful choices over what to do with limited time. Therefore, continued mission statement work actually became a defense against grappling with the realities of their current situation, providing a pseudo-leadership, severing goals discussions from the means of achieving them.

Similarly, at the next level up, the president of the technical and research arm had developed the mission statement for that level and planned to "launch" a new mission statement with video, buttons with a logo, and a fancy brochure. Many of the members of this organization who had participated in the development of the mission statement had felt that much of it was drawn from a similar statement that the same leader had developed in another organization. Despite his considerable talk about developing it collaboratively, many felt its main features were taken from his prior experiences.

Evidence that in the leader's mind the mission statement developed was loosely coupled to local realities was his reaction to a question the consultant posed about a key point on the "people-centered" section of the mission statement that stated "avoid serious injury to anyone." When asked if he regarded the 100 people who had been laid off as "injured," amazingly, it appeared to be the first time that he had made the connection. He seemed quite taken aback and reflected thoughtfully on the harm the organization had done to these individuals. This slippage of the defense of embracing mission development as a way of avoiding the painful realities of the situation suggest its dominant defensive function.

In looking at the search for heroic leadership as a social defense, we are referring to the ways in which many organizations are taking in the ideas about leaders and managers, not necessarily about the meanings and intentions of the original authors. For example, Peters and Waterman (1982) in *In Search of Excellence* talk about vision and values, but also stress the attention to details and follow through, arguing for the necessary linkage between the vision and the controls to make it happen. Yet, in the way the ideas are taken in by many organizations, they are often served, with some organizations taking in techniques, e.g., MBWA, close to the customer, and others taking in the broad leadership themes of excellence.

What is being defended against?

To the extent that these managerial ideologies are used by members of organizations as social defenses to reinforce and supplement individual-level defenses against anxieties, then the question must be raised as to the specific nature of these anxieties. While we have pointed several times to the painful difficulties involved in the profound innovations required to adapt to the emergent social fields in which organizations must now operate, the strength of our ideas will ultimately depend on the deeper understanding of the unconscious dimension of responses to these challenges and the anxieties they elicit. Here, we identify a set of anxiety-laden issues cutting across many organizational sectors which can begin to address the question of what is specific about this contemporary situation and why this particular set of issues might well evoke a distinctive set of primitive, painful doubts and anxieties.

Not only is more change required, but it is occurring at an accelerated rate (Ackoff, 1974). Under any conditions change is difficult and upsetting. Facing the unknown and uncertain future is in itself anxiety producing (Menzies, 1979). Furthermore, any organizational change threatens to disturb extant social defense systems, rendering members vulnerable to painful feelings from which they were being protected (Jacques, 1955). Change inevitably involves loss and mourning (Marris, 1975), evoking both angry and depressive responses in organizations (Trist, 1981).

In the shift from industrial to post-industrial forms of organization, demands are being made on organizations to innovate in profound ways, and in ways which penetrate deeply into members' ways of thinking and relating. Beginning with Burns and Stalker's (1961) distinction between the organic and mechanistic approaches to organizing, many have identified, categorized, and listed the emerging properties necessary for organizations if they are to thrive in modern times. Many of the adjustments called for can be understood to require type II learning, involving changes in the calibration of the system, its values, orientations, assumptions, and basic frameworks (Argyris & Schon, 1975). To name a few of those which, it can be hypothesized, are likely to be experienced as a threat to comfortable ways of being and stimulate severe anxiety:

1. In moving from a more placid to a more turbulent operating environment, organizations must cope with far greater complexity. Following Ashby (1956), the complexity internal to a system must match the complexity in its environment. Thus, members must contend with heightened complexity within as well as without, must live with and sustain the need for active, ongoing adaptation, and must sustain the capacity for continuous organizational

flexibility. The cult of the hero serves as a nostalgic defense against realizing the need to acknowledge the more complex, often painful ways in which leadership will be exercised.

2. The current emphasis on competition and service point to an increasing emphasis on close, individualized, and responsive relationships to customers across the enterprise boundary. Customer contacts which are less buffered by standardized procedure and routine make a far greater demand on organization members. It is far easier to champion the customer abstractly from high-up in an organization than concretely in a service encounter with a difficult, aggressive consumer.

3. As environments become more complex and turbulent (Emery & Trist, 1965), strategies must be more cooperative and collaborative as opposed to competitive. Paradoxically, collaborative relationships can be more anxiety producing than competitive ones. Just-in-time inventory systems, for example, make the company dependent on supplies outside of its direct control. Other examples include an emerging emphasis on labor-management cooperation and more self-management, public-private cooperation in community economic development. All call for major reorientations in the mindsets with which managers approach their work, acknowledging one's interdependence.

4. An increasing number of stakeholders are making a greater number of demands on organizations and those who manage them. The goals and purposes of a wide variety of enterprises are called into question as groups claim legitimate interests with respect to the resources used by particular organizations. As one labor leader commented, "twenty years ago I needed two concepts in my head—labor and management. Now when I make a decision I feel like I have 100 people in my head."

5. In connection with these changes, many of the former aspects of organizational life which met certain basic security and dependency needs are being removed (Miller, 1986; New York Times, 1987). Along with such turbulent conditions and seemingly constant reorganization efforts, many executives at high levels no longer enjoy the same level of job security as was previously customary (New York Times, 1987).

6. While an increasing number of people occupy professional roles, the rules governing professional life and behavior are

undergoing profound transformation. The historic norm of professional autonomy and practice orientation of technical rationality are giving way to vastly different professional roles in which professionals are increasingly embedded in their organizations and must increasingly struggle with value-laden issues underlying their technical expertise (Schon, 1983).

These features of the emerging post-industrial world are undoubtedly destabilizing expectations, creating massive uncertainty about the feature, and calling into question former patterns of family, work, and community life. Given what we know about the conditions under which anxiety is stimulated (Menzies, 1979; Hirschhorn, 1988), it is hard to imagine how current demands for innovation being made on our organizations and the concurrent demands for change and reorientation made on their members could fail to elicit deep, primitive, and painful anxieties.

This situation can be expected to yield, in many instances, an increase in the degree and potency of basic assumptions (Bion, 1961) functioning within these systems as the intense and volatile pressures will often overwhelm established ways of dealing with and modifying work-based anxieties (Krantz, 1985). Predictably, social defenses geared to these pressures are likely to emerge. Because the social forces we are considering here are on the level of the widest social ecology (Trist, 1976), it is not surprising that the social defenses erected to manage the associated anxieties will select from themes in the wider society rather than being differentiated by particular organizations or sectors. Managerialism, as a defense, enables people to evade those anxieties by creating an experience of technical mastery in a delimited area. Heroism, in contrast, binds anxiety with the comforting image of the person or idea that will magically deliver the organization to the future without its having to grapple with the real complexities and differences that surround it.

Conclusion

The challenges facing organizations to adapt and thrive in the turbulent environments of post-industrial society are daunting, and the potential stumbling blocks and barriers equally formidable. In this essay, we have been concerned with one such barrier, the emergence of a paired set of social defenses, appearing as managerial ideologies.

In both instances, we hypothesize that this domain-based defensive process represents a response which organizations are now having to make, in common, to the features of post-industrial society. In particular, the accelerating rate of social and technological change, far denser interdependences which yield uncontrollable environment turbulence, and the conflicting demands being made on institutions by diverse groups are posing painful realities in managing enterprises which we suggest are being evaded by the enactment of these two defensive stances.

The effect is one of surface innovation, but at a deeper level creating the conditions for maintaining the status quo at a time in which this systemic inertia is becoming increasingly maladaptive. We propose that this splitting stems from the anxieties inherent in attempting to lead/manage complex organizations in today's changing world, and comes to serve as a social defense against confronting many of these painful realities. Rice (1963) has argued that unless a leader has the competence to make a contribution to the primary task, he or she is ultimately confined to an administrative role. Conversely, unless leaders have access to the administrative apparatus, their visions cannot be realized.

While there is no rule that says leadership must be provided by a single individual who embodies all traits (leadership is often provided by a team in tandem), it is our hypothesis that the *overall* leadership of any enterprise, whether it is an organization or a unit of one must combine both the leadership and managerial aspects to be effective. Even when the roles of leader and manger are held separately, they both need to be respected and need to be integrated. The splitting of them, or dramatic ascendancy of one over the other creates a dangerous situation and puts the organization at risk, though this may not be immediately felt. Yet, on a different level, we suggest this splitting is inherently conservative. That by splitting apart leadership and management one is separating the new idea from the means to realize it. We suspect that an unconscious aspect of the split is the encapsulation and containment of the creative innovative ideas.

In sum, the splitting apart of leadership and management, with the concomitant idealization of one and denigration of the other leads to two distinct manifestations. One is mangerialism, the magical investment in technique and method. The other is heroic leadership, the magical hope for a savior from fossilized organizations. We believe both represent a societal level defense against the anxieties inherent in realizing the need for a deep restructuring of contemporary organizations in the face of emerging post-industrial society and in confronting the different world in which we live.

Acknowledgment

The authors would like to express their appreciation to Clayton Alderfer, Jonathon Gillette, Laurence Gould, Larry Hirschhorn, Eric Trist, Victor Vroom, and Abraham Zaleznik for their thoughtful comments concerning this paper.

Notes

1. Splitting, in a psychological sense, refers to a defense that is used by people to cope with doubts, conflicting feelings, and anxiety. It is a defense which enables the individual to separate the negative and positive feelings toward something, thereby reducing the complex and contradictory feelings associated with it. This is an intrapsychic maneuver commonly used to evade painfully ambivalent feelings people typically have toward important people, events, or objects.
2. Note that this is always in the future when the participants return, when they really master the techniques. Much of the disappointment that follows such events reveals the unrealistic hopes that were invested in them.

References

Abodahen, D. (1986). *Iacocca*. New York: MacMillan.
Ackoff, R. (1974). *Redesigning the future*. New York: John Wiley & Sons.
Argyris, C. & Schon, D.A. (1975). *Theory in practice: Increasing professional effectiveness*. San Francisco: Jossey Bass.
Ashby, W.R. (1956). *Introduction to cybernetics*. London: Chapman & Hall.
Barnard, C. (1938). *The functions of the executive*. Cambridge: Harvard University Press.
Bell, D. (1973). *The coming of post-industrial society*. Boston: Harper Colophon.

Bennis, W. & Nannus, B. (1985). *Leaders: The strategies for taking charge.* New York: Harper and Row.

Bion, W. (1961). *Experiences in groups.* London; Tavistock Publications.

Boguslaw, R. (1965). *The new utopians.* New York: Prentice Hall.

Botero, L. (1987). *Accidental millionaire: The rise and fall of Steve Jobs at Apple Computer.* New York: Random House.

Burns, T. & Stalker, G. (1961). *The management of innovation.* London: Tavistock Publications.

Chandler, A.D. (1962). *Strategy and structure.* Cambridge, Massachusetts: MIT Press.

Emery, F. & Trist, E. (1965). The causal texture of organizational environments. *Human Relations, 18*:21–32.

Emery, F. & Trist, E. (1973). *Towards a social ecology.* New York: Plenum Publishing Co.

Galbraith, J.K. (1967). *The new industrial state.* New York: Houghton Mifflin.

Geneen, H. (1984). *Managing.* Garden City, NY: Doubleday.

Heimann, P. (1952). Certain functions of introjection and projection in earliest infancy. In *Developments in psycho-analysis.* London: Hogarth Press.

Hirschhorn, L. (1988). *The workplace within.* Cambridge, Massachusetts: MIT Press.

Iacocca, L. & Novak, W. (1984). *Iacocca: An autobiography.* New York: Bantam Books.

Jacques, E. (1978). Social systems as a defense against persecutory and depressive anxiety. In M. Klein, P. Heimann, and R.E. Money-Kryle (Eds.), *New directions in psychoanalysis.* London: Tavistock Publications, 1955 (reprinted in *Analysis of Groups.* San Francisco: Jossey-Bass).

Kanter, R.M. (1983). *The changemasters.* New York: Simon & Schuster.

Kernberg, O. (1980). *Internal world and external reality.* New York: Jason Aronson.

Kouzes, J. & Posner, B. (1987). *The leadership challenge.* San Francisco: Jossey-Bass.

Krantz, J. (1985). Group process under conditions of organizational decline. *Journal of Applied Behavioral Science, 21*(1):1–17.

Lawrence, P. & Dyer. (1983). *The revitalization of American industry.* New York: Basic Books.

Leavitt, H. (1986). *Corporate pathfinders*. Homewood, Illinois: Dow Jones-Irwin.

Levinson, H. & Rosenthal, S. (1986). *CEO: Corporate leadership in action*. New York: Basic Books.

Marris, P. (1975). *Loss and change*. Garden City, New York: Anchor Books.

Menzies, I.E.P. (1960). The functioning of social systems as a defense against anxiety. *Human Relations, 13*:95–121. (reprinted in M. Kets de Vries (Ed.), *The irrational executive*. New York: International Universities Press, 1984).

Menzies, I.E.P. (1979). Staff support systems: Task and anti-task in adolescent institutions. In Hinshelwood and Manning (Eds.), *Therapeutic communities*. London: Routledge & Kegan Paul.

Michael, D. (1973). *On learning to plan and planning to learn*. San Francisco: Jossey Bass.

Miller, E. (1986). Making room for individual autonomy. In S. Srivastva and Associates (Eds.), *Executive power*. San Francisco: Jossey-Bass.

Miller, E. & Gwynne, G. (1972). *A life apart*. London: Tavistock.

Miller, E. & Rice, A.K. (1967). *Systems of organization*. London: Tavistock.

Morgan, G. (1988). *Riding the waves of change*. San Francisco: Jossey-Bass.

New York Times. (1987). Remaking the American C.E.O. (Section 3). p. 1.

Peters, T. & Waterman, R. (1982). *In search of excellence*. Newark: Harper & Row.

Pfeffer, J. The ambiguity of leadership. (1977). *Academy of Management Review*, 104–112.

Plamenatz, J. (1971). *Ideology*. London: MacMillan & Co.

Reich, R. (1985). The executive's new clothes. *New Republic*, 23–28.

Reich, R. (1987). Entrepreneurship reconsidered: The team as hero. *Harvard Business Review*, 77–83.

Rice, A.K. (1963). *The enterprise and its environment*. London: Tavistock.

Schein, E. (1985). *Organizational culture and leadership*. San Francisco: Jossey-Bass.

Schon, D. (1971). *Beyond the stable state*. New York: W.W. Norton & Co.

Schon, D. (1983). *The reflective practitioner*. New York: Basic Books.

Schwartz, H. (1993). Totalitarianism and symbolic management: Implications for organizational practice. 1985 Unpublished paper. [cf.

Schwartz, Howard S. (1987), On the psychodynamics of organizational totalitarianism. Journal of Management 13, 1, 41–54. Republished in The Psychodynamics of Organizations, Larry Hirschhorn & Carole K. Barnett (eds.). Philadelphia: Temple University Press.]

Selznick, P. (1957). *Leadership in administration*. New York: Harper & Row.

Shoenberg, R. (1986). *Geneen*. New York, NY: Warner Books.

Trist, E. (1976). A concept of organizational ecology. *Australian Journal of Management*, 2(2):161–175.

Trist, E. (1981). The evolution of sociotechnical systems. In A. Van de Ven and W. Boyce (Eds.), *Perspectives on organization design and behavior*. New York: Wiley.

Trump, D. (1987). *Trump: The art of the deal*. New York: Random House.

Tushman, M., Newman, W. & Romanelli, E. (1987). Convergence and upheaval: Managing the unsteady pace of organizational evolution. *California management Review*, 29(1).

Weber, M. (1947). *The theory of social and economic organization*. New York: The Free Press.

Wyder, P. (1987). *Iacocca: The unauthorized biography*. New York: Morrow.

Zaleznik, A. (1974). Charismatic and consensus leaders: A psychological comparison. *Bulletin of the Menninger Clinic, 38*, 222–238.

Zaleznik, A. (1978). Leaders and managers: Does it make a difference? *McKinsey Quarterly*, 2–22.

To explore the unconscious dynamics of transition as it affects the interdependence of individual, group and organizational aims in paradigm change

Harold Bridger

> *"The fish only realises that it lives in water when it is already on the bank."*
>
> —Old French saying
>
> *"A basic principle of groups ... how any given person was reconciling personal ambitions, hopes and fears with the requirements exacted by the group for its success."*
>
> —W.R. Bion
>
> *"The main emphasis today is that people want to arrive without the experience of getting there."*
>
> —Daniel Boorstin

Introduction

As this paper is intended to provide a basis for discussion I am writing in a form which represents more closely the fluid state of my thinking and working situations and not a definitive closely argued position.

I have always felt, and attempted to demonstrate, that psycho-analytic knowledge and psycho-analytic experience (as analysand and as analyst) can be of immense and significant value in the consultative practice of enabling organizations and communities to review themselves, adapt to change and continue maintaining their own further development (i.e., action-research). This conviction has increased and intensified as organizations and communities have become more open to their environments and those environments have become more uncertain, complex and turbulent than ever before. [1]

But, for me, psycho-analysis refers to the work being carried out by analysand and analyst on an individual basis. I doubt if we can use the term 'psychoanalysis of an organization' unless we are going to invent a method which would *specifically* enable that organization to examine its unconscious processes as well as its more conscious strategic, planning and operational behaviour under conditions involving transference, counter-transference and other aspects of psycho-analytic practice. The trap in which we may find ourselves—and this is pertinent to the main approach of my work and paper—is similar to that which pertains in contrasting 'occupational health' and 'organizational health'. In the former, the doctor and nurse tend to treat people in a captive practice and offer specialist advice in respect of the working environment, stress, etc. In the latter, the health team has also to accept responsibility for working on the ways the organization-as-a-whole with its mission, strategy, objectives, practices, activities and processes, is functioning to enable the individuals, functions, divisions etc., to exercise responsibility for their own health. (Fig. A)

Until recently, the interplay of the personality, psycho-pathology of the Chief Executive and other key figures in a variety of roles have, together with stress-research of various kinds, received most attention. This has allowed the use of psycho-analytic knowledge and experience most directly. However, if we are to recognise 'the organization-as-a-whole-with its tasks-in its environments' as our-client system then we need to face learning about such open systems and discovering, in the course of our practice (action-research), how this particular institution is functioning—consciously and unconsciously.

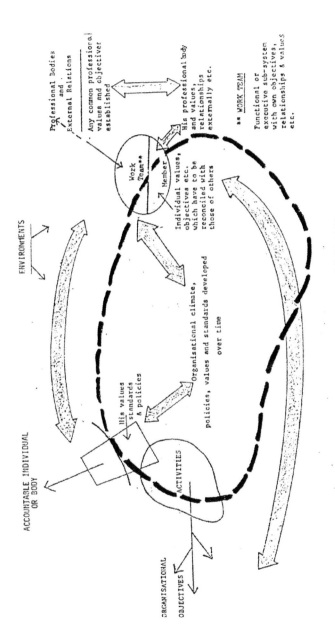

FIG. A: TENSION SYSTEM FOR A WORK TEAM MEMBER IN AN ORGANISATION*

* Adapted from: 'The value of the organisation's own systems in coping with stress.' H. Bridger, May 1977.
In: Reducing Occupational Stress, eds. A. McLean, G. Black & M. Colligan. The Proceedings of a Conference,
New York Hospital-Cornell Medical Center, May 10-12, 1977. Washington, D.C.: U.S. Dept. of Health, Education & Welfare

Such an approach demands more, much more than our current psycho-analytic knowledge and experience and our knowledge and experience of group therapy and group relations training equips us to fulfil.

In the War Office Selection Boards of World War II and in the First Northfield Experiment, Bion designed and very clearly stated the dynamics of groups-with-a-task and defined the roles of those observing or working with them. He distinguished these, as many have not done since, from the group therapy task and the role of the therapist. [2]

In the first instance we need to recognise that whilst the group-with-its-task comprises a number of individuals, the group organism is distinctively different from the individual one—for example, it is born and dies quite differently. And, despite volumes of books, theories and researches, we know little about the processes in the development of the 'group-with-its-task' organism compared with our knowledge of individual development. When we move to inter-group and the greater complexity of the organizational organism we are in deeper waters still. It is not surprising therefore that a certain rush of attention has been given to 'corporate culture' and this, at a time, when mergers, de-mergers and stock exchange power and intrigue have become rife. Survival for many—and not just in the business and commercial area, depends on criteria which have little to do with organizational health. But those that do address themselves to organizational viability through a self-viewing mode may, we hope, stand a better chance both internally and externally. We will certainly need to consider the various reality processes involved as well as the unconscious ones, if we are to appreciate how these interact, affect each other—and are used in different ways.

The institution, the organization and their leadership

Perhaps the most effective attempt to clarify and differentiate the concepts of institution and organization was that of Philip Selznick. [3]

> "The term *organization* suggests ... a system of consciously co-ordinated activities .... It refers to a rational instrument engineered to do a job .... It has a formal system of rules and objectives. Tasks, powers, procedures are set out according to some officially approved pattern. This pattern purports to say

how the work of the organization is to be carried on, whether it be producing steel, winning votes, teaching children or saving souls ... . We allocate tasks, delegate authority, channel communication and find some way of co-ordinating all that has been divided up and parceled out."

"An *institution*, on the other hand, is more nearly a natural product of social needs and pressures—a responsive, adaptive organism. This distinction is a matter of analysis, not of direct description. It does not mean that any given enterprise must be either one or the other. While an extreme case may closely approach either an "ideal" organization or an "ideal" institution, most living associations resist so easy a classification. They are complex mixtures of both designed and responsive behaviour ... . But when an enterprise begins to be more profoundly aware of dependence on outside forces (and on an internal socio-technical-political world—HB.), its conception of itself may change." [3]

Thus the process of adapting, of projecting and internalising, of learning and acting, unconsciously as well as consciously, is the *institutional* characteristic. The institutional leadership as distinct from personal leadership would require being *accountable* for developing the overall mission, ensuring its fulfillment through building the "distinctive competences" (another Selznick tern) in a committed critical mass of key people at all levels and functions, managing the boundaries of the institution with its environments and, not least, developing and disseminating modes of managing conflict. The latter being the natural concomitant of obtaining agreed decisions and actions from a wide diversity of interdependent functions and roles. A diagrammatic form attempting to illustrate some of the main *institutional* characteristics of an open system with its organizational components and inter-connections is set out in Fig. B.

For convenience and in deference to present day usage of "organization" in both senses, the term "organization" will, predominantly, be used. It is important, however, that the distinction of meaning should be clear.

It should also be noted in the footnote of the model that such an institution is both "purpose-oriented" and "learning and

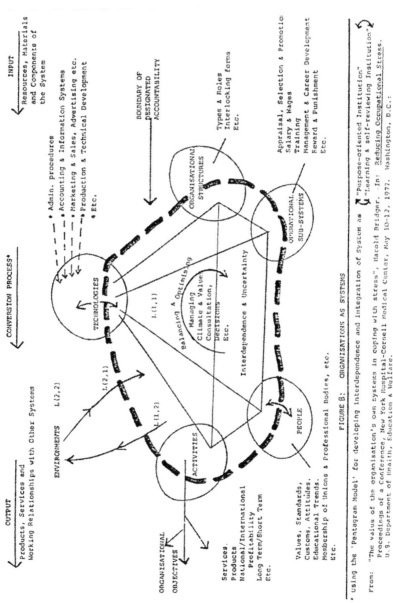

FIGURE B: ORGANISATIONS AS SYSTEMS

* Using the 'Pentagram Model' for developing interdependence and integration of system as ⤵ "Purpose-oriented institution" ⤴ "Learning & self-reviewing institution"

From: "The value of the organisation's own systems in coping with stress", Harold Bridger. In: Reducing Occupational Stress. Proceedings of a Conference, New York Hospital-Cornell Medical Center, May 10-12, 1977. Washington, D.C.: U.S. Department of Health, Education & Welfare.

self-reviewing". It is this *'double-task'* that I consider lies at the heart (and/or root) of effective, healthy and viable institutions today. The capability of carrying out this double-task at appropriate times and in the course of normal working when relevant will, it is suggested, become an essential feature in interdependent multi-disciplinary work forces. It is already a normal feature in sophisticated decision-making, strategy building and planning situations.

It has been my contention that where an organization and the professionals related to it conceive their tasks to include a better understanding of the working systems, and are prepared to learn about those organizational situations that give rise to conflict and stress, they also develop methods for preventing or working through these issues and problems. Where the professionals are also prepared to review their own organizational maps and work through variances shown up in their working with other functions and within their own, greater readiness will be shown by other parts of the organization to engage in collaborative re-thinking—and greater respect accorded to that profession.

The individual, organization and community— the characteristics of change

The boundaries of individuals, institutions and communities are so open to their various environments—and to the changes, uncertainties and complexities in them—that revised concepts of 'identity' (which include definition of associated contexts and environments) are required. For example, not so long ago the man who changed his job or organization to suit his interest or development was regarded as 'something of a rolling stone'. Today it is not infrequent for the question to be raised about the man who remains for a stretch of time in a function or side of affairs: "Has he certain limitations or did anything go wrong for him?" Even more recently governments as well as institutions and professions have demonstrated, with increasingly thin disguises, how 'out of control' the regulation of their boundaries and the management of their internal and external affairs have become. Economic, political and technical planning, changing values, attitudes and worth of resources have made that management of internal and external affairs more complex, uncertain and inter-dependent. The new dimension of 'turbulence' in the environment is not a temporary phase. It implies that groups and institutions as well as individuals will need to learn how to live as 'open systems' and derive identities in vastly different ways from the past. [4]

Similarly the educational and health systems whether national or local, whether in government or business, are having increasingly to be perceived not as quasi-permanent 'establishments' but as instruments or means for effectively carrying out national and community or institutional objectives. They are therefore required to be far more adapted to changing socio-psychological, economic and political situations as well as to changing technical developments. This holds true both in the external world as well as in the internal functioning of the particular social organism.

Implications for organizational processes, values, culture and roles

The individual thus finds himself, consciously and unconsciously, looking around for aspects of that society, or of institutions in it, which have a continuity of stability with *values, standards and cultural norms* that mirror those acquired and patterned in his own development and experience. Every human being has, over time, internalised a system of object-relationship configurations derived from his development and life experience—based on a combination of sound, fantasy and false premises. Similarly, he has built an external "identity" of knowledge, *roles*, skills, aspirations, hopes and fears. It has always been true that 'person', 'role' and 'value system' are concepts which are inextricably inter-related in any individual. E.g., a 'role' needs a person to fill it and the 'person' has been significantly developed by the roles he has carried in the past and the ones he is filling in the present; the value system permeates both. The last will, of course, be profoundly affected by the defences against anxiety which have been built in the course of establishing relationships, beginning with parental figures of earliest times; finding or failing

---

* *For, this reason, too, professional, functional and specialist institutions and networks also become more significant for that individual who, increasingly in his career pattern, is more mobile and less permanently related to a particular organization.*

to find membership in a variety of groups, filling roles with greater or less appropriateness and also with greater or less degree of successful outcome.

With the *increasing "openness"* of the boundaries of individual, group and institution to the changing, complex and sometimes turbulent environments in which they exist, the significance of roles, values, standards and cultural norms will become increasingly important for the person as a means of making initial contact and establishing forms of communication.* Greater and more intense difficulties and anxieties associated with recognising an 'identity' in others as well as resolving doubts and uncertainty about his own can therefore be understood as *realistic* and, at the least, not be regarded as an irrational element in the people concerned and in their relationships with each other. [5] Accompanying this phenomenon, and related to it, is the increasing tendency for people to 'belong' to many more groups and to have partial and temporary membership of others, whether for work, to benefit from various social services or for leisure activities.

With this tendency there is the increased mobility, and the psychological as well as social distance which affects those who 'stay put' as well as those who 'travel' in the course of fulfilling such assignments and activities. There will be varying and differing qualities of anxiety-driven elements in these societal changes and in the search for a new kind of security. It needs to be recognised and appreciated that rational and appropriate adaptations to change are taking place, internally as well as externally, in individuals, groups and organizations. The mode and culture of young people's parties, music and dancing have changed radically to counter anxiety as well as to gain new freedoms. It is not expected, therefore, that we should see some pro-active "explosions' in this process (e.g., demonstrations and student riots), some primitive reactive measures such as some business mergers and take-overs, and some planned innovations—such as super-markets, discount stores, and comprehensive schools. Professions are having to rethink their philosophies and values while there has been a general increase in the demand of people to have a relevant say in the decisions which affect them. The distinction between 'growth and development' on the one hand and protecting boundaries and resources on the other, has become blurred. Conflictual forces and attitudes have become part of existence and working life in ways which differ considerably from the days when the function of structure was to eliminate them. The need for a deeper understanding and analysis of the circumstances and processes within and between the human organisms of institutions or groups and their environments is reminiscent of the psycho-analytic model.

Perhaps one of the most striking examples of such multiple purposes inherent in the organizing of an institution was demonstrated in the Hospital Study conducted by I.E.P. Menzies [6] one purpose was clearly directed achieving hospital aims, the other, operated as a defence against the anxieties relating to nurses' involvement with patients suffering pain, ill-health and possible death. Unconscious collusive processes ensured that working through could not take place and a deeper order of stress led to poor morale and sickness absence among the nurses themselves.

Transitional processes

It is in these distinguishable yet inter-connected dimensions that 'entering' and 'leaving' groups become more highly significant reciprocal processes in which entering one culture, value system or set of role relationships may imply leaving another temporarily or permanently. This is happening at a rate and frequency which creates its own specific stress on individuals, families, and on the organisations and communities to which they belong. It may be that the "looseness" or "vagueness" of the group which is entered or left is not a sign of its 'openness' but rather an indication that it is not really a group but an 'aggregate' with a greater or lesser degree of social cover. This will occur not only in international settings and networks but in the growth of loose-knit communities which are trying to develop their own rationale for living.

The need for particular attention to be paid to the understanding and use of the "settling-in" process and "leaving" process in organizational life, training courses and conferences, group treatment and so on, is not a plea for some better or extended form of induction procedure. It is being suggested that in group therapy, group relations and other training situations, whatever the technique or approach used, there is, and will be, an increasing need to be aware of the roles and values which individuals bring with them into the group and which they use in their relationship with one another. These roles and values are important, too, in building the "institution" of the group which will provide them with the opportunity to develop further roles, and create another value system. It is also suggested that whether the technique used is concerned with the study of tensions either through inter-personal relations in a group setting or through a group-centred approach, the chances of hardening inappropriate defences or of intensifying unworked-through anxieties are likely to increase if the group itself is only deemed to consist of "people" without the roles they carry and the values they have built over the course of time—and if attitudes and behaviour of group members to each other are the main basis for expression and feedback. As a means of providing a basis on which aspects of roles and values can also emerge and be used in the service of the therapeutic or group training objectives, the writer has for some time used the "entering" process (which will, in varying degrees and depending on circumstances, entail leaving other groups) as the *task* of the group in its first phase. At other times group work may be "suspended" to explore methods of working, values, standards, norms and customs which the group has evolved so far. In the terminal phase the "leaving process" has also been used as the task of the group.

If we are not to create or use our organizations as defenses against anxiety when we can better develop inner resources and capabilities for more appropriate competences, then we need to acquire more suitable 'transitional objects' (Winnicott) (5) in our organizational settings—not just to bridge a painful gap or episode, but one that provides the awareness on which the individual or group can build further. From earliest times in the child's life we have various forms of a transitional object to act as 'cover' for the inner work such as sorting out the 'me'/'not me' confusion in the earliest months of life.

Just as the teddy bear itself is a necessary appropriate 'clothing' for the "area of illusion" (Winnicott) within which the child can try-out, test-out and work-through issues, problems, tensions and reactions going on *within* him/her in the *context* of a puzzling, helpful, frustrating, loving, rejecting, triumph-offering, humiliating etc., world, so we need at all later stages appropriately 'clothed and coloured' objects or situations to enable us to learn to cope with increasingly complex phases or stages. We also have to unlearn some of those coping modes and methods of behaving which stood us in good stead in the past but which become (whether recognised or not) inappropriate for the present and future. Residues of past resolved and unresolved 'settlements' together with a greater involvement and pressure from environmental forces of many kinds may well interfere, warp or blur our preparatory planning and speculating about the future. We require more sophisticated 'transitional objects' and 'transitional systems' to deal with such increasingly complex phases and stages. At the community and organizational level, however, the groups and institutions themselves become organic entities in their own right and we need to incorporate the appropriate dynamics into our working or social system.

Dynamics of the psycho-analytical situation and those of groups and organizations

In psycho-analysis the group of two [7] begins by the patient being given the task of "saying what comes into his mind as far as he can". The conscious and unconscious implications of all that is said at the beginning cannot be comprehended to the extent which will be possible as the analysis progresses. On the other hand, characteristics and difficulties associated with beginning a relationship with another person do become apparent in the transference and counter-transference. The different forms which this initial dominant theme of "beginning" may take represent a basis on which the analyst-patient relationship grows. This relationship becomes the temporary or transitional institution which is itself used as an instrument for enabling the patient to develop his insights, understanding and personal resources. Freud's genius in recognising and developing the concept of transference and P. Heimann's [8, 9] contributions and those of others to the development of the concept of counter-transference as means of effectively engaging those 'institutional components' in the service of the objectives of the analysis also had another important consequence. While the an alytic situation could be seen as an "organization of two" for fulfilling certain purposes, meeting at a certain hour in the day, for so many days a week, and its own reality within the lives of the patient and analyst, the 'institution' was effectively being regarded as subject to continuous re-appraisal. It was treated as existing for finite time, finite in the sense of being dependent on reality factors in the lives of analyst and patient as well as on the time required for the analytic task to reach appropriate termination. [10]

The insight and learning which is by confronting the loss of 'institution' and its implications in the life and relationships of the patient—past, present and future—gives the termination phase a special place in the analysis. The reality-testing which has been a continuous feature of the analytic work will, we expect, develop new dimensions in the patient himself through which he will be able to take over some of the sensibility and 'instrumental' aspects of the transference and counter-transference when the 'institution' is terminated. The internalised 'learning-institution' with its growing points continues with its values to help the individual in his development.

One of the first attempts to apply principles and concepts corresponding to the dynamics of the psycho-analytic process through an organizational rather than in a group setting alone, was made in 1943 when the nature, characteristics and processes of a large hospital institution were themselves employed in the therapeutic task. This entailed engaging all levels, roles, functions and services in recognising and confronting a situation which had dynamic equivalence to therapeutic tasks being conducted by psychiatrists in individual and group treatment. [11]

Another attempt took place almost simultaneously in the growth of an organization of twenty combined civilian and army transitional communities to assist in the social re-connection of repatriated prisoners-of-war. [12]

Since that time there have been many further experiences developed from this early work in establishing more effective methods in collaborating with organizations in their efforts to adapt more insightfully to change—and to maintain the reviewing process.

Research, training, therapy and the wider society

It has, however, been a striking feature of the contemporary scene that it has been the industrial organization rather than academic institutions and centres which have engaged in research and development along these lines. They increasingly began to recognise the organization as an organismic dynamic structure of roles, values, etc., to be kept under review and adapted to change in the light of the social needs of the wider society as well as their own objectives. In some cases, they have taken the step of building "internal institutions" whose function it is to collaborate with external professional social scientists in continuing and deepening the value of the work. [13] It is perhaps not, after all, so surprising when one realises the accelerating rate of change in the many facets of society today.

The psycho-analyst, in particular, has to contend with understanding this world in which his patients are working, living and developing values and standards so different from the past. Whatever changes in theory or technique may arise in the future with developing research and creative practice, it is certain that even today it is important to understand the changing cultures and to recognise group, community and institutional processes that affect awareness and communication between patient and analyst.

Without this understanding the very nature of the transference and counter-transference can be adversely affected while the free associations of the patient and the interpretations of the analyst will be that much less relevant.

The various researches and developments which have taken place over a number of years have certain implications for the roles of the group therapist and social scientist and the techniques they employ in group therapy, group relations training and training institutions more generally. [14] Unfortunately and all too frequently, psychoanalysts assume that their field pre-empts any necessity to study external social change. Indeed it is often felt to be a "dilution" of skill and commitment.

There is an overdue need for psycho-analysts and social scientists in particular to engage in much greater collaboration and mutual learning in joint tasks, as well as in the need to acquire appropriate understanding and knowledge from the different disciplines employed. Only in these ways will more integrated approaches and methods be developed to meet the changing nature and characteristics of the groups, including the psycho-analytic group of two, with whom we may be working, and in the changing environments of which the individuals and those groups are themselves part. [15]

Otherwise we will find ourselves unable to comprehend the gropings of young people in their searching out new career patterns, and of younger patients seeking health in present day and future society. We shall find, as in all other careers undergoing changes today that there will need to be an "education permanente" for us all which we will have to allow for as a continuous feature ('institution') of our continued work in these fields.

It will be a process going far beyond the limited learning we might derive through some academic study in each other's disciplines but might, as has been indicated above, develop out of greater collaboration.

References

1. Emery, F.E. and Trist, E.L. (1965). "The causal texture of organizational environments." *Human Relations, 18*:21–32.
2. Bion, W.R. (1946). "The Leaderless Group Project." *Bull. Menninger Clin., 10*:77–81.
3. Selznick, P. (1957). *"Leadership in administration."* Harper & Row.
4. Bridger, H. and White, S.F.T. (1972) *"Towards a policy for health of the manager": In:* Hacon, R.J. (ed.) *Personal and organizational effectiveness.* New York: McGraw-Hill, pp. 240–255.
5. Winnicott, D.W. (1971). *Playing and reality.* Tavistock Publications.
6. Menzies, I.E.P. (1970). The functioning of social systems as a defence against anxiety. London: Tavistock Institute of Human Relationships.
7. Rickman, J. (1957). "The factor of number in individual and group dynamics." Selected contributions to Psycho-Analysis, London 1957.
8. Heimann, P. (1950) "On counter-transference". *Int. J. Psycho-Analysis, 31.*
9. Heimann, P. (1960) "Counter-Transference." *Brit. J. Med. Psychol., 33.*
10. Bridger, H. (1950) "Criteria for the termination of analysis." (Short paper in a Symposium), *Int. J.-Psycho-Anal., 31*: –203.
11. Bridger, H., Main, T.F. and Bion, W.R. et al (1946). "The Northfield Experiment." *Menninger Bulletin,* May 1946.
12. Trist, E.L. and Curle, A. (1948). "Transitional Communities." *Human Relations, Vol. 1,* Nos. 1 & 2.
13. Bridger, H., Miller, E.J. and O'Dwyer, J.J. (1963). "The role of the doctor and sister in industry." *Occupational Health, 15.*
14. Higgin, G.W. and Bridger, H. (1965). The psychodynamics of an intergroup experience. *Human Relations, 17*:391–446, 1963. Reprinted as Tavistock Pamphlet No. 10, 1965.
15. Bridger, H. (1971) A viewpoint on organizational behaviour. In: Wolstenholme G. and O'Connor, M. (eds) *Teamwork for World Health.* London: J. & A. Churchill, Ciba Foundation Blueprint.

Psychoanalytic frameworks for organizational analysis and consultation: An overview and appraisal of theory and practice

Laurence J. Gould, Ph.D.

Introduction

It may be said that within psychoanalysis the application to organizational life began with Freud's (1921) consideration of the Church and Army. In this connection Freud linked certain dynamic aspects of these organizations to his earlier hypotheses regarding the origins of social process and social structure—namely, the primal horde (1913). While Freud never directly followed this line of thought further, except generally in his later sociological works (1927, 1930, 1939), there is, by now, a rapidly growing and impressive body of literature on psychoanalytic conceptions of organizational behavior (e.g., Baum, 1987, Bion, 1961; Hirschhorn, 1988; Jacques, 1951, 1955; Kernberg, 1979; 1984; Kets de Vries, 1984; Kets de Vries and Miller, 1984; Lawrence, 1979; Levinson, 1972; Menzies, 1960, 1988, 1989; Miller, 1976; Miller and Gwynne, 1972; Miller and Rice, 1967; Rice, 1958; Trist and Murray, 1990; Zaleznik, 1967, 1984). However, despite this rich and abundant interest, little work has been reported with respect to developing techniques and methodologies for the practice of organizational consultation which derive from these conceptions. The reasons are numerous and can be briefly adumbrated.

Psychoanalytic organizational psychology is still in its infancy compared to clinical psychoanalysis. Further, many of those interested in applying psychoanalytic viewpoints to their organizational consultation work are not clinicians, much less psychoanalysts. Hence, such practitioners usually have little knowledge of, or direct experience with the sorts of technical issues, questions and dilemmas that are at the heart of psychoanalytic treatment. Equally, most practicing psychoanalysts do not do organizational consultation work, and indeed the majority have little experience working with groups of any sort, to say nothing of large formal organizations. In consequence, the different backgrounds and experiences of psychoanalytically trained clinicians, and organizational practitioners, have a counterpart in the almost non-existent area of psychoanalytic practice and technique in group and organizational work settings.

A related factor is the strong and pervasive intrapsychic and narrowly interpersonal (dyadic and triadic) biases of psychoanalysis—even among many of those who practice psychoanalytic group psychotherapy! Therefore, at best, trans-individual psychoanalytic methods and perspectives have been slow to develop. Another issue is the rather marked differences in the culture of psychoanalytic clinical practice compared to that of organizational consultation. The core clinical modes in psychoanalysis are the *processes* that result in healing and transformation. In the organizational sphere an emphasis on *results* or *outcomes* is the prevailing norm—among practitioners as well as clients. What this means, in effect, is that in organizational work a more pragmatic attitude prevails, with little concern about process or the "purity" of the intervention. Therefore, instead of developing psychoanalytic strategies with the inevitability of technical variations and parameters (e.g., Eissler, 1953, 1958) to accommodate special circumstances, as is most often the case in clinical work, even the psychoanalytically oriented organizational practitioner usually feels free to do whatever seems to work, using many sorts of non-psychoanalytic techniques, strategies, and interventions, (as well as invoking many non-psychoanalytic viewpoints [e.g., open-systems theory; family systems theory; communications theory; a variety of sociological and social psychological viewpoints, etc.]). The effectiveness of an eclectic approach notwithstanding, the result is that little is developed in the way of psychoanalytic technique, or more precisely a theory of psychoanalytic practice in work group and organizational settings.

Finally, the major obstacles to developing such a theory are the different temporal expectations, and the relatively "uncontrolled" nature of the organizational setting, compared to that of clinical practice. Here the issue is not simply one of complexity, but rather the stability and constancy of the environment within which the work is being conducted, and the control of the relevant boundaries. In clinical work the patient comes to the psychoanalyst's office, and in accepting treatment agrees to the conditions which the analyst outlines such as fee, schedule, time-frame, technical procedures, and "psychological contract" (e.g., the analyst's "neutrality," the sanction to interpret, the use of the couch, etc.). By contrast, the organizational consultant enters the client's setting and system, and attempts to negotiate a viable work contract. But "turbulence" in the client system, the necessity for working with groups whose composition may vary, individuals whose schedules may vary, and the exigencies of the client's coping with the press of day-to-day demands, all conspire to make the likelihood of setting up and maintaining a regular, predictable and "protected" work environment extremely small. To even suggest then that there may be organizational analogues to the technical procedures of psychoanalysis, that can be utilized for more than the span of one meeting, may itself be viewed as a naive fantasy in the work context, where it is often difficult to simply keep one's wits about one, and remain "right side up." Such "buffeting" is a far cry indeed from the sheltered, controlled and relatively enduring character of the psychoanalytic situation. And it is precisely these qualities and characteristics of the psychoanalytic situation which, in fact, defines the core of psychoanalytic practice as originally articulated in Freud's (1911–1915) papers on technique.

In summary, if "the couch is at sea" (to slightly paraphrase the felicitous title of Kernberg's (1984) paper on organizational psychology) what, in fact, remains of technique? Has it, to continue this metaphor, been swamped or left to languish on a distant shore? In any case it is not much in evidence in psychoanalytic approaches to work group and organizational consultation. In what follows, therefore, a necessarily selective overview and appraisal of psychoanalytic theory and practice related to work group and organizational consultation will be outlined and developed. It should be noted, however, that the intention is not to provide answers for the many obvious questions as to the feasibility and utility, if any, of developing organizational analogues to the technical procedures of psychoanalysis. Rather, a conceptual "typing" will be used to locate and assess the current state of work group and organizational consultation techniques and strategies informed or directly guided by psychoanalytic theory. This will be followed by a brief commentary and discussion, with an emphasis on the advantages of utilizing psychoanalytic perspectives and consultation techniques to work with organizational disturbances and conflicts at the individual, group and systems level. It is hoped that this discussion may provide a useful starting point for a more extended and systematic consideration of the issues related to furthering this enterprise, which for reasons suggested earlier, have generally been neglected.

Psychoanalytic theory and types of practice

While quite oversimplified, two types of work group and organizational consultation practice can be distinguished within a psychoanalytic context as shown in Figure 1. Type I practice utilizes the technical procedures and methods of psychoanalysis, while Type II practice uses psychoanalytic theory to guide an eclectic array of methods and procedures which may include, but are not restricted to those considered psychoanalytic. It should be explicitly noted that these types are distinguished for heuristic purposes only. In practice they most often overlap or shade into each other. Finally, in order to provide a more complete perspective on these types, examples of some psychotherapeutic and educational modalities that are comparable to, or analogues of work group and organizational interventions, will also be indicated and briefly discussed.

Type I (utilization of the technical procedures and methods of psychoanalysis)

This type includes, of course, psychoanalysis proper, and the variations of psychoanalytic psychotherapy. The major training modality of this type is the group relations conference which derives from a tradition developed at the Centre for Applied Social Research of the

Type I Utilization of the Technical Procedures and Methods of Psychoanalysis	Type II Utilization of Non-Psychoanalytic Methods and Techniques

Δ Psychoanalysis and Psycho-
    analytic Psychotherapy
# Group Relations Workshops 	
    and Conferences
• In-House Group Relations
    Conferences
• Psychoanalytic Process
    Consultation
• Organizational Role Analysis
	Δ Psychodynamic
	    Psychotherapy
	# Levinson Institute and
	    Menninger Seminars
	• Socio-Technical
	    Interventions
	• Active Process Consultation
	• Multi-Modal/Multi-Level
	    Intervention

Δ Psychotherapeutic Interventions
Training and Educational Methods
• Organizational Interventions

Figure 1. Types of work group and organizational consultation based on psychoanalytic theory.

Tavistock Institute of Human Relations in London, under the leadership of the late Dr. A. K. Rice (1965) and his colleagues. The primary task of these conferences is to provide members with opportunities to study the nature of leadership and authority, and the interpersonal, group and intergroup problems encountered in their exercise. To implement this task, participants are involved in a number of group events (e.g., the small group, the large group, the intergroup, the institutional event, etc.) that provide opportunities to experience and examine their membership and behavior in varying group configurations, and in the conference as a whole. The basic staff role is to provide consultation *vis-a-vis* taking up a psychoanalytic stance of neutrality, and offering interpretations of covert and unconscious group processes, with an emphasis on transference and countertransference manifestations as these may illuminate the vicissitudes of authority relations. The hope is that the ability to exercise leadership and authority effectively in one's back-home work roles will be enhanced by a heightened awareness and understanding of how these processes and forces operate in group and organizational situations.

One major example of an organizational intervention strategy based on the above is the in-house group relations conference. While little has been published to date on such events, several have been held. However, an example of an abbreviated version can be found in Gustafson and Hausman (1975) in which they utilize the paradigm of the intergroup event (e.g., Astrachan and Flynn, 1976) to examine and clarify conflict in a small psychiatric organization. The basic model for designing such an intervention is to utilize one, or a combination of several events derived from group relations conferences, with a membership composed of individuals who are a natural work group, or groups, or the totality of an organization. This contrasts to the typical situation in the group relations conferences offered as training, in which the participants are, for the most part, strangers from different organizations.

Another example of the application of the group relations conference methodology is to be found in Miller's (1977) work in Belfast. A group relations conference was designed for interested individuals "representing" major political and/or sentient groupings (see, Miller and Rice, 1969) such as: Catholics and Protestants; working and middle-to-upper classes; youth and adults; and, males and females. The hope was that an exploration and understanding some of the powerful unconscious individual and group level phantasies at work in the relative safety of the conference setting, and the ways in which these were projected onto others, would generalize, and thereby enhance the leadership potential of the participants in reducing conflict and fostering community development in the back-home environment.

Finally, there are also variants of the group relations conference approach to be found in the creation of in-house analogues to the various group events. For example, a number of psychiatric institutions have adopted a form of the large group event (Turquet, 1975) by holding regular patient-staff community meetings which are conducted as self-study groups (e.g., Edelson, 1970a and 1970b). The purpose of such meetings is to examine the covert forces in the unit or service which may impede (or facilitate) the therapeutic task.

In addition to the above, there is another approach to organizational development which is based on systematically providing group relations training for key staff of an organization. Typically, in this approach, small groups of staff members are selected over a period of time to attend group relations conferences until there is a critical mass who are "trained" (Menninger, 1972, 1985). A variation is to do the training in-house in a series of workshops until the whole staff has been through the experience (e.g., Johnson and Fleisher, 1980). The rationale for this approach is that the "training" of a sufficient number of staff in key positions of authority will *naturally* facilitate constructive organizational change and development as a function of increased awareness of destructive covert processes and authority relations, a lowering of anxiety and resistance to change, and an increased capacity for sophisticated leadership and followership.

Another organizational application of psychoanalytic theory and technique is exemplified in what may simply be termed psychoanalytic process consultation—or in Bion's (1961) terms "therapy of the group," (as distinct from "group therapy"). The general model is for a consultant to join the regular meetings of a natural work group (or an organizational group specifically created for the purpose of fostering organizational change) and to interpret process in much the same way that a consultant would function taking a small study group in a group relations conference. It is more usual, however, that in consultations to an organizational work group, there is some shift away from interpretations that specifically and systematically focus the group's relationship to the consultant (although these would be made if necessitated, for example, by manifestations of excessive dependency) to relations between the group members themselves and their approach to the task at hand. This shift in emphasis highlights the fact that the approach is different when the task is consultation, as distinct from training.

Finally, there are a variety of consultations to individuals, focusing specifically on how they take up their work roles, that combine psychoanalytically based theories of individual and group behavior, and psychoanalytic methods. One such approach typically takes the form of a time-limited series of consultations with an individual (Reed, 1976). In these consultations (generically called "organizational role analysis" [ORA]), techniques that derive from projective or semi-projective methods (e.g., the production and analysis of "mental maps"), the solicitation and interpretation of dream material and fantasies, and supportive/interpretive interventions are all utilized. This form of consultation can be especially useful in situations in which a key executive or manager in the client system has either taken up a new role, needs to reassess role performance in light of changing organizational circumstances, or is experiencing chronic difficulties in functioning effectively. With regard to the latter, time-limited consultations may also be useful in helping an individual more clearly recognize major characterological issues and tendencies which may impinge on role performance (Kernberg, 1979, 1984), if they are not so severe as to be uninfluenced by insight, which can be translated into more adequate self-management.

Type II (utilization of non-psychoanalytic methods and techniques)

Therapeutically, the whole gamut of eclectic and/or psychodynamically informed modalities are included in this type. These are (most often) characterized by the selected use of psychoanalytic concepts and explanations to either design more "active intervention strategies" (e.g., Wachtel, 1977), or simply as the backdrop for helping a patient or client focus on, or clarify an issue which is the source of emotional distress. In organizational work, many interventions are an analogue of the former—namely, the use of a psychoanalytic understanding of human behavior to design an intervention strategy. It can be said that much, if not most, of the socio-technical work developed originally at the Tavistock Institute is of this variety. Parenthetically, it should be noted here, that on the psychological side, this work is largely based on the object-relations theories of Klein (1948), Bion (1961), and their colleagues, in contrast to the organizational work indigenous to the United States, which has its origins more in classical and ego psychological viewpoints (e.g., Levinson, 1972a; Zaleznick, 1967, 1984). In this connection it should also be noted that Kernberg (e.g., 1980, Part 1) has attempted to integrate these perspectives.

An essential element of the Tavistock perspective is to differentiate between behaviors and activities geared toward rational task performance (Bion's "Work [W] Group"), and those geared to emotional needs and anxieties (Bion's "Basic assumption [ba] Groups"—Fight/Flight [baF], Dependency [baD] and Pairing [baP]), which are viewed as being rooted in early experiences, and having manifestations in unconscious phantasies. Specifically, this view posits the existence of primitive anxieties (of a persecutory and depressive nature), and the erection of individual and "social defense systems" (Menzies, 1967; Jacques, 1955) against them. Such defenses are conceptualized as either impeding or facilitating task performance, adaptation, and response to change. Bringing this view to bear is at the heart of the Tavistock socio-technical approach to organizational analysis and development strategies. Interventions based on such strategies typically involve redefining and redesigning some, or all, of the following: tasks; work sequences; administrative procedures; and, organizational structure. Major early exemplars of this approach are to be found in the works of: Trist and Bamforth (1951) on the psychological consequences of technological changes in a British coal mine; Rice's (1958) efforts to re-organize the work relationship structure in the weaving room of an Indian textile mill; Menzies' (1967) study and action research in a hospital nursing organization; and, Jacques' (1950) and Jacques, Rice and Hill's (1951) attempt to change the method of wage payments in a department of a light engineering factory. In all of the above, organizational change efforts were geared toward providing a better fit between work tasks, work activities, organizational structures, and administrative procedures on the one hand, and the social defense system on the other. Typically, as noted, these efforts, while guided by a psychoanalytically informed appraisal of the situation, involved some form of reorganizing and redesigning work including, for example, the creation of new groupings such as autonomous work groups (e.g., Rice, 1958).

In the United States, organizational applications of psychoanalytic perspectives more typically take the form of active and focused process consultation to work groups, directive and supportive consultations with key individuals, or a variety of large-scale multimodal, multi-level interventions which may overlap with the socio-technical systems work outlined above.

The most common form of Type II process consultation differs from its Type I counterpart in that it is usually more active, supportive and directive, and rarely make explicit, (through interpretation), transference material. The focus is almost exclusively on the group itself, and again, compared to the Type I model the interpretations are more didactic, developed, and generally aimed at the manifest level of group process. Awareness of the primitive, covert or less conscious aspects of the process are used by the consultant to guide the group, and to more sensitively facilitate its work through an appreciation of the underlying anxieties, conflicts and dilemmas.

A well-developed example of the kind of large-scale, multi-modal, multi-system intervention, noted above, is to be found in the work of Kets de Vries and Miller (1984). They provide a case study of a family lingerie business in which powerful unconscious dynamics were creating and intensifying organizational difficulties. The intervention methodology they ultimately adopted, based on a careful assessment and diagnosis of both individual and organizational difficulties included: helping to rationalize the organization (e.g., by providing clearer definitions of responsibilities and lines of authority); suggesting personnel changes and reassignments; offering supportive and/or insight-oriented psychotherapy and counseling for key individuals; giving common-sense business advice; and encouraging appropriate executives to participate in a psychodynamically based management training program with senior executives from other companies.

In effect then, the psychoanalytically informed consultant uses psychoanalytic theory, conceptualization and insight to diagnose and identify emotional "hot spots" on the individual, group and/or organizational level, and designs consultations and/or multimodal intervention strategies based on these assessments. In this approach the consultation strategy takes into explicit account the ways in which the system is "driven" and distorted by powerful unconscious processes and anxieties, and the concommitant defences against them, but it neither attempts to interpret these, nor work them through, directly.

Finally, there are several management development and management training programs that are directly based on psychoanalytic theory, but compared, for example, to the group relations conference model outlined under Type I, they either use more conventional educational methods such as lectures and discussion groups, or modified experiential learning approaches. Examples of the former include the well known executive development programs offered by the Menninger Foundation (B. Rice, 1979) and the Levinson Institute. Examples of the latter (which are usually more structured and focused versions of group relations conference events—particularly the small group event)—are to be found in a wide variety of training programs such as those originally developed for post-graduate social workers and general practitioners (e.g., Balint, 1959; Gosling, et al., 1967).

Summary

It should be apparent from the foregoing discussion of each of the Types, that psychoanalytic theory and procedures applied to work group and organizational situations can be used, separately, or in combination with non-psychoanalytic methods and techniques in a wide variety of ways. As noted in the introduction, this state of affairs generates a large number of obvious questions and issues regarding the circumstances, conditions and criteria for making critical decisions when planning and implementing an intervention. In the next section, both some general and specific points related to these concerns will be briefly enumerated and discussed, in order to clarify and provide a focus, for beginning an appraisal and consideration of the issues germane to advancing the practice of a psychoanalytic organizational psychology.

Discussion

As a starting point for discussing the implications of the foregoing account of the practice of a psychoanalytically-based organizational psychology, and the issues alluded to above, I will use, as an organizing framework, the familiar triadic nature of psychoanalysis: as a theory of human behavior; as a method for the in-depth investigation of mental processes; and, as a treatment for mental and emotional illness. In what follows I would like to discuss these three interrelated aspects of psychoanalysis in turn, as they apply to the theory and practice of organizational consultation.

Psychoanalysis as a theory of human behavior

I believe that the richness and diversity of many of the contributions, noted previously, are more than ample testimony to the generative power of psychoanalytic theory when used as a basis for describing and understanding significant aspects of organizational behavior at many levels, including: the dilemmas of an individual manager; the impact of small group processes on task performance; and, how the culture and character of the organization as a whole may have a profound influence on the behavior and emotional well-being of its members. Further, I believe that a psychoanalytic perspective can be viewed, in general, as having considerable utility in guiding our interventions, of whatever variety. In this connection two broad considerations may be offered as examples. First, as Levinson (1972b) argues, the failure to diagnose adequately, as a basis for planning interventions, may have serious and unintended consequences. These can occur when an intervention does not take sufficient cognizance of the depth and complexity of the psychological forces at work on individuals and groups. A similar point is made by Jacques (1955) who notes that "the character of institutions is determined and coloured not only by their explicit or consciously agreed and accepted functions, but also by their manifold unrecognized functions at the phantasy level." Since such functions include important individual and social defenses against anxiety, interventions that do not take this into account may have little enduring impact, or worse yet, may catalyze considerable anxiety and concomitant decompensation, if these defenses are inadvertently breached. It is my contention, therefore, that the sort of fundamental appreciation and comprehension of the power of unconscious processes that a psychoanalytic perspective affords us, is a useful general antidote to all sorts of inadvertencies, even if it does not yet help us to design our organizational interventions with more technical precision.

Psychoanalysis as a method for the in-depth investigation of mental processes

While I believe that the foregoing conclusion is arguably demonstrable, it begs an essential question related to the issues of psychoanalysis as a methodology for investigating the mental life of individuals and collectives, as well as a consideration of what constitutes psychoanalytic data. As Kaplan (1984), for example, points out " ... the empirical realm of psychoanalytic theory is its clinical situation—the psychoanalysis of patients ... ." He goes on to note that the major discoveries of psychoanalysis were made in the treatment room, and thereafter applied by analogy to other realms such as art, literature, culture, etc.

While one may disagree with his basic premise, in most instances the same may be said of organizational behavior and character, as when, for example, one asserts that a manager's difficulties with his supervisor are the result of unresolved Oedipal conflicts. In an organizational situation what are the data for making such an assertion? Surely not the manager's free-associations. How were the data—whatever they are—collected? How were they analyzed and interpreted? By what rules or criteria? The broad issues raised by such questions are fairly obvious. In clinical work we are able to construct a carefully controlled and regulated structure for using our investigative methods like free-association, dream analysis, etc. Despite whatever forms patients' resistances may take—also data, of course—psychoanalytic methods also require considerable motivation on their part and their painstaking and continuing cooperation for a long period of time. By contrast, in complex natural settings, the situation is entirely different—we generally have neither the psychological contract, structure, opportunity, nor the level and kind of cooperation necessary to investigate the situation psychoanalytically. We are, therefore, usually "stuck" with analogizing based, at best, on limited data which may either be erroneous or too general to be of use. Thus, Kaplan (1984) argues, for example, that when one claims Moby Dick is Ahab's mother, one is making "too bland a statement to be worth asserting." I suggest that the term blandness is equally apposite when one asserts that a manager has Oedipal difficulties with his supervisor.

My purpose in making the foregoing remarks is neither to daunt the reader, nor to convey an overly pessimistic view about the possibilities of developing adequate depth-psychological organizational diagnoses and assessments. Rather, these remarks are offered in the spirit of underscoring several caveats. First, our diagnoses must remain fluid. We need recognize that we run the risk of erroneously or crudely imposing a formulation based on an initial assessment, if we do not fully appreciate the inevitable limitations of our data. Further, we need always to be fully open to the emergence of new or contradictory data. Our assessments are, at all times, simply working hypotheses, rather than fixed, neatly integrated diagnostic formulations. In this connection it may also be observed, that in diagnosing or assessing patients, their responses to treatment (e.g., trial interpretations) are an important source of data for understanding the nature of their ailments. The same is true in organizational work. How a client responds to our initial interventions—whatever they may be—is an important source of diagnostic data. That is, *linear* or *a priori* diagnostic models are usually either simplistic or misleading at worst, or what, in fact, may amount to the same thing in the end, incomplete at best. Perhaps another way of making this point is to note, that compared to the nature and structure of the clinical inferences we make in the treatment room, those we make in organizational situations are likely to be considerably more tenuous and fragile yet. An appreciation of the inevitability of this state of affairs will hopefully allow us to avoid the worst excesses of "wild" interpretations (Freud, 1910) as in "the organization is experienced as a devouring whale," or in the mounting of clumsy, premature and counterproductive interventions of other sorts. Finally, following Levinson's (1972a) pioneering lead, much more work is needed to develop diagnostic criteria, assessment methods and strategies, and to test formulations based on them against an evaluation of process and outcome. It is only in this manner that we will begin to define more precise and conceptually coherent linkages between theory, diagnosis and practice (see below) than we have at present.

Psychoanalysis as a treatment for mental and emotional illness

It should be obvious, as Levinson (1984) points out, that we do not psychoanalyze organizations. For the most part, opportunities and suitability for Type I practice are quite limited. On the other hand, the psychoanalytically informed practitioner, as noted in the discussion of Type II practice, utilizes psychoanalytic theory and a general psychoanalytic perspective to plan and guide organizational interventions. In this regard, to paraphrase Sullivan "[in organizational work] we are all more eclectic than otherwise." Must we be content to settle for such a general derivation of psychoanalysis, or may there not be, for example, more direct and better articulated linkages between theory and practice, between diagnosis and intervention, and between client characteristics and the nature of our intervention strategy? Put another way, there ought to be something between interventions "driven" by some form of psychoanalytic methodology (e.g., the in-house Tavistock group relations conference), which often does not sufficiently consider client needs, resources, preparedness, etc., on the one hand, and interventions merely informed by psychoanalytic theory, on the other. This is precisely the sort of issue which I believe we need to address. Even in clinical psychoanalysis we can observe that such issues are very much in the forefront of current concerns. At a recent panel discussion (Richards, 1984), Wallerstein, for example, noted that counter to the prevailing view that theory and technique "lock securely together" is the fact, that despite significant theoretical changes and advances in almost nearly one hundred years of psychoanalysis, it is difficult to state with any precision how technique has been correspondingly modified. A similar assertion regarding technique in the organizational realm can easily be made. I would suggest, therefore, that despite the obvious practical difficulties of working with many, if not most of our organizational clients psychoanalytically, we need to continue our attempts to do so. That is, we need to develop interventions and techniques that are truly analogues of our clinical methods, in addition to those simply informed or guided by psychoanalysis. I would argue that even if only an occasional client may be suitable for such an approach, both theory and the theory of practice would be enriched. I believe that all too often we have shrunk back from developing a psychoanalytic strategy, and taking a psychoanalytic stance in our organizational work because of our own anxieties in the face of client resistance and practical difficulties.

In summary, I would like to note the extent to which the field of psychoanalytic organizational practice has been noncumulative. I do not know what forms a more authentic psychoanalytic approach may take, but I believe that with almost forty years of psychoanalytic organizational psychology already behind us, the time is ripe for attempting to advance our theory of practice more directly, more self-consciously and more systematically. The hope is, of course, that we may be able to produce the kinds of "structural" change (in the psychoanalytic sense) in organizations that are comparable to the mutative and salutary results of successful psychoanalytic work with patients.

References

Astrachan, B.M. and Flynn, H.R. (1976). "The Intergroup Excercise: A Paradigm for Learning About the Development of Organizational Structure." In: E. Miller (ed.), *Task and Organization*. London: John Wiley & Sons.

Baum, H.S. (1987). *The Invisible Bureaucracy*. Oxford University Press.

Bion, W.R. (1961). *Experiences in Groups*. New York: Basic Books.

Balint, E. (1959)."Training Post-graduate Students in Social Casework." *British Journal of Medical Psychology, 32*:193.

Edelson, M. (1970a). *The Practice of Sociotherapy*. New Haven: The Yale University Press.

Edelson, M. (1970b). *Sociotherapy and Psychotherapy*. Chicago: University of Chicago Press.

Eissler, K.R. (1953). "The Effect of the Structure of the Ego on Psychoanalytic Technique." *Journal of the American Psychoanalytic Association, 1*:104–143.

Eissler, K.R. (1958). "Remarks on Some Variations in Psychoanalytical Technique." *International Journal of Psycho-Analysis, 39*:222–229.

Freud, S. (1957). *Wild Analysis* (1910). *Standard Edition of the Complete Psychological Works of Sigmund Freud*. Vol. 11. London: The Hogarth Press.

Freud, S. (1958). *Papers on Technique* (1911–1915). *Standard Edition of the Complete Psychological Works of Sigmund Freud*. Vol. 12. London: The Hogarth Press.

Freud, S. (1955). *Totem and Taboo* (1913). *Standard Edition of the Complete Psychological Works of Sigmund Freud*. Vol. 13. London: The Hogarth Press.

Freud, S. (1955). *Group Psychology and the Analysis of the Ego* (1921). *Standard Edition of the Complete Psychological Works of Sigmund Freud*. Vol. 18. London: The Hogarth Press.

Freud, S. (1961). *The Future of an Illusion* (1927). *Standard Edition of the Complete Psychological Works of Sigmund Freud*. Vol. 21. London: The Hogarth Press.

Freud, S. (1961). *Civilization and its Discontents* (1930). *Standard Edition of the Complete Psychological Works of Sigmund Freud*. Vol. 21. London: The Hogarth Press.

Freud, S. (1964). *Moses and Monotheism: Three Essays* (1939). *Standard Edition of the Complete Psychological Works of Sigmund Freud*. Vol. 23. London: The Hogarth Press.

Gosling, R. et al. (1967). *The Use of Small Groups in Training*. The Codicote Press.

Gustafson, J. & Hausman, W. (1975). "The Phenomenon of Splitting in a Small Psychiatric Organization: A Case Report." *Social Psychiatry, 10*:199–203.

Hirschhorn, L. (1988). *The Workplace Within*. Cambridge, Massachusetts: The MIT Press.

Jacques, E. (1950). "Collaborative Group Methods in a Wage Negotiation Situation." *Human Relations*, 3:223–249.

Jacques, E. (1951). *The Changing Culture of a Factory*. London: Tavistock Publications.

Jacques, E. (1955). "Social Systems as a Defense Against Persecutory and Depressive Anxiety." In: M. Klein, P. Heimann, and R. Money-Kyrle (eds.), *New Directions in Psychoanalysis*. New York: Basic Books.

Jacques, E., Rice, A.K. and Hill, J.M.M. (1951). "The Social and Psychological Impact of a Change in Method of Wage Payment." *Human Relations*, 4:315–340.

Johnson, J.L. and Fleisher, K. (1980). "Reactions of Teachers to Emotionally Disturbed Children to Group Relations Conferences: A New Application of Tavistock Training." *Journal of Personality and Social Systems*, 2(2–3):11–25.

Kaplan, D. (1984). Review of *Literature and Psychoanalysis* by E. Kurzweil and W. Phillips (eds.). New York: Columbia University Press. In: *Contemporary Psychology*, 29(9).

Kernberg, O. (1979). "Regression in Organizational Leadership." *Psychiatry*, 42:24–39.

Kernberg, O. (1984). "The Couch at Sea: The Psychoanalysis of Organizations." *International Journal of Group Psychotherapy*, 34(1):5–23.

Kets de Vries, M.F.R. (1984). *The Irrational Executive*. New York: International Universities Press.

Kets de Vries, M.F.R. and Miller, D. (1984). *The Neurotic Organziation*. San Francisco: Jossey-Bass.

Klein, M. (1948). *Contributions to Psychoanalysis 1921–1945*. London: The Hogarth Press.

Lawrence, W.G. (1979). *Exploring Individual and Organizational Boundaries*. New York: John Wiley & Sons.

Levinson, H. (1972a). *Organizational Diagnosis*. Cambridge: Harvard University Press.

Levinson, H. (1972b). "The Clinical Psychologist as Organizational Diagnostician." *Professional Psychologist*, Winter.

Levinson, H. (1984). Review of *The Psychoanalysis of Organizations* by R. de Board. London: Tavistock Publications, In: *Journal of the American Psychoanalytic Association*, 32:3.

Menninger, R.W. (1972). "The Impact of Group Relations Conferences on Organizational Growth." *International Journal of Group Psychotherapy*, 22:415–430.

Menninger, R.W. (1985). "A Retrospective View of a Hospital-Wide Group Relations 'Training Program: Costs, Consequences and Conclusions." A.D. Coleman and M.H. Geller (Eds.) In: *Group Relations Reader 2*, The A.K. Rice Institute, 285–298.

Menzies, I.E.P. (1975). *The Functioning of Social Systems as a Defense Against Anxiety*. Tavistock Pamphlet No. 3. London: Tavistock Publications, 1967. Also in, A.D. Coleman and W.H. Bexton (Eds.) *Group Relations Reader*, The A.K. Rice Institute, 281–312.

Menzies Lyth, I. (1988). *Containing Anxiety in Institutions*. London: Free Association Books.

Menzies Lyth, I. (1989). *The Dynamics of the Social*. London: Free Association Books.

Miller, E.J. (1976). *Task and Organization*. New York: John Wiley & Sons.

Miller, E.J. and Gwynne, G.V. (1972). *A Life Apart*. London: Tavistock Publications.

Miller, E.J. & Rice, A.K. (1967). *Systems of Organization*. London: Tavistock Publications.

Miller, J.C. (1977). "The Psychology of Conflict in Belfast: Conference as Microcosm." *Journal of Personality and Social Systems*, 1(1):17–38.

Reed, B. (1976). "Organizational Role Analysis." In: C.L. Cooper (ed.), *Developing Skills in Managers*. London: The MacMillan Press, 89–102.

Rice, A.K. (1958). *Productivity and Social Organization: The Ahmedabad Experiment*. London: Tavistock Publications.

Rice, A.K. (1965). *Learning for Leadership*. London: Tavistock Publications.

Rice, B. (1979). "Midlife Encounters: The Menninger Seminars for Businessmen." *Psychology Today*.

Richards, A. (1984). "The Relation Between Psychoanalytic Theory and Psychoanalytic Technique," (panel report). *Journal of the American Psychoanalytic Association*, 32(3):587–602.

Trist, E.L. and Bamforth, K. (1951). "Some Social and Psychological Consequences of the Longwall Method of Coal Getting." *Human Relations*, 4, 3–38.

Trist, E.L. and Murray, H. (1990). *The Social Engagement of Social Science Volume 1: The Socio-Psychological Perspective*. Philadelphia: The University of Pennsylvania Press.

Turquet, P. (1975). "Threats to Identify in the Large Group." In: L. Kneeger (ed.), *The Large Group: Dynamics and Therapy*. London: Constable.

Wachtel, P.L. (1977). *Psychoanalysis and Behavior Therapy: Toward an Integration*. New York: Basic Books.

Zaleznik, A. (1967). "Management of Disappointment." *Harvard Business Review*.

Zaleznik, A. (1984). "Power and Politics in Organizational Life." In: M.F.R. Kets de Vries, *The Irrational Executive*. New York: International Universities Press.

Institutional consultancy as a means of bringing about change in individuals

Isabel Menzies Lyth

I begin with a statement by a wise and perspicacious psychoanalyst, Otto Fenichel (1946). He stated that social institutions arise through the efforts of individuals to satisfy their needs, but the institutions then become external realities comparatively independent of the individuals that affect the personality structure of the individuals, temporarily or permanently. Fenichel was using the term 'institution' in a wide sense to include customs, practices and the culture of society as well as the organisations in which we consultants work. I shall be using the term mainly in the latter sense.

Institutions have an extraordinary capacity to sustain their most important characteristics over long periods of time even when significant changes have taken place in the environment, in the demands on them and in the resources available to meet those demands. Individuals who initiate the institution or who join it later must somehow adapt themselves to 'fit' since their chance of basically changing the institution is not great, although not non-existent, and consultancy may help. The main process through which the individual's adaptation takes place is by introjective identification, one of the major ways by which children develop and form their personalities. The possibility of change by introjective identification remains

87

throughout life, even for mature adults. On entering an institution, an individual must take in and identify with the main characteristics of the institution if he is to stay there. If he cannot, and so does not become sufficiently like the institution and the other members, he will find himself under overt or covert pressure to leave. He may find the effort and the effects of trying to adapt himself too stressful and leave of his own accord.

I will give some examples from institutions whose influence on their members was detrimental to their mental health and to their growth and maturation. The first is from a study of the nursing service of a general teaching hospital in London, England (Menzies Lyth, 1988). The level of stress among the nurses was extremely high. At first glance, this seemed hardly surprising. Nurses are in constant contact with people who are physically ill, injured or dying. They are confronted with the reality of suffering and death as few people are. Their work involves tasks that, by ordinary standards, are distasteful, disgusting and frightening. Intimate physical contact with patients arouses strong libidinal and erotic feelings that may be hard to control. The nurses' feelings are strong and mixed: pity, compassion and love: guilt and anxiety: hatred and resentment of the patients who arouse such strong feelings: envy of the care given the patients. The nurse also has to cope with the feelings of patients and relatives and other nurses. The feelings are deep, powerful and primitive, picking up and drawing strength from many memories and fantasies, both conscious and unconscious. However, this did not seem sufficient to explain the high level of stress. Why had the nursing service and the nurses not come more effectively to terms with their work situation and their stress?

Among the needs that people have of institutions is to use them as a defence against anxiety. This leads to the development of socially structured defence systems which arise through an attempt by individuals to externalise and give substance in external reality to their characteristic psychic defence mechanisms. A social defence system thus develops over time as the result of collusive interaction and agreement, often unconscious, between members of the organization as to what form it should take. When facing powerful and primitive anxieties like the nurses', people tend to regress in terms of the defences used. This appeared to be what had happened in the nursing service.

For example, such regressed defences appeared in the sometimes manic denial of the suffering of patients and relatives and, indeed, of the nurses themselves. The nurse-patient relationship was in a sense fragmented by the work-organization in which all the nurses looked after all the patients indiscriminately, multiple indiscriminate care-taking, so that close, intimate and lengthy contact between them was limited. There were attempts to 'depersonalise' both patient and nurse and to deny the significance of the individual, by emphasising uniformity and by putting people into categories which defined their rights, privileges and responsibilities regardless of their own needs or capacities. Attempts were made to avoid the stress of decision-making by eliminating the need for decisions as far as possible by ritualisation, and by constant checking and counter-checking. Tasks and responsibilities tended to be located at a hierarchical level above that which was really appropriate and/or in people whose capaci-ties were notably above those necessary for the job they were doing. This was a complicated interacting and interdependent system of defences which, however, had in common the attempt to deal with anxiety by avoiding it or trying to eliminate situations that might stimulate it. The system made little provision for confronting anxi-ety and working it through, the only way in which a real increase in the capacity to cope with it and personal maturation would take place. As a social defence system, it was ineffectual in containing anxiety. Returning to Fenichel, the social defence system which the nurses had to identify with and operate if they stayed in the service was immature and regressed. The effect of the system on person-ality was to inhibit maturation and growth. This situation was not peculiar to the hospital studied. It was characteristic of nurse train-ing schools at the time and it is interesting that 30–40% of student nurses did not complete their training. Those who stayed were on the whole those most able to incorporate the system. A significant number of those who left were the more mature students who could not or would not do so. Thus the system became self-perpetuating. Those who remained accepted it and continued it. Those who did not accept it and would have wanted to change it left.

My second example comes from a study in a day nursery con-ducted by my colleagues Alastair Bain and Lynn Barnett to which I was a consultant (Bain & Barnett, 1986). They described the discon-tinuity of care provided by even a single caretaker in a traditionally run day nursery. The children's intense needs for individual atten-tion tend to mean that they do not allow the nurse to pay attention to any one child for any length of time. Other children pull at her skirt, want to sit up on her lap, push the child who is receiving attention away. Further, during the periods between intervals of attention, the young child experiences his fellows receiving moments of atten-tion. He experiences as the predominant pattern of relationships between adult and child a series of discontinuities of attention, a nurse momentarily directing her attention from one child to another. He and his moment are part of a series of disconnected episodes.

A follow up of these children into school showed them to have identified with and to be operating that model, a model of episodic and discontinuous attention, forming a series of episodic and discon-tinuous relationships with their world through fleeting superficial attachments, episodic discontinuous play activities and difficultly in sustaining continuous attention in school. I came to call this the 'butterfly phenomenon', the child flitting apparently aimlessly from person to person and activity to activity.

Children are, of course, more malleable and more susceptible to institutional influence than adults although the general point holds throughout the age groups. And, sadly, unlike the 'refugees' from nursing, children did not usually have the option of leaving the nursery and escaping from its adverse effects on personality development.

Fortunately, such situations are not inevitable. In particular, it is sometimes possible through the use of institutional consultancy to change the institution in such a way as to improve the mental health of its members, as happened in both those examples. The improve-ment in the hospital was minimal but in the day nursery it was con-siderable. Children going to school after the consultancy showed little evidence of the 'butterfly phenomenon'. My main concern here is not with those comparatively few members who are psychiatri-cally ill but rather with raising the level of mental health through-out the membership and facilitating further growth and maturation. Incidentally, this would be likely to decrease the incidence of actual breakdown.

In moving on now to consider institutional consultancy, I begin by acknowledging the debt we consultants owe to Psycho-analysis when we see as our aim facilitating change in institutions which not only benefit the institution per se, but will incidentally improve the mental health of individual members, sociotherapy being psychotherapeutic. Psycho-analysis was in itself a major breakthrough in improving the mental health of individuals, the clinical work being the first significant 'institution' devoted to doing so.

Wherein then, lies our debt? First, perhaps, in the insights that psycho-analysis provides into the human personality and object-relationships together with the conviction of the significance for experience and behaviour of the unconscious mind. From Freud and later psycho-analytic research we have come to understand the particular importance of anxiety and related defences both to the mental health of the individual and to the functioning of institutions and the health of their members. Psycho-analysis has contributed a great deal to our knowledge about the environmental conditions that further mental health from the young baby with his mother in his family to the adult in larger institutions. Health improves as defences are modified or abandoned and replaced by better adaptations and sublimations. Of great significance also is the growing appreciation of both transference and counter-transference and from that, the use of ourselves as an invaluable resource in understanding what is going on between our clients and ourselves and in the client institution. In institutions, making contact with the implicit as well as the unconscious is important, things quite conscious in individuals but kept secret or shared with only a few others sometimes only outside the institution. The implicit is thus not immediately available for work. Whichever, unconscious or implicit, we share with psycho-analysis the task of searching out and making available for work the hidden factors that are impeding healthy development.

In this context, I thought of the title of a paper I have not written: 'Self-diagnosis and Prescription as a Defence against Institutional Change'. The client himself tells us what the problem is and what he expects us to do about it. Usually the prescription implies minimal involvement in the core of the institution and often, indeed, doing something right outside. Thus, the client tries to avoid change that would be experienced in anticipation as catastrophic (Bion, 1970) even if it is potentially beneficial, because it means disruption of established modes of behaviour, traditional attitudes, established relationships. It is part of our responsibility as consultants to explore the situation, revise the diagnosis and facilitate appropriate change in the core of the institution. In this, consultancy is like psycho-analysis. For example, the Tavistock Institute was hired by the London Fire Brigade Committee who told us that the Brigade was suffering from a man-power shortage and needed more recruits. The diagnosis, our given task, the prescription, was to devise a recruitment campaign that would ensure sufficient numbers of appropriate recruits (Menzies Lyth, 1989).

There truly was a man-power shortage but when we looked into the situation with the men and women of the Brigade we found that the problem stemmed mainly from the loss of existing staff who found conditions of work in the Brigade unduly stressful and unsatisfying: if this loss could be reduced there would not have been much problem In getting enough good recruits. But dealing with the loss would have meant a considerable modification in the whole way the Brigade operated. Sadly, in this case, the Committee could not face our re-diagnosis and prescription, a Committee that was itself far removed from and largely ignorant of the conditions of work within the Brigade. I believe we could have worked with the Brigade itself could we have gained the necessary access.

Alas, people never learn. The British Government has just spent a vast sum on a recruitment campaign for nurses which produced very very few recruits. The shortage of nurses is truly desperate but the remedy lies in reducing wastage by modifying the core of the work situation not in 'enticing' new recruits who are likely soon to leave again. I am sad and perhaps rather ashamed that I predicted in about 1960 that if something basic was not done about the conditions of work for nurses the situation that now exists would arise (Menzies Lyth, 1988). Sadly, we have not yet found a way to do anything about it.

My colleague, Alastair Bain, had a similar experience when be was asked to deal with problems in a computer firm, including high wastage, low productivity and general worker dissatisfaction (Bain, 1982). The operatives themselves told him what they thought was wrong, generally rather dreary conditions of work and the prescription was more flexible hours, being allowed to chat to each other as in an ordinary office job, free tea and coffee, more holidays—things to make life more comfortable. Bain was quite unconvinced that this was the substance of the matter. Upon further exploration a rather terrible picture emerged: loss of the sense of self or fears of this, loss of awareness of what was going on around them although they continued to function, feeling like an automaton or like the machines they worked on, irritation, boredom, alienation, depersonalisation. This was much more convincing and led to the need for action in the job-situation itself, not just additional fringe benefits. Bain's work led to a major reorganisation of the work-situation which completely changed the operatives' experience and incidentally increased productively and decreased wastage.

Sadly, mistaken self-diagnosis and related unrealistic prescriptions occur over and over again. The fact that the remedies have not worked in the past does not seem to deter people from repeatedly trying them and each time attributing some magic to them. 'This time it really will work.' This is very true of nursing, improved training courses to achieve higher status and more pay have peen tried over and over again. In the meantime, the job of nursing itself has not been appreciably upgraded to match the upgraded training. The discrepancy between the level of training and the level of job has thus been increased. The nurses' complaints about their jobs remain much the same and wastage remains excessive. The remedies do not touch the core of the problem and are repeatedly ineffectual.

Bain's case demonstrates what I think often happens in such a situation. The defensive manoeuvres seem to have been something like this, defences that are familiar in patients. There is a focus of deep anxiety and distress in the institution associated with despair about being able to tackle the situation directly. The defensive system collusively set up against these feelings consists, first, in fragmenting the core problem so that it no longer exists in recognisable form in the minds of those concerned. The fragments are then embodied in aspects of the ambience of the work-situation which are honestly but wrongly experienced as the problem about which something needs to be done usually by someone else—responsibility is also projected. Hope for a real remedy only exists if the fragments can be re-integrated and the core problem recognized again and confronted.

We are indebted to psycho-analysis and particularly to Freud himself for technical help and for models of working that both facilitate the exploration that may lead to more effective diagnosis and show how, having made the diagnosis, we can work with our clients to tackle the problem at the heart of the matter.

From Freud's technical papers we learn much that is relevant to our own work. Derivatives from the psycho-analytic clinical method give us our own most useful tools (Freud, 1911–15). Freud recommends evenly suspended attention, a very open mind, we should try not to direct our attention to anything in particular, to avoid premature selection and prejudgment of the issues. That would block our receptivity to what might emerge as being significant. If one can hold to that attitude one can hope that gradually the meaning of what one's client is showing one may evolve. Later psycho-analysts have learned the value of this attitude and have clarified it further. Bion, for example, recommends eschewing memory and desire: that is to not deliberately summoning up conscious memories of what has previously happened—even yesterday, the 'facts' one knows about the clients (Bion, 1970). Dismissing such memories from one's mind leaves one's mind free for the spontaneous emergence of memories, rather like dreams, evoked by what the client is telling us in the here and now, memories more likely to be relevant to the understanding of the current situation. Similarly, desires for the client or the progress of the work, or for that matter for oneself, may seriously interfere with helping the client to find his own way through the change that is appropriate to his circumstances and his resources. We, too, can sometimes be caught in the trap of false diagnosis and unrealistic prescriptions.

The strain of working in this way is considerable for the consultant as it is for the psycho-analyst. One has deliberately knocked away one's traditional props, memory, consciously set objectives and theory. Consequently, one exists for a great deal of one's working lime in a state of ignorance, uncertainty and doubt, often not knowing for the moment where one's client stands, or oneself, a state that may be profoundly frightening to one's belief in one's own competence to understand and help one's clients. One needs faith that there is light at the end of the tunnel even when there may seem not much hope.

This experience is compounded by being repetitive. If one is lucky, or perhaps skilful, and holds to ignorance, meaning may evolve, some partial understanding and some idea of how to proceed. But this will serve usually to show how much more of the unknown still surrounds us and how far there is still to go. It sometimes feels unrelenting. Our clients themselves may precipitate us further into the unknown if they accept our partial interpretation of the situation and are prepared and able to go on.

Nor need we suppose that our clients will necessarily accept or like our rather strange way of working, especially those who want, or are used to, the kind of 'expert' who will give them a definitive answer quickly rather than help them evolve a solution for themselves. So we may have to 'teach' them how to use us, work with their resistance and support them through the early distrust and frustrations aroused by our methods. In working through these problems with our clients we will also be helping them to see the value of learning to work in a similar way themselves: not to make prejudgments about relevance, for example. but to cast the net wide: not to be over influenced by such common attitudes as loyalty to colleagues, tact and discretion, often used as defences against engaging in difficult explorations. It took some time in a hospital where I worked to help the staff understand that an unwritten rule that one did not talk about colleagues in their absence even, or especially, when the absence itself was a key issue was defensive and obstructive. One is coming close to helping one's client towards free association, though neither we nor psycho-analysts today would think it of much use to ask people to free associate. Rather one has to work to remove resistance to free speech and help the client to appreciate its value. One can also give permission and offer oneself as a model. In the first nursing study, although the set problem was the deployment of student nurses to practical training which also provided most of the nursing services in the hospital, we asked our respondents to discuss any features of their nursing experience that seemed significant to them. The discussions were quite discursive and helped to put the deployment problem into the wider context of institutional anxieties and defences. Clients can learn to work this way, increasingly so in the later stages of a study when one is sharing data and its understanding, working through resistance to its acceptance, correcting or modifying one's own interpretations if necessary and working towards change.

The method we use to further such work again owes much to psycho-analysis, basically interpretation: making the unconscious and implicit explicit, working with resistance against accepting unwelcome insights, helping the client to think more freely and laterally, using the transference and counter-transference and at times interpreting them, helping the client to modify his defences, exploring important projection systems, helping him move towards significant change and sustaining him through the difficulty and stress of implementing it. This is challenging and rewarding for both client and consultant. This is analysis.

In institutional terms, Bain has described this analysis as tri-partite, work culture analysis, role analysis and structure analysis (Bain, 1982). All three types of analysis prove on examination to owe a great deal to insights from psycho-analysis. This is most obvious in work culture analysis which deals with attitudes and beliefs, tra-ditions, patterns of relationships, the context within which work takes place. But analysis of roles and structure show them also to be permeated with content and dynamics with which psycho-analysts are also familiar. For example, institutionally sustained projection systems and anxieties and defences contribute to role-definition, to role-relationships and so to structure. These are quite as influential in the experience and personality structure of members as work cul-ture. The three types of analysis are theoretically separable but in practise are and must be carried out together.

There are dangers in institutional consultancy that only one or two types of analysis may be used. Quite frequently, consultants particularly in 'humane' institutions, only undertake work culture analysis, commonly described as sensitivity or support groups for staff, aimed at increasing their sensitivity to their clients and them-selves. Psycho-analysts and members of related professions who are not also social scientists are prone to do this. The objectives of this work are not too difficult to achieve within the groups themselves: the group members both want to and are quite able to become more sensitive. But they usually return to a work-situation where roles and structure have not been modified. This may make it impossible for them to deploy their new insights in action. A nurse cannot be more sensitive and intimately related to her patients when a nursing system based on multiple indiscriminate care-taking prevents her from ever really getting to know them well.

Non-psycho-analytically oriented consultants may do only role and structure analysis and suggest changes that cannot effectively be implemented because parallel changes in work culture have not been achieved. In fact, attention to work culture might well have shown that the suggested changes in role and structure were inap-propriate. This is what appears to have happened in the British Health and Social Services where repeated consultancy seems to have produced little significant benefit.

In either case, the consultancy is likely to prove ineffectual and the hoped for benefits will not materialise. The client is disappointed, frustrated, disillusioned. The consultant and what he stands for may be discredited.

To return now to the change-process in institutions and to a point made above, another parallel with psycho-analysis. The initiative for taking action as insights and meaning evolve lies with the client just as It does with the patient. The consultant's responsibility is to be available to collaborate in this task: to help clarify objectives and plan change and to bear the stress of carrying it out.

This latter is, I am sure, established practice among psycho-analytically oriented consultants although it is by no means accepted by all consultants. Some make their diagnostic explorations, and send a report to their client, often a blue-print of what they think should be done. They then leave the client to do what he can about it, dodging out of what may well be the most stressful part of the consultancy. This is an important aspect of the failure of consultancy in many cases, contributing especially to the relative failure of consultancy in the British Health and Social Services. It would be unthinkable to assess a patient, give him a detailed report about his psychopathology and instructions as to what he should do about it and send him away to carry them out on his own. I would find It just as unthinkable to treat a client that way.

My final point in drawing the parallels between psycho-analysis and consultancy practice concerns termination; the difficult question both of when termination is appropriate and how it should be accomplished. When termination is appropriate concerns more than simply that the institution has gained from the consultancy, in particular that the problems tackled in the joint work have reached resolution, and that one can be reasonably certain that the gains will be sustained. One would also hope that the client has 'learned' a way of tackling problems that will survive when the consultant has left and can be applied to new tasks and problems as they arise. This is particularly important in present-day society where the need for continuous institutional change is both great and immediate to match rapidly changing circumstances. A crucial aspect of management is the management of innovation (Rice, 1963). As consultants we can help increase such management skills. This is in some ways analogous to the capacity for self-analysis one hopes a patient will develop and continue to use to meet new situations in his life as they arise.

Sustaining the learning requires that the process of termination be carried out effectively. In psycho-analytic terms, this could be described as helping to establish the consultant and the consultancy method as a 'good object' within the client so that they continue to be used consciously and unconsciously as a resource when needed. One important requirement is that the consultant and the client have time to work through together what termination means. A process of mourning is appropriate and needs to be facilitated: to face anger about deprivation of further consultant help, to work through anticipatory anxiety about being left on one's own, to face feelings about the loss of people who are withdrawing, to speculate and fantasize about whether some sort of continued relationship might be appropriate institutionally or personally, and if so what. Nor are the feelings all on the side of the client. The loss of a rewarding project and of the friends one's client almost inevitably become may also be hard for the consultant. He too needs to be able to work this through in himself if he is to be able to help his client mourn. After the Tavistock team left the Royal National Orthopaedic Hospital the ward sister, Mavis Young Remmen, and her staff brought about significant improvements in the unit for latency children where the team had not worked. What was exciting was that this was not a slavish copy of the care system in the Cot Unit where we worked together but was developed from first principles as it were, taking realistic account of the different needs of latency children and the very different staff resources in the two units. (Menzies Lyth, 1988).

However, one should not perhaps push the analogies with psycho-analysis too far. There are differences too between psycho-analytic and consultancy practice some of which are to the consultant's advantage, some to his disadvantage. It is more difficult in consultancy to sustain analytic anonymity: one has to mix socially to some extent with clients or even with their families. Holding the balance between social and professional relationships can be difficult. Holding a neutral position between different members and groups in the institution can also be difficult. These factors greatly complicate both transference and counter-transference and require great sensitivity from the consultant. However, those difficulties may be mitigated by the fact the consultant need not, often cannot, work alone. Consultancy is not quite so lonely as psycho-analysis. Fellow consultants are invaluable in helping sort out transference and counter-transference. Working with others also gives added richness to the interpretation of data, bringing different perspectives and different field experiences to bear.

Freud discouraged the taking of notes during sessions since it would interfere with free-floating attention. But one consultant may work with free-floating attention while the other takes notes, inevitably selectively. Together they may produce a better record of the complex data we handle. One may also have to write reports for a client, for those who provide research funds or for publication, as the psycho-analyst does not. How does one avoid the consequences I discussed earlier of sending blue-print type reports? I think only by reporting first verbally to clients and working through the report with them before writing so that the report becomes a distillation of work already done. This is also necessary to get agreement for publication. This is very stressful and time-consuming. It may in the end mean, frustratingly, that one cannot publish. The Tavistock Institute is a graveyard of unpublished reports. But I am sure there is no way round this.

In concluding this paper I would like to return to Fenichel and the view that institutions affect the personality structures of their members temporarily or permanently (Fenichel, 1946). I think that our work in consultancy supports this view: as the institution changes, so also do the members: their attitudes, their behaviour, their relationships with the institution and with each other. These changes can become fixed and may be carried outside the institution as well. The success of a consultancy may be judged perhaps in two interrelated ways. Firstly, it may be judged by the success of the institution itself: has it become more effective in carrying out the task it was set up to do? Has productivity gone up? If it is a humane institution like a school, hospital, or children's home, has the care given become better and more realistic, and has it lead to real growth and maturation in those who are cared for? The second concerns the staff members of the institution. Have there been changes for the better in their personalities: has the quality of mental health improved: have the members grown and matured? The connection between the two criteria is to some extent circular. An institution is likely to become more task-efficient if the members grow and mature and orient themselves more realistically to their own part in the common task and co-operate in a more healthy way with others also involved in the common task. From the other side, efficient task-performance is itself rewarding, it reduces anxiety and guilt and the defences against them which stem from bad task performance: it increases confidence and self-esteem. Task-effective institutions tend to be healthy for their members and vice versa.

There are some fairly simple measures of institutional health: productivity, if that should be simple to measure, and others which used to be known at the Tavistock Institute as morale indicators, for example, labour turnover, absenteeism and sickness rates. These give some indication of the mental health of members, of their satisfaction or dissatisfaction, the strength of the need to escape from a situation which is too stressful, perhaps to save themselves from breakdown. Going to conferences might be another such measure in some institutions. A senior civil servant at a Leicester conference indicated that part of his motive for being there was to get away for a time from an almost intolerable work-situation so that he could go back and cope again. These measures are also some indication of the loyalty that members feel towards the institution and their esteem for it. Institutions that can otherwise be judged as unhealthy tend to show high figures on all the indices. I have already mentioned the 30–40% wastage of student nurses during training, the high wastage in the London Fire Brigade. The wastage of staff in the day nursery. The damage to mental health indicated by such figures is considerable. Other measures of mental health are more complicated but the evidence on an intuitive level is unmistakable when one gets to know the members. There is no mistaking the high level of anxiety and the inadequate defences among nurses and the danger to their growth and maturation. Likewise, there was no mistaking the confusion, disorientation and low self-esteem of the men and women of the London Fire Brigade. Similarly, one is aware when members of an institution are confident about the institution and themselves, are enjoying being there, feel and are valued and feel themselves to be growing and developing. Rewardingly for us consultants, we can watch one kind of situation change into another as our work develops. Not only did we see it in the Royal National Orthopaedic Hospital, but staff themselves noticed it as shown in a typical remark by a senior nurse: 'This has been the most definitive learning experience in my whole life.' The atmosphere and the people change, changes that are also marked by the morale indicators.

A great deal of my own work in recent years has been in institutions caring for children where the main objective was to improve the care of the children. In the Royal National Orthopaedic Hospital we were particularly concerned to develop a care method which would mitigate or prevent the classical bad effects of hospitalisation on personality development and mental health as described in the early hospital studies of the Robertsons (Robertson, 1970). A follow-up of the children and families showed that none of the children suffered from the effects of hospitalisation described by the Robertsons.

At the Cotswold Community which cared for very disturbed and often delinquent boys from disturbed families, the results were not so encouraging: the task was much more difficult. But, nevertheless, the improvements in the boys' personalities and in their subsequent life-performance were significantly better than those of similar boys cared for in other communities which operated on a different model of care.

These results were impressive, but perhaps more impressive were the beneficial side-effects for other people. The adults concerned also grew and matured as the care-system changed, often involving them in more challenging but more rewarding work and stretching their capacities as they has never been stretched before. Most apparent was the change in the young nursery nurses in the Orthopaedic Hospital as they took on increasingly difficult tasks, for example in family support, and through case-assignment came more directly into contact with the children's and families' distress and their own. Senior nurses were often understandably anxious lest the changes were imposing too much strain on the nursery nurses. They need not have worried: the nurses took to the new tasks like ducks to water and thrived on them. I have already mentioned how senior nurses felt. Other adults who spent time in the Unit also grew, particularly the children's mothers. Their confidence and skill in their mothering increased as did attachment to their child. In fact, implicit in devising a better care system for the children was to help the adults become better models for the children to identify with. Role and structure changes gave the adults more authority and responsibility which helped the adults mature and made them better models for identification. As before, one may note that better task-performance in child care went hand in hand with maturation in the staff providing the care.

Finally, one can begin to establish principles, or theories, about what constitutes a healthy institution that performs well and furthers the mental health of its members—principles, not blue-prints. Each institution has to be helped to implement the principles in its own way, with its own tasks, problems and resources. These principles quite closely match the criteria for a healthy personality as derived from psycho-analysis. They include avoiding dealing with anxiety by the use of regressed defences, more use of adaptions and sublimation: the ability to confront and work-through problems: opportunities for people to deploy their capacities to their full, not more nor less than they are able for: opportunity to operate realistic control over their life in the institution while being able to take due account of the needs and contributions of others: independence without undue supervision: visible relation between effort and rewards, not only financial. But having outlined the principles one forgets them in the field, in the here and now relation with clients. The principles evolve over and over again in the work: they cannot be imposed. The principles are not so new. Implementing them is what is so difficult and I suppose that to date our failures have been as great as, or greater than, our successes. We have been more successful when we have worked in rather small self-contained units where face to face contact is easy.

What has proved much more difficult and we still have much to learn about is to work with very large organisations and multiple organisations which are subject to a great deal of central control and aim at uniformity. One can build a model in a sub-institution such as the Orthopaedic Hospital but how does one transfer the learning to other hospitals? How does one get beyond a central committee to the operating units as in the London Fire Brigade? I think this is a serious problem now and for the future.

References

Bain, A. (1982). The Baric Experiment. Occasional Paper No. 4, Tavistock Institute of Human Relations, London.

Bain, A. and Barnett L. (1986). The Design of a Day Care System in a Nursery Setting for Children under Five. Occasional Paper No. 8, Tavistock Institute of Human Relations, London.

Bion, W.R. (1961). Experiences in Groups and other papers. Tavistock: New York Basic.

Bion, W.R. (1970). Attention and Interpretation. Tavistock Publications, London.

Fenichel, O. (1946). The Psycho-Analytic Theory of Neurosis. Routledge and Kegan Paul Ltd. London.

Freud, S. (1911–15). Papers on Technique. Standard Edition, Vol. 12, Hogarth Press. London.

Jaques, E. (1955). Social Systems as a Defence against Persecutory and Depressive Anxiety. In: Klein. Heimann & Money-Kyrle Eds. 478–498.

Kernberg, O.F. and Arner, J. (1986). Institutional Problems of Psycho-analytic Education. Psycho-analytic Association, 34:4, 79–83.

Levinson, H. (1990). Freud as Entrepreneur: Implications for Existing Psycho-analytic Institutes. Paper read to the International Society for the Psychoanalytic Study of Organisations Symposium, Montreal 1990.

Menzies Lyth, I. (1988). Containing Anxiety in Institutions Selected Essays. Vol. I Free Association Books, London.

Menzies Lyth, I. (1989). Containing Anxiety in Institutions. Selected Essays. Vol. II Free Association Books, London.

Menzies Lyth, I. (1989). The Dynamics of the Social: Selected Essays. Vol. II Free Association Books, London.

Robertson, J. (1970). Young Children in Hospital. Tavistock Publications, London.

Social dreaming as a tool of consultancy and action research

W. Gordon Lawrence

'We are such stuff as dreams are made on;
and our little life is rounded with a sleep.'

—Shakespeare, *The Tempest*, Act IV, Sc. 1, 156–58.

'I will get Peter Quince to
write a ballad of this dream.
It shall be call'd "Bottom's
Dream," because it hath no
bottom.'

—Shakespeare, *A Midsummer Night's Dream*,
Act IV, Sc. 1, 220–22.

Action research, the unconscious and dreaming

When I worked at the Tavistock Institute there was no frame of reference with which to incorporate dreams into thinking about action research and consultancy. Nevertheless there were experiences that caused me to start to think. In 1975, for instance, I was interviewing managers as part of an action research study of management development in companies in Britain. One manager volunteered that he had a repeated dream, which was that he had to come to work each day through a graveyard. No matter which route he took he always had to pass through a cemetery. The associations we had in the interview were that his particular company was going to enter into a financial crisis that could be terminal. He felt depressed because most of his colleagues were denying this probability. It led me, subsequently, to think about the mortality of individual managers and the place of the idealization of careers in the lives of individuals. As important was the fantasy that the business enterprise was immortal in that it would exist forever in the future. This seemed to be a shared fantasy which role holders projected into the business 'in the mind', irrespective of the current trading and commercial realities. Whatever uncertainties they had of the future were projected into the business, which acted as a 'container', and they could introject, in turn, certainty.

The other example comes from about 1980 when I had an interview with a civil servant in the then Department of Employment. At one point he seemed to slip into a reverie and said that he had a repeated dream that England in the future would become a nation of city-states as in Mediaeval Italy. He himself was of Italian descent so that might have explained his metaphor. What he said as he developed the idea of communities being in some kind of tension and self-protective posture, if not in actual conflict, echoed with experiences of living in Britain at the time. We had begun to experience yet another recession and already people were beginning to be unemployed. The difference from the past was that it was the members of the traditionally, safe managerial occupations who were now vulnerable. There was a sense of social classes defining themselves more sharply and different racial groups self consciously emerging in England with each of them having the characteristics of a beleaguered minority. Their anxiety for the future fuelled a growing sense that people had to be more and more narcissistically preoccupied with their concerns for survival (Lawrence, Bain and Gould, 1996). It was with these and similar experiences, coupled with what I had learned in my own psychoanalysis, that I realized that dreaming could be an area for exploration in the context of action research and consultancy projects.

The discovery of social dreaming

In another place the history of how Social Dreaming emerged has been described (Lawrence, 1991). To date, the work has been done in the context of Social Dreaming Programmes convened for that purpose. These Programmes have allowed my consultant colleagues and I to understand further the processes involved in Social Dreaming in the context of a Matrix.

One programme has been pivotal in helping to shape Social Dreaming as a tool of action research and consultancy. This Programme, entitled 'Social Dreaming as Memoirs of the Future; an Action Research Project', has been held for three years at the William Alanson White Institute in New York. There the membership of the organizational development course are students in an institution which has a continuous life so there is a sense of a community of shared interest which lasts for a number of years. It has been clear from these particular Programmes that Social Dreaming can be used to enable participants to clarify the nature of the work relations among them and the transferential and counter-transferential issues that inevitably occur between the faculty and the students. By exploring the content of members' dream conflicts, which sometimes have been too painful to surface in everyday discourse, have come to be understood and resolved through the process of amplification. So Social Dreaming started to have an action research dimension because it was seen that the dreams could be used to illumine the communal life of the students and the faculty, at the very least.

Social Dreaming does not question the use and value of dreams in the classic, psychoanalytic tradition but, like Bion's work on groups, affirms that dreams have also a social dimension though there needs to be a dreamer to give expression to them. The primary task of a Social Dreaming Matrix is now:

> To transform the thinking of the dreams, presented to the Matrix, by means of free association to make links and connections among the dreams and be available for new thinking and thought.

Excerpts from a social dreaming matrix

For the past four years I have organized a seminar for the president and managing directors of a group of companies. In 1994 I introduced a Social Dreaming Matrix to the seminar. The companies all trade in mail order and they have a substantial turnover running into millions of pounds. All the companies are experiencing some difficulties because of their respective national economies, increased competition and a general downturn in consumer spending. The phrase that emerged during the seminar to capture their current situation was that they conduct business in a *'Casino des incertitudes'*.

I introduced Social Dreaming because I felt that awakening and speaking with their unconscious through dreams might help them to think how they could engage with business uncertainty in a more confident way. I was trying also to find ways into revealing what 'unthought known(s)' might be present in the group of companies. Consultants or action researchers work in institutions where the role holders face both the private troubles and public issues, to borrow C. Wright Mill's phrase, engendered by living and managing in contemporary, unpredictable environments. The role holders are living in what they experience and understand to be a real world full of real problems. They relate to these with a nagging fear that a wrong decision will bring catastrophic consequences—an institutional world of chaos. Consequently, they think and act very often from a psychic position of defending themselves from the psychotic anxiety that would be engendered by chaos. This results in the political fabrication of organizational systems to hold this anxiety at bay. At the same time, role holders know that they are participating in, what I call, a 'rational madness', i.e. that the structure and form of the organization when examined does not make sense particularly in circumstances where events and happenings in the external environment are lurching from one discontinuity to another. But, often, this cannot be thought of and articulated because of the fear that there will be chaos if the form of the organization is deconstructed.

Since Christopher Bollas's formulation of the 'unthought known (Bollas, 1987) action researchers and consultants, led by David Armstrong, have come to see that an investigatory aspect of their work is:

> '... bringing into view at an organizational level of something known in the organization, known in the emotional and physical and perhaps imaginal life of the organization which has resisted formulation: something primary and ordinary, that is

lived, but only as a shadow. And once formulated, once brought towards thought paradoxically creates a difference which makes a difference to how every decision, policy, action is understood. It does not make things easier; it does not show a client what to do. But it discloses meaning: introduces the client, as it were, to the organization-in-himself and himself-in-the organization. And this disclosure sets a new agenda' (Armstrong, 1994, p. 5).

This commitment to revealing the 'unthought known' is consistent with the view that action research and consultancy in the original Tavistock tradition is grounded in the 'politics of revelation' rather than those of 'salvation'. (Lawrence, 1994) Revelation of the unconscious functioning of groups, institutional life and life as it is lived in societies which exist in the context of an eco-systemic environment has emerged over the years as the agenda of action research. This has to be contrasted with consultancy as 'salvation', i.e. as a social variant of the 'rescue phantasy' which can operate in the therapeutic situation when the practitioner is caught up in trying to offer salvation to the client. The 'politics of salvation' are geared to saving the 'client' organization from its problems or, for instance, expertly introducing new technology, such as a new IT system, whereas the politics of revelation are centred on the idea that the clients can take their responsibility and authority to disentangle the nature of realities for themselves in order to manage themselves in their roles in their particular systems. The consultant working in such a revelatory mode has a preoccupation with the infinite, the unconscious, with socially induced psychosis, with the unthought known, with the social phenomena that rational madness brings forth.

The dream is the classic link between the finite and the infinite; conscious and the unconscious. 'A night dream is a spontaneous symbolic experience lived out in the inner world during sleep. Such dreams are composed of a series of images, actions, thoughts, words, and feelings over which we seem to have little or no conscious control.' (Savary, 1984) Dreaming makes the dreamer aware that what is taken-for-granted in waking life can be made non-sense of during sleep when rationality is suspended. Action research, which is postulated on the revelation of the unconscious mind, would be expected to have made use of dreams and dreaming. Even though the methodology is based on psychoanalytic thinking, access to the role holders' dreams has never been part of the discourse of action research. This, probably, is because in the popular imagination dreams have come to be understood to be a personal, private experience rarely to be shared except with a therapist who would have the skill to 'interpret' them.

Each day, mostly in the mornings, we had a Social Dreaming Matrix that lasted for an hour. The Social Dreaming was introduced with some trepidation for I was unsure what would be realized and how it would evolve. I always have an anxiety before a Matrix opens that no dreams will be made available, but on this occasion I had the added anxiety that dreaming would be rejected as being not relevant to the participants' work. The title of the seminar was 'Memoirs of the Future.' It was conducted in French. Working with me was a young French manager, Dominique Guisiano, who is marketing director of a chain of retail clothing shops. Previously he had been a participant on a weeklong programme of Social Dreaming in England.

I have made a selection of the dreams with his help to try to illustrate the potential of Social Dreaming by showing that people with pressing business problems can benefit from the experience. The selection is as representative of the whole experience of the Matrix as we can make it. In this account I wish to preserve confidentiality so contributions are anonymous.

The first Matrix opened with one participant saying that he felt angry at being present in a seminar on a Sunday evening. (The seminar began on a Sunday and ended on the following Wednesday after the last Social Dreaming Matrix from 9 to 10 a.m.) There were some observations made on the nature of dreaming and some participants wondered if they did dream in fact. They concluded that they dreamed more when they were on holiday, and particularly when staying at high altitudes, than when they were at work. One manager who had a dream of being on an escalator expressed the doubt about the value and possible risks of dreaming. He had the feeling of being off balance and that he was always trying to keep in balance. It was not an unpleasant feeling but, at the same time, it was not a pleasure. I took it that the escalator symbolized links between waking and dreaming, reality and dream, between the conscious and the unconscious which is always putting one off balance but, ideally, could be in a symbiont relationship.

Another manager followed by saying that normally he did not remember his dreams but he had had one the night before and after some effort when he awoke he was able to recall some elements. His dream, he said, was in relation to the catalogue of his company. (The catalogue for a mail order company is the key selling tool and thus its quality is critical.) *There was a fashion presentation that was taking place on the gangway and the ladder of a boat. The presentation was being photographed. The feeling of the place was of elegance with a lot of people present. It was, however, cold. The people present were fashion designers and the atmosphere was a little mad, even bizarre. There was a lot of light from the sun and much movement among the people present.* The dreamer ended his description by saying that they were not dealing with issues of fashion in his company.

I was intrigued that one of the first dreams should be about work and I assumed that the gangway (*passerolle*) symbolized the catalogue issued by the company with its marketing strategies to sell its goods to potential customers either on the 'boat' or the 'quay'. In actuality the company has an attractive catalogue and even has what are called 'best sellers', but the amount of turnover needed is not yet present so, therefore, it is very worrying for all the people in the company. There is stress in the company and a sense of persecution has grown because of their comparative lack of success. The market is a cold place in reality. (The theme of water was to reappear in subsequent dreams of the Matrix that can be assumed is a reference to the unconscious.)

The fact that the act of dreaming was engaging participants and causing them to reflect on its nature was made clear by one participant who described that he had two kinds of dreams: first, a *reve lancinant* and, second, a *reve d'envol*. The first kind of dream he said was like listening to music which goes on for a long time and which occurs when he has difficulties. The second kind of dream happens during periods of social excitement or when he is experiencing good, affective relationships. This kind of dream he likened to a bird flying from island to island. He added that he had not had the second kind of dream when he was appointed a managing director.

Someone, at this point, observed that we create a story with our dreams, perhaps to restore ourselves?

A dream was given about the group that was members of the seminar.

All were visiting the Souk in Marrakech. It was full of colour and smells. The dreamer said that it was a very rich and vivid dream for him. At the edge of the Souk there were wooden barriers. Alongside one of these barriers was a collection of furniture made from olive trees. The wood was rich, heavy and colourful. The barriers halted the group. They wanted to go out by the left because they wished to go and visit another place or do something else from the left children appeared and the air was filled with an extraordinary smell. A small open-top car appeared. (Later we established that it was an 'Alpine' made by Renault a few years ago.) The car had bumpers but they were dented on the left-hand rear side. (I was never to understand the amount and significance of references to 'left' in this and subsequent dreams except in the sense of 'sinister'.) By the car was a salesman who had blond hair. The dreamer kept wondering if he was honest but he had the look of a Norseman so he felt that he must be trustworthy. By the side of the dreamer was Nicholas his son.

The car transforms into the back wheel and the rear of a motor-cycle. In front is the head of a dog, called a chien des avalanches (St. Bernard). The dog is licking Nicolas, who reciprocates by licking the dog. The dreamer does not like this because the dog may not be clean. He says so to Nicolas, who replies, 'I have the money and I need two places.'

The dream was followed by what the participants called a 'flash'. (This was their word.) This dreamer had two. The first one was *Ta foi t'a sauve*. Faith saves one; and the theme of faith had been running through the seminar in other events. His second was that he is wondering where Lawrence is to put any new books into his library. We were sitting in a large room where there are a few thousand books around the walls.

This dream had considerable importance but the full meaning is not yet clear. As the associations were being offered it was established that the barriers were formed from cross beams shaped like a cross of St. Andrew. The top executive of the group, who was not present, is called Andrew and the role of the dreamer is to work closely with him arranging, for example, the acquisition of new companies (attractive olive wood furniture?) and selling those which are no longer viable. The theme of 'alpine' occurs twice. There is the motor car and the dog. The company has strong associations with Switzerland. The motor car transforms into something else. Is this one of the problems of mail order that the old methods are no longer working with the same efficacity? The dog is a benign and helpful one. Does this represent how companies should treat their customers? What is the relation of the dreamer to his work in the companies in the group as indicated by his son who has the money. Where are the two places? Is the relationship purely a calculative, instrumental one and what is the place of faith in business? The Souk, fairly obviously, could symbolize the market environment but it was pointed out to me that the Souk is also a *bordel*. Since this word is often used to describe a total mess or shambles it might mean something about the state of the market.

I jump to a later dream in the sequence.

> *The dreamer is walking on the left side of a road. Coming towards him is his President who is also on the left of the road. The right hand side of the road is piled high with stones. The dreamer is not sure if these stones are the result of a rock-fall, or if they are waiting to be used in the rebuilding of the road. He says that he is not sure if they are there as a result of destruction or if they are waiting for use in construction. The road itself is well marked but is the line marking the centre of the road or marking the edge of it?*

The dreamer gives his second dream that is erotic. *Along with another fellow, he meets two gorgeous women. There is a little house that is a sauna.* He says he cannot give the end of the dream; whether because he forgot it or out of delicacy I'm not sure. He remarks that in the hotel he is sleeping in an old-fashioned iron bed that has brass balls on the bed ends. All night as he moves in bed they go 'kling-kling'.

This dream echoes the actual political situation of the dreamer as a new managing director working with the President whom, up to now, has also held the role of managing director. We thought that the stones on the right—one of the President's names is Pierre (pierre- = stone)—represented the company which has experienced a downturn in trading. Could the company be turned round, i.e. is reconstruction possible or is it in a disastrous, ruinous state? Where are the limits to any future growth of the company? The unasked question around for all the members of the seminar were: can the new managing director work with the President? Will they have a confrontational, conflictual relationship or work in harmony? Who is the other fellow in the erotic dream—the President?

Another dreamer is on the gangway of a boat. *He cannot see anything because there is fog but everyone assures him that when the weather is good it is a very nice view.* Our association was to the present state of the companies seeing the gangway, again, as the commercial link between the companies and their customers. While matters now may be bad perhaps better trading conditions will come when the fog lifts.

Again, I jump in the sequence. The other consultant says he has had a dream *in which everyone is at a big table with large quantities of food. There are a lot of people around it. He feels joyful in the dream but worried because nobody is available for serving the food.* Later he and I talked and we thought the dream was a reflection of his anxiety of how I managed the seminar. My aim was to create conditions for thinking and thoughts to be available, and so I rarely intervened in events except to press this aim forward. By the dream bringing the anxiety forward we were able to talk about our work relationship and the place of reflective 'containment' in an educational setting.

Another dreamer said he dreamt of working with a woman director.

> There are about fifteen people around a big table which he thought was located in the building of the company in Paris where he had worked before. The purpose of the meeting is the presentation of a collection of clothes. A woman who is either a director or the owner's wife is managing this. She is aged about forty and he is thirty in the dream.
>
> She says, 'I found these tiles (carreaux de sol) in the selection room.' Another women replies, 'They would be perfect for me.'
>
> 'May I add them to your purchases?' asks the vendeuse.
>
> The dreamer was very angry in the dream because these tiles belonged to the fabric of the building and were not part of the collection for sale, and he said that while he was employed in the company nothing would be taken from the enterprise. He realized in the dream that he was the guardian of l'ethique, and that he saw this woman as an enemy because she was always saying the contrary to him.

In many ways this dream expressed the dreamer's dilemmas in the group of companies in which he often feels in disagreement about the long term policies of the selling and the acquisition of companies. He is very concerned that the French group is partly owned by a German shareholder and he has anxieties that ultimately the French group will become, in effect, a German commercial colony and then no one will know the real identity of the French group.

A subsequent dreamer recounts his dream. *He is sailing down a river in a boat. The torrent is very powerful and there are rocks. While he is travelling in the boat he is working on the translation and explanation of a fable by Goethe. When his work is completed another manager, who is also in the dream Matrix, reads his text to an audience.* To add a note, the reader is the most recent appointee to the managing director role. He is not present in the boat going down the river. In reality the dreamer is the most senior director of Human Resources for the group of companies.

For French people it would be Fontaine who is the obvious author of fables but we assumed that Goethe represented the other substantial shareholder in the group of companies. Perhaps the dreamer's role in the future would be to give explanations of German policy to French managers who would give voice to it and act on it?

In the last session of the Social Dreaming Matrix the other consultant said that *he had had a dream in which he found himself to be the only spectator and was not eating with the others.* He said that this might reflect perceptions of his role in the seminar.

Another dreamer said

> that he had a dream but in the dream he experienced himself as conscious and awake. He is speaking to another managing director about a new marketing manager who is being transferred from one company in the group to another. (This was true.) The dreamer finds himself saying that this marketing manager speaks English very well—indeed would have an A grade. The President reacts to this by saying, 'You see you don't have enough confidence in people. Leave me, I am going to read the Bible.' He does so and in the dream he is facing Lawrence who is reading the Bible but in English.

The President is reading the book of Baruch, which does not appear in the King James Version but in the Apocrypha, having been excluded from the Protestant canon at the time of the Reformation. Baruch appears in French Bibles. As far as I have been able to check,

Baruch was important for giving a message to the conquered people who were under Babylonian rule. He also saved the religious furnishings of the temple after a Holocaust. The President is Catholic while it is well enough known that I am not. So I took it that the dream expressed something of the difficulty that the dreamer has in understanding why a French president should have an English-speaking consultant. And what is the nature of the transference between them? Who has access to what kind of knowledge? The possible reason for the selection of Baruch was that it might express something of the phenomenal role of the President in the group, i.e. trying to celebrate and maintain its French identity in an international context.

The next dream, which I will make the last in this account, was a fable of the 'Fat Duke and the Little Vassal'.

> *There is a town in which lives a Little Vassal. The Fat Duke comes to visit and the Little Vassal welcomes him to the town. There is in the place a big armchair, which could also be a throne   and it is used for that purpose on occasion. When the little Vassal sits in the armchair the whole town is illuminated and the longer he sits in the chair the more intense is the light. In order to have the very best light possible it is suggested that the Fat Duke also should sit in the armchair with the little Vassal.*
>
> *While the two are sitting in the chair the son of the little Vassal, who is an architect, is installing a spiral, which is in the form of a mobile, to the ceiling of the room in which the Fat Duke and the Little Vassal are seated. It is a very innovative and attractive spiral. The Little Vassal finds that there are two ways to sit in the chair with the Fat Duke. If the little Vassal is on his own he can make his body be flat shaped—like a slice of bacon—and so spread himself over the greatest area of the chair to provide his fellow townspeople with even more light. When the Fat Duke is present, however, he finds that if he is not quick enough the Fat Duke sits on top of him and squashes him. When the Fat Duke is in the chair with him he still has to shape himself like a slice of bacon but sitting upright like a piece of toast in a rack.*

There is a terrible scream from outside with someone shouting, *'Douleur, frustration cholere!'* The dreamer says that the Little Vassal is very *sympa* but the Fat Duke is *antipathetique* What the Little Vassal felt was great frustration and the experience of being made ashamed in front of his son the architect in the presence of the Fat Duke.

This dream summarizes much of the frustrations and feelings of being in this group of companies—pain, frustration and anger. I suspect the Little Vassal and the Fat Duke represent the shareholders. All of this cannot be spoken about publicly so it comes forward in the dreams and so falls into the domain of the 'unthought known'. The French-German axis tends to be construed in contemporary European terms which is fashionable. Furthermore, the differences between a French mode of managing and a German one are easily denied because all the companies have the same work, structures and methods which are the universal ones of mail order. My speculation was that the mobile spiral might symbolizes the DNA of the group, when DNA is represented as a double helix, and that the future, company successors (son as architect) might have to give the group a new identity which, at present, could only hang suspended in space and time. The Fat Duke and the Little Vassal sitting on the throne symbolized the German and French hidden struggle to control the companies in the future. Likely this may be shaming for older French managers in front of their younger compatriots. The Little Vassal could give light—leadership and employment—but it was assumed that the Fat Duke could give more if he added his bulk to the throne. The result, however, would be that the Little French Vassal would have to be squashed or squeezed out. All this, as I have indicated, is known at some level in the organization but it is never articulated through thought because it would result in rode holders having to think through the political version of the organization they carry 'in the mind' and their own psychic perception of themselves in that organization. Through the dreams, however, these issues have now been revealed.

I have given this lengthy extract, but nevertheless considerably shortened version, from a sequence of dreams and associations in a Matrix in order to give the feeling of what can happen when people with a shared work interest come together to dream socially. Essentially, I am trying to show that Social Dreaming can be used as one tool of action research, though always in conjunction with the other methods which traditionally have been used. In this way the repertoire is extended.

Working hypotheses on social dreaming

As more and more colleagues have joined me in the activity of Social Dreaming we have come to learn increasingly since 1982. The most important insights I give in the form of working hypotheses.

1. The first hypothesis, that it is possible to have dreams that have a social content and significance, was substantiated through the experiences of the first Social Dreaming Matrix in 1982. From the extract above it can be seen that people in roles in companies do dream about themselves in role and in the context of their business. And they dream of issues and conflicts that often cannot be voiced and debated publicly.

2. The second hypothesis is that if the dreams were received in a group rather than a Matrix there would be different social processes present. The mental space of a Matrix is different from a group—not better or worse, but different. In a Matrix the dreams of the participants are the 'currency'. In a group it would be the nature of the relationships between them. In particular transference and counter transference issues would be expected to be dealt with in the 'here and now' of a group. By having a Matrix such issues come to be dealt with through the dreams, e.g. the President and myself reading different Bibles, to cite from the sequence above. Indeed, colleagues' experience is that if such issues are discussed in the Matrix they are talked away and so rob the dreams of the residues on which to work.

   There is, I shall take the opportunity to add here, what could be called a 'meta' transference issue. One dreamer in an American Matrix dreamt that she had to swim between tow islands. One was marked 'Tavistock Group Relations' and the other 'Social Dreaming.' The writer was encouraging her to swim from the former to the latter. This, in actuality, does not represent my position because I see Social Dreaming, just as the Praxis Event has been, as being a development of the Tavistock tradition of understanding unconscious social processes, suffused as they are with psychosis. (Lawrence, 1985)

3. The third hypothesis is that the existence of a Matrix to receive the dreams alters the nature of the dreams compared with a

classic psychoanalytic situation. In short, a change in container alters the nature of what is contained and so the content of Social Dreaming is different. The dreams recounted in this paper probably would be different if the participants had been taking part as individuals in an analytic session.

4. The fourth hypothesis is that the idea of a Matrix alters the nature of the thinking processes and of how meanings are arrived at by the participants. Whereas in a group the concern is to create a universe of meaning, otherwise mutual understanding would be felt to be impossible, in a matrix a plethora of meanings can coexist for a particular dream. If one thinks about it there are as many associations to a dream as there are participants in a Matrix. In a Matrix it is possible to live with a multi-verse of meaning. It can be argued that such an experience is psychotic-like but it may be that the desire to have one interpretation for an event or dream is also a manifestation of psychosis. There can be a tyranny in preemptive interpretation. It is the act of mental association that is the creative element in Social Dreaming.

5. The fifth hypothesis is that Social Dreaming questions the notion that dreams are personal possessions. This is true in the psychoanalytic situation, to be sure, because of the nature of the dyadic relationship. In a Matrix people dream of the Matrix and anticipate their experiences of it. Will it be an unbalancing ride on an escalator? The idea of the 'social' dream has led my colleagues and me to think that just as Bion postulated that there are thoughts in search of a thinker so there may be dreams in search of a dreamer.

6. The sixth hypothesis is that the dreams in a Social Dreaming Matrix alert participants to the tragic aspects of life and intimate the horrendous that is to come. Often such issues cannot be spoken of directly because they are so frightening. Examples come from American programmes where a good deal has been surfaced through dreams as to what may happen to the country in the future. In the sequence I have offered in this paper the dream of the Little Vassal and the Fat Duke has tragic tones and it may be that in the future of this particular group of companies the Little Vassal will be squashed flat like a slice of bacon.

7. The seventh hypothesis is that dreams experienced in a Social Dreaming Matrix are a threat to ordinary awareness. The dream

has its own logic, embedded in its manifest and latent content, which questions the rationality experienced in waking life. The logic of a dream, if accepted and followed, may question the illogicality of existing in contemporary civilizations and their institutions. As I have observed for years, often our organizations are an expression of 'rational madness' as their role holders strive to avoid the anxiety of psychosis. There is evidence since the very first Matrix that what is unconsciously known about the institutions of the dreamers and the societies in which they live out their lives comes to be present in their dreams. While they consciously may make their knowledge absent in their waking lives their experiences come to be present in their dreams. The dream gives the lie to ordinary awareness.

8. The eighth hypothesis is that Social Dreaming is a tool of action research that is in the making. I suspect that this process of becoming will be arrested by moves to convert Social Dreaming into an activity taking place in groups because Social Dreaming in a Matrix is very open-ended and difficult to tolerate. (Cf. Baird, 1994) To be a consultant to a Matrix is to be never certain, always speculative. This is unlike being in a group where, with what has become distortions of the Tavistock 'technology', there is always the fantasy that one is right, at least some of the time. The dream, however, can be understood to be the almost undisturbed activity of the unconscious and, as Freud pointed out, censorship, which is the activity of the conscious mind, can be used to forget dreams and so negate the insight of the unconscious. The method used to work with dreams in a Social Dreaming Matrix needs to be congruent with a respect for the unconscious and alive to the possibility of censorship. At present, I think that there should be only sparse intervention by the consultant and then only to lead into association so as to further the discovery of the meanings of dreams by participants. I try to have faith in the dream and faith that the dream carries its own meaning and interpretation enshrined in it.

9. The ninth hypothesis is that provided we can remember our dreams we can have confidence that we are in touch with our unconscious and if we can associate to them mentally to find out their meanings we are on speaking terms with our unconscious. If that is made possible we can minimize the possibility of being

caught up in psychotic-like social processes because we can speak with our own psychosis. The dream itself, it can be postulated, is a natural, primordial form of action research by the psyche, on the psyche, for the psyche to unravel its relations with the external world of other people and natural phenomena.

10. The tenth hypothesis is the most disturbing. Unamuno says that we ourselves are 'a dream, a dream that dreams' (Unamuno, 1954). There is sufficient evidence in the literature to show that inventors and discovers dream what they are puzzling out. What we do in our daily lives may well be rehearsed during the time of dreaming. The Australian aborigines refer to the 'dream time'; a time when the land and its features and its peoples and gods were dreamt into existence. If, however, we do not listen to our dreams and rely totally on our consciousness, we may be cutting ourselves off from the roots of our unconscious, both good and bad.

The Social Dreaming Matrix which I have described in part had an unexpected denouement The managing directors left the seminar in France feeling that it had been a liberating experience in terms of thinking. All of them, I repeat, are facing exacting commercial challenges. All are competent and know their metier intimately. Each had been able to give the others confidence that they had to be continually reinventing the business of mail order if their companies were to survive and prosper in the future. They had recognized that Social Dreaming would never give them a direct answer to the issues they were facing but that the experience of searching for meanings would have direct consequences on the way that they thought about problems.

One of them had mentioned during the seminar that he had lost a notebook that he had been keeping while he was waiting to take over his new role as managing director. In the notebook he had been recording his observations of the company, disentangling issues he had to address and reasoning out decisions he had to make. Before the seminar he had lost the notebook which he could not find anywhere. The others had commiserated with him on his loss.

The night after the seminar he had a dream. In the dream he placed the notebook in the drawer of a black desk. On awakening he thought of black desks. He had one neither in his office nor his home. The only one he knew was the President's desk but it would have been unrealistic to place it there. As he thought about it he remembered that the desk had been an antique one with a not entirely smooth surface to its top. He thought more and remembered that he had been in a hotel with such a desk. He telephoned the hotel and the manager said, 'Yes we have your notebook but we did not know who to mail it to. We shall send it to you! ' And so the managing director was restored to his lost transitional object. Social dreaming may be useful, at least, for finding our lost properties that are contained in our dreams even though, like Peter Quince, we may not always get to the bottom of them.

References

Armstrong, D.G. (1994). *The 'Unthought Known'*. London: The Grubb Institute.

Baird, N. (1994). *The Dream Team Group; Members Sharing Dream as an Organizational Development*. Swinburne University, Australia: MBA thesis.

Bollas, C. (1987). *The Shadow of the Object*. London: Free Association Books.

Lawrence, W.G. (1985). Beyond the frames. In M. Pines (ed) *Bion and Group Psychotherapy*. London: Routledge & Kegan Paul.

Lawrence, W.G. (1991). Won from the void and formless infinite: experiences in social dreaming. *Free Associations*, 2 (Part 2, No. 22); pp. 254–266.

Lawrence, W.G. (1994).The politics of salvation and revelation in the practice of consultancy. In R. Casemore, G. Dyos, A. Eden, K. Kellner, J. McAuley, & S. Moss (eds.) *What Makes Consultancy Work?* London: South Bank University. Reprinted in Lawrence, W.G. (2000). *Tongued With Fire*, London: Karnac Books.

Lawrence, W.G., A. Bain & L. Gould (1996). The fifth basic assumption *Free Associations*, 6 (Part 1, No. 37); pp. 28–55.

Unamuno, M. de (1954). *Tragic Sense of Life*. New York: Dover.

Death imagery and the experience of organizational downsizing *or, is your name on Schindler's list?*

Howard F. Stein*
University of Oklahoma Health Sciences Center

Experiential realities of downsizing, reductions in force, restructuring, outsourcing, and cognate terms are often at wide variance with their touted and expected promises of increased productivity, profit, rationality, realism, efficiency, teamwork, and role interchangeability. Vignettes cited suggest that downsizing is not primarily about economics or business but, instead, myth and ritual. Downsizing is explored as a symbolic form and action, rationalized and masked by euphemism. Downsizing implements devastating planned social change, one that takes the form of sacrifice to purchase organizational life via symbolic death. Downsizing is experienced as a metaphoric Holocaust, one driven by the need to perform sacrifice (a) to separate bad from good parts of oneself and (b) to secure organizational rebirth through the expulsion of death. The link between the popular 1993 movie Schindler's List and organizational themes in the language of

---

* Many of the ideas in this article owe their existence and testing to lengthy telephone conversations with Michael Robin, M.S.W., whom the author gratefully acknowledges. I am likewise grateful to an anonymous reviewer of this manuscript who pressed me to explain the "But why?" choice of sacrifice and Holocaust symbolism in downsizing.

the Holocaust is explored and takes us to the heart of the conscious and unconscious emotional experience and meaning of downsizing.

Introduction: Downsizing, economics, and American culture

Whatever the ideological chasms between positivism, modernism, constructivism, and postmodernism, they at least agree on the position that things are rarely what they seem to be, or are officially declared to be. Life is more than meets the eye or ear or nose. It is the additional, and disturbing, legacy of the century of the Freudian revolution to teach us that our thoughts, feelings, and decisions are made from unconscious stuff to which we have rare and ambivalent access, let alone over which we exercise complete control. We act, but we do not know wherefrom we are acting—a although we insist we are consciously and rationally in charge of our thoughts and destinies. In a sense—and I shall say this over and again in different ways about the subject of *downsizing*—our depths and breadths of meanings and emotions elude us because we unconsciously wish them to do so.

Here is precisely where a psychoanalytic perspective on workplace and wider cultural organization is essential: both retrospectively over the past decade and prospectively toward the millennial year 2001. The contribution of the present study will be to show how an apparently rational-seeming action such as downsizing is being driven by unconscious motives. I conclude that if we paid more attention to unconscious motives, we could avoid much grief and long-term social costs, as well as economic costs. Yet it is of the very nature of unconscious resistance, especially when buttressed by group consensus, to wreak havoc on reality testing in the name of preserving psychological—and including organizational—structure.

I shall make an effort to reclaim more of the story of downsizing than Americans (of the United States) are used to or are comfortable with. Although I am a citizen of American culture, I cannot turn away from what I have learned through a decade of consulting and writing on the triad of social change, loss, and grief in workplace organizations, including one of its most widespread manifestations, the mass firing of workers.

In this article on American downsizing, I situate "economics" within culture rather than outside as its "engine." That is, I locate it within a broader ideological structure of what life is all about, and within the shared unconscious substrate of such ideological systems, rather than uncritically accept economics as the driving force of our society. In many circles, this is secular heresy. However, I come to this interpretation inductively and inferentially—not deductively from theory—from 25 years of ongoing fieldwork inside biomedical training institutions and from consulting. My views take exception from much of our received, official, and even obligatory wisdom about American's health care institutions, corporate decision making, and their link to the wider national culture.

I do not ask the reader to accept this counterintuitive, against-the-cultural-grain view on faith but on data—data different from spreadsheets and computerized profit/loss/production statements. I shall question our own business-related cultural presuppositions, most of which are not articulated in mission statements and strategic plans, *to wonder why getting rid of people on a large scale in the workplace via upper management decision making is the first and final solution (the latter, a term upper management often uses) we now offer and implement to organizational problems of profit, loss, productivity, and global competition.* Why this? Why now? I ask these on a large cultural scale, much as a physician wonders why a patient develops a particular disease at a particular time and why the patient comes to the office or to the hospital emergency room at this time instead of some other.

I should state my premises from the start. Downsizing, reductions in force (RIFs), restructuring, reengineering, rightsizing, outplacement, out-sourcing, and trimming fat, to name but several core euphemisms, are not primarily business decisions determined by economic rationality, enlight-ened self-interest, pragmatism, realism, empiricism, and objectivity—although our American cultural rule is that we *should* if not *must* see them as motivated this way and only this way (see 't Hart, 1991). I hope to show through five vignettes that *downsizing* and cognate terms are cultural maps and euphemisms. Through them we direct ourselves and are directed by others toward some things and away from others. These maps make some things explicit and blur others. I describe how downsizing and related ostensibly business terms are deeply embedded in unstated values (workers as machines and expendable units of production), perception of time (short term rather than long term), and unconscious conflict (e.g., about aggression, dependency, and identity). I argue that downsizing as a mode of decision making and of induced social change is opaque to comprehension if we do not first recognize that it rests on unstated values placed on human life, well-being, and loyalty, to name but three dimensions.

Far from being the pinnacle of rational, enlightened self-interest, objective judgment, downsizing is driven by destructively irrational forces. Even the *Wall Street Journal* and the *Washington Post* (e.g., Grimsley, 1995) now feature articles that raise skeptical "second thoughts" about the heady promises advocates of downsizing made in the 1980s era of corporate leveraged buyouts, raids, takeovers, and mergers. The cover story of *Newsweek Magazine's* 26 February 1996 issue is titled "Corporate Killers." David M. Noer's (1993) book is tellingly titled in euphemism-free English: *Healing the Wounds: Overcoming and Revitalizing Downsized Organizations*. Sometimes sacred, culturewide solutions turn out to be recognized as problems in disguise—or at least safely so in retrospect.

In our zeal to "de-layer" and "horizontally flatten" workplaces (a paradoxically "vertical" act), and to brand those "cut" ("axed," as many newspaper and magazine cartoonists depict) as nonessential "fat," we forget that in the 1970s and 1980s we regarded increasing administrative, managerial vertical layers as solution rather than as problem. We could not produce and hire MBAs (masters of business administration) fast enough. We once believed in the "fat" we now disdain, cut, and discard. They were to be our organizational "muscle," a police (external superego) to help corporations gain better control. Now "bloating" is our enemy, and "anorexia" is our salvation: Yet these both are our own organizational ideologies.

Downsizing was an inescapable reality and constant threat in the United States during the past decade. There is scarcely any American whose life has not been directly touched or at least threatened by it, often multiple times. Many executives as well as workers have been through two, even three, mass layoffs. Many now hold two, three, even four jobs to make ends meet for themselves, their families, and their lifestyles. Downsizing as reality, as memory, as anticipated event, as emotion-charged fantasy, casts many shadows. Having said this, I wish also to be clear that I am not engaging in "downsizing-bashing." The culprit is not a specific mode of organizational change but is rather unrecognized and disavowed influences that drive workplace life. Following on the pioneering work of Diamond (1984, 1985, 1988) and Diamond and Allcorn (1985), I argue that business and other workplace organizations in our mixed-capitalist economy, like larger ethnic groups and nations, are largely unconsciously constituted and constructed. Downsizing is a special, and current, instance of this process. Business, policy, economics—from day-to-day bureaucracy to upheavals—are not sufficient unto themselves; they rest on volcanoes.

What downsizing *is*, is inseparable from what it symbolizes, what it feels like, to all involved. In a formula: Downsizing (and related terms) is a cultural idiom of problem definition and problem solving in the language of economic necessity. If in the 1960s, the image of abundance and generosity prevailed in political economy, in the 1990s, the image of scarcity and deprivation dominates. There is not enough of anything (resources, money, love, caring, commitment) to go around in order to survive: This is the central, unstated dread of our time.

Downsizing is a single institutional form taken by bloodless as well as bloody *domestic, internal wars* now occurring between groups inside the United States (Stein, 1990a, 1994a, 1995a). Since 1990, the cold war has ended, and the "evil empire" of the Soviet Union is but memory. The aggression, though, that bipolar world contained is now let loose among us. In an article on the U.S. defense budget, Stephen S. Rosenfeld (1995) astutely tied current pressure to increase military defense to free-floating anxiety:

> Leading congressional Republicans have seized upon his [President Bill Clinton's] discomfort to define a post-Cold War global environment of pervasive danger and struggle. In this fevered vision, a fear of chaos replaces the old fear of communism. The outcome is a similar sense of embattlement and crusade, and a certain increased readiness to spend more on the military (p. A25).

We all live in Bosnia now. Our equivalents to "ethnic cleansing" and Balkanization are conducted in gang wars, in racial and ethnic strife, and in ruthless business competition, to name but three ways we strive to keep a sense of goodness inside and to expel badness outside, to create decisive local boundaries in an era of collapsing global boundaries.

Historically, I would situate downsizing as one expression of our domestic internal wars against a myriad of internal enemies. These wars erupted in the wake of the end of the cold war and the emotionally destabilizing effect of the loss of the Soviet Union as our "shadow," or evil double, that served so well as a focus and vessel of Americans' disavowed aggression (Stein, 1993, 1994a, 1995a, 1995b, 1995c; Volkan, 1988). With the boomeranging return of the repressed, and of what we had dissociated and projected outside our national group self to feel good and whole, we now shatter into alliances and oppositions, corporate and clinical camps of enemies and allies, as well as ethnic and political ones. "We" are now uncomfortably "they" as well—unsure of our internal boundaries, as we continue to try to expel the "bad" from ourselves in groups as well as individually. In corporate businesses and academic biomedicine alike, our computers and spreadsheets conduct bloodless wars. But death and thoughts of death abound—as the vignettes below illustrate vividly.

Before I turn to a detailed narrative account of downsizing and to illustrative vignettes, let me state my qualifications and limitations. My experience rests on paying careful attention to the language, the metaphors, the images, the idioms, the emotions, the clichés, and the euphemisms that people in organizations use to describe, to explain, to understand, and to justify their day-to-day work. Much of my organizational experience comes from academic health sciences centers and community health care practices. Clinical faculty meetings, case conferences, curricu-lum meetings, team meetings, quality assurance meetings, departmental retreats, and regional and national medical conferences are all treasure troves of the ordinary that hold keys to our understanding of downsizing. For the past 17 years, I have offered an annual graduate seminar on "Behavioral Science in Occupational and Environmental Medicine" to physicians and to physicians' assistants (PAs). They have taught me to pay close attention to workplace culture. Much of my data come from news magazines and newspapers, from medical economics journals and in-flight magazines, and from television and radio.

Lastly, as a culmination of these experiences, in November 1994, the CEO of a large metropolitan hospital complex invited me to become the ongoing consultant to its three-wave downsizing and subsequent internal reorganization. This role has given me an often harrowing intimacy with the day-to-day preparation for the mass firings and with the long-term consequences of the firings for morale and task performance among those people who remained behind to pave the way for the world of managed care and hospital mergers. From them, I have learned more what I needed than what I wanted. For me, there is no turning away, no turning back, from what they have taught me.

I owe the reader a brief note on my methodology or modus operandi. I conduct all my research as an applied medical and organizational anthropologist. That is, organizational consulting is a form of applied fieldwork. I do not know beforehand what I shall or should "study." I am a naturalist. I am nosy. I often discover disparities between social realities people espouse and those that I observe or infer (Richards, 1956) from others' words, deeds, and emotions. Much of my most reliable data come from my own emotional reaction ("countertransference") during the process of consulting. The observer or consultant's own subjectivity can be a powerful instrument of greater objectivity, even as it can be a source of massive distortion.

Schindler's list as parable of the downsizing of America

This article takes its inspiration from a movie, Steven Spielberg's (1993) *Schindler's List*. For all its historical inaccuracies and understatement, this movie was both a box office success and won an Academy Award in 1994 for best picture. It disturbed me enough to see it three times—not only because it allowed me, an American Jew, to safely visit once again a still raw historical trauma. The more I watched it, the more I saw it also as allegory for our America of the 1990s, not only as a quasi-documentary of Europe between 1933–1945. Are there any "essential workers" left in America? "Business," ours or that of dandy-porcelain industrialist Oskar Schindler, is high drama, opera, cinema, and grueling reality.

Now, I am aware that for an employer to layoff a large number of employees is not the same as to murder them by firing squads and in gas chambers. Symbolic murder is *not* actual murder. Equivalence at the unconscious level is *not* identical with equivalence at the level of reality. I only ask that the people whom I quote here be heard in their own voices, that we begin to wonder why so many people articulate their experience in the catastrophic symbology of the Holocaust, and that we not be quick to dismiss their idiom as exaggeration. If an entire nation uses downsizing as a preferred way to problem solve, many people will be unemployable, uninsurable. Many will be left out in the cold—placed at great risk, to disappear, to go away and die. The presence of the Holocaust as a constant occupant of the inner representational world makes psychodynamic sense.

Certainly "older" workers (those nearing or over 50 years) are among those at high risk of being regarded as expendable. What are experience, loyalty, the sense of organizational history—for example, what has been tried before and succeeded or failed?—informal networking, and the girth of one's rolodex if one is viewed by management and younger co-workers as "dead meat" or "corporate fat"? Yet, are the "lean and mean" younger, less expensive competitors any more secure when upper management begrudges them all benefits and perks?

In this article I try on my fantasy that as an American culture we have become our own death camp, one where we hope some CEO Oskar Schindler or Daddy Warbucks (the industrialist in the Broadway musical *Annie* popular a decade and a half ago) will protect us with our jobs, our health insurance, and our dignity. But in the movie, even a person with the proper documentation, "papers," an "essential worker," could be summarily pulled out of the work line and shot point blank dead in the head. In our movie fantasies, we are now all Jews, wandering the corporate halls, industries, and campuses. Even upper management, whom we might fantasize as Nazi torturers and butchers, is not exempt. We are both Jews and Germans; we vacillate between poles of victim and victimizer. There is no place to hide. We who protect ourselves one day by consuming others might soon become the consumed. Spreadsheets and profit-loss figures are symptoms in the guise of impersonal solutions. Downsizing is bloodless, but we know that we have created a trail and a pool of blood. Symbolic murder harbors the wish to kill.

Schindler's List is parable. What the Nazis did to the Jews is allegory for what we Americans now do to our own. Sometimes cinematic and other artistic fiction are truer than official sociological fact. In the Vietnam War, the memory of which still haunts us over 20 years later, we Americans did not know who was friend or foe. All Vietnamese became potentially dangerous "Gooks"—things, not people—depersonalized menaces. Today in our American hospitals, corporations, banks, research and development institutions, industries, universities, and even government, we do not know from one day to the next who is ally or enemy. Many upper management have said to me: "The person or board whose firings I execute today could fire me tomorrow, no matter how productive or loyal an employee I have been." The living are all disposable waste.

The scale of destructiveness is emotionally overwhelming even to consider, as a Department of Health and Human Services (1995) an-nouncement describes,

> If the 1980s are remembered as the decade of mergers and acquisitions, the legacy of the 1990s will be the decade of downsizing and reorganization. The trend toward downsizing began in the late 1980s, but increased substantially in the 1990s, and widened its focus from blue-collar jobs to include white-collar jobs. The result has been a virtual epidemic of job loss due to downsizing across all industries and forced career changes, especially among professional and white-collar workers. It has been estimated that two-thirds of all large firms in the United States (U.S.)—more than 5000 employers—reduced their workforces in the latter half of the 1980s. From 1983 to 1988, approximately 4.6 million U.S. workers were displaced, with 2.7 million (57.8%) resulting from plant closings. An estimated 300,000 jobs will be lost in the banking industry alone in the 1990s, and over 200,000 jobs are being eliminated as part of the federal government's *"Reinvention"* effort (Announcement No. 572, p. 3).

Questions that come immediately to mind are why for nearly a decade we as a nation have been in the thrall of the beliefs that (a) the primary motives behind downsizing are economic, (b) that the only victims have been those who have lost their jobs, and further (c) why we as members of workplace organizations have been so slow to notice that in the workplace and outside, downsizing is everyone's business. It is culturally significant, and disturbing, that we are surprised by how widespread the suffering might be. Our self-blindedness—not unlike tragic Oedipus's own—takes us to the heart of the matter. *The bottom line (as culture) is not only about the bottom line (as economics).* As a way of thinking, the bottom line cries out for careful dissection. *Schindler's List* is a warning about what our all-American bottom line is coming to—a point to which I shall return in the vignettes.

We must listen carefully to people's images, words, metaphors, and feelings as they describe downsizings and their roles. They are not inconsequential, epiphenomenal, "icing" on the cake. If organizational RIFings are indeed bloodless, if borrowing from what Lucy Dawidowicz (1975) called "the war against the Jews" is allegorical, we must still take seriously the fact that *annihilation by Holocaust is a recurrent frame of reference by which people undergoing downsizing articulate what it feels like to experience RIFing.*

Ultimately, no one is secure from damage in this devouring process. No one is truly exempt, and everyone in some way becomes complicit. Boundaries are unclear and constantly shift in the liquid world of down-sizing. Everyone is a potential Jew and a potential Nazi. Everyone is at risk. Perpetrators, victims, and bystanders (Hilberg, 1992) are not fixed categories. Much of the Holocaust's systematic degradation, dehumani-zation, of non-"Aryans" (non-us; persons manufactured into disposable nonpersons, "them") commends analogizing precisely because at the unconscious logical level, if not at the behavioral, the two had similar goals.

There is still another level one might characterize as the phenomeno-logical, the way people *experience and make sense of* the event and process of downsizing and of being downsized. *To live through down-sizing, to witness it firsthand, is so horrible, so devastating, so inducing of regression, that the only consistent image that can do it justice is the Holocaust.* The first questions are: "Was it *real?"* "Did this really happen at our organization, to us?" "Did *we* really do this?" To answer in the affirmative—whether one be consultant, outside observer, or employee—one must be able to experience enormous guilt, shame, anxiety, even terror, rage, remorse, and sadness. It is to feel regression's disorganization and desperate effort to reorganize the inner and outer worlds. The next question is: "What image(s) condenses and sustains those feelings, wishes, fantasies, and the defenses against being overwhelmed by them?" Those who insist on analogy with the Nazi Holocaust have much to teach us about removing the shroud of euphemism and unreality from the face of downsizing. Use of the Holocaust metaphor commits the fallacy of misplaced concreteness only if we take the metaphor literally. An extension to this question is the "why" of motivation behind the selection of the Holocaust as the central story line, and of Nazis and Jews as the inseparable protagonists. I shall address this latter question of *analysis* via the vignettes and following them.

Downsizing and its victims

What happens to the morale, the spirit, the soul of an organization, when it is guided by such imperative mottoes as "No margin, no mission," "The only bottom line is the bottom line," "Don't tell me what you did for me yesterday; tell me how you're going to benefit the company tomorrow"; or when, after a major series of layoffs, an executive or mid-level manager upbraids a worried worker: "What are you whining about? You weren't RIFed! You've still got your job! You should be relieved, grateful, not worried. Forget this nonsense and concentrate on productivity. We've a job to do." What happens to profit and to productivity when morale is assaulted by the degradation of "survivors"? What are the consequences of calling oneself, or of being called, a survivor? What happens to profit and to productivity both in reality and in expectation?

As in a drama, enter now, from the wings to center stage, the downsizing corps of consultants and consulting teams who live out the prevailing military metaphor and competitive, warlike, atmosphere. These corps serve the symbolic function of "SWAT" (Special Weapons and Tactics) teams and "Special Forces," even "hired guns." Economic and military metaphors condense. Business comes largely to be a military operation in disguise, one in which only the fit survive. The creation of a new, radically different future takes the unmistakable form of annihilation to prepare its way.

Downsizing in business, industry, health care, education, and gov-ern-ment is a "logical" cultural extension of the widespread *eradication of all pasts* and of an *arrogant monochromatic and foreshortened vision of the future*. This new vision is one often imagined and imposed by upper-level executives isolated and self-isolated from the rest of the organization. Further, often the owners or largest investors consist of high-risk leveraging financiers who are virtually unacquainted, and who have little interest in becoming familiar, with the day-to-day details of the very industry or type of work done in the place they have acquired.

Downsizing is an institutionalized solution that is, in turn, embedded in a worldview that defines human life as nothing more than a globally competitive marketplace. It is a Hobbesian image of all social life (not only the workplace) as driven by sudden-death economics. It is also Social Darwinism in corporate rather than (or in addition to) nationalist guise. The reified body with whom we symbiotically fuse our own fate is the workplace. In the fantasy underlying this work world, there are no people here, only products, producers (robots), and wished-for profit in the shadow of dread, loss, and death.

What is the view of the world in which downsizing and restructuring make sense and become orthodoxy? If I propose downsizing to be a problem rather than a solution—or as well as a solution—my point of departure is to understand the view that downsizing and reengineering are the *preferred* solution. Can a whole society be wrong (see Edgerton, 1992; Endleman, 1995; La Barre, 1972; Stein, 1994a)? And wrong in what ways? Is downsizing itself inherently evil (dehumanizing, degrading, destructive), or is it the way in which it is implemented that is evil? We are creating by result, if not by design, an emotionally vulnerable, unprotected, starved, regressively dependent, and enraged workforce, and we are rationalizing the entire process by insisting that it is necessary for organization economic survival.

Downsizing's Orwellian 1984 "Newspeak" euphemisms and cognates include an entire, obligatory vocabulary of self-deception. The emotional reality is of abrupt firings, staged as surprise attacks, layoffs, betrayal, abandonment of everyone, and plummeting morale. Downsizing is one contemporary expression of what I have come to call "murder of the spirit," an ubiquitous but little-explored nonphysical act of violence in the workplace in which people are experienced and experience themselves treated as things, as commodities, as objects, producers of products, and themselves parts of production lines. Those unnecessary for the perfor-mance of functions are simply thrown away. For all the official, facile rhetoric of Total Quality Management, the 1990s come close to resembling Frederick Winslow Taylor's early 20th-century ideal of a totally controlled, impersonally efficient, American industry governed by principles of "scientific management." More so now than ever before in my experience, medical practice buildings, their standardizing architecture and decor, and their human interactions are coming to resemble nothing so much as *a factory.*

In downsizings, who are the victims? Of course, the answer hinges on how victimhood is defined, and by whom. Ostensibly, it is those who are fired. On the other hand, officially, often by fiat, it is no one. There are no victims, only market forces. In today's entitlement-ridden society, virtually no one is left who does not claim some sort of victimhood: ethnic, national, racial, age, class, gender. I would insist that everyone is involved, from the CEO, chief financial officer (CFO), chief operating officer (COO), midlevel managers who do the actual face-to-face firing, the surviving rank-and-file workers "in the trenches," to the security guards who are summoned to escort those fired to their cars. Upper management might "only" be the psychological casualty of its indifference, its psychic numbing, rationalization, and denial; but more often than not, even upper management is eventually consumed by its own relentless revolution. Some of the most decisive, accomplished, arrogant, swashbuckling, intimidating CEOs and CFOs I know were fired by the very corporate board and stockholder supporters who had hired them to do the axings in the first place.

The experiential reality of downsizing: Some vignettes

Vignette 1

Leaders, researchers, and consultants alike cannot help but be struck by the ubiquity of death imagery and feelings experienced and articulated by people going through downsizing. For this first vignette, I draw on an example a consultant colleague told me at an organizational consultation conference. He had been working at a prominent national research and development (R&D) laboratory in the early 1990s. The widely shared image of the RIFing within the corporation was "sudden death." The image took and spread like a prairie grass fire.

The hapless supervisors who did the actual firing were called "angels of sudden death," a bitter twist on the celestial realm: Expected mercy becomes unexpected terror. In this context, it will be remembered that the infamous Nazi concentration camp physician, Dr. Josef Mengele, who had "experimented" on thousands of Jews, had been known as the "Angel of Death" (Lifton, 1986).

Those who were laid off were fired summarily. They were given absolutely no preparation or anticipation (except, of course, rumor). Security guards escorted the RIFed persons to their cars or other vehicles in the parking lot after they had cleaned out their offices and desks immediately the same day as they had been notified of their firing. Out of upper management's fear that computers and other vital equipment would be sabotaged or stolen, none of those fired were let back into the building after the security guards had led them this one final time to their motor vehicles, and after their company keys had been turned in. The manner or style of the firings was itself traumatizing. Soon its memory, amplified in further fantasy and dread, came to terrorize the R&D laboratory, even as everyone aspired and was exhorted to return to business as usual, only with redoubled effort. This style of forced "recovery" based on the "inability to mourn" (Mitscherlich & Mitscherlich, 1975) makes inner recovery difficult if not impossible.

Vignette 2

Organizational metaphors and similes serve as a path to understand how members of a work group imagine themselves and their situation, what it is like to be there (Stein, 1990a, 1990b, 1994b, 1995a; Stein & Apprey, 1987). They also serve as one "Royal Road" to an organizational unconscious, to widespread fantasies and affects that underlie and organize recurrent images.

Organizational metaphors express and reflect shared intrapsychic social reality (Diamond, 1993). "This is what it feels like to work here" is what management and workers say through their metaphors. *Downsizing, RIFs, rightsizing, restructuring, reengineering, outplacement,* and *outsourcing* are widely used metaphors for causing, or participating in, great suffering and at the same time gaining vast emotional distance from that suffering. Through euphemisms in the idioms of mechanics and architecture, we can borrow our conscience from others; cede personal responsibility to "the Organization"; diminish the feeling that we are causing harm; and therefore diminish our own sense of responsibility, anxiety, guilt, and shame (Alford, 1990). Socially shared and justified defenses do not feel like defenses at all: They feel like reality. We "restructure" people who we have made into the image of cold, dead things, not real, whole people.

At one Roman Catholic-sponsored urban hospital long known for its service to the poor, upper management announced and unilaterally executed large-scale firing without including department heads or chiefs of hospital services in the decision. Many employees called these layoffs "Pearl Harbor"—and this in an institution whose entire hierarchy had professed the Vatican II values of dignity and subsidiarity (i.e., allocating decision-making authority and responsibility not only to the top leaders of church, parish, or hospital but to the bottom as well). Issues of economics and job security became inseparable from the sense of sham and betrayal, and the consuming rage and despair that shadowed the hospital's future among those who retained their jobs.

In a nutshell, the secular R&D organization in Vignette 1 and the sacred church hospital I just briefly described were equally suffused by the same narrowly "bottom-line" official ethos that made downsizing compelling and unquestioned. But images of the devastating surprise attack of Japanese airplanes on Pearl Harbor on 7 December 1941, and of sinister angels of sudden death—and its implicit allusion to the Nazi doctor, Dr. Josef Mengele—tell a different narrative tale, one we dismiss at great peril.

These metaphors are not difficult to detect. They are difficult to recognize only if we defend ourselves from taking them in and taking them seriously. For example, as I read a transcript of interviews from a study of the downsizing of a large urban hospital (in Allcorn, Baum, Diamond, & Stein, 1996), I wrote down a succession of metaphors and similes.

> Rumors are running amok; I'm afraid that when problems arise, my department will be scapegoated; "Am I the one?" [targeted to be fired]; hospital as the target; Black Friday; D-Day [invasion]; how long can a gun be held to someone's head before they say "shoot"? [reductions]; It was important to hear that the ship was not going down and a message like, 'This too shall pass";

flatten the organization [administrative layers]; Everyone was herded like cattle to slaughter into the auditorium [to announce the layoffs]; It is almost like the university and the medical center are in a glass bubble. People do not know what is going on in the outside world [boundary issues]; Everyone is feeling vulnerable. There is the feeling that we will never let this (the layoffs) happen again, like the Holocaust.

The reader might say that in so enumerating and isolating core metaphors, I am taking them out of their narrative context. I agree. I do not discount the more obvious sequential, narrative context of the detailed interviewing of hospital managers. On the other hand, the official context can be seen as a kind of "smoke screen" to divert attention from the "fire"! The fire is itself clearest when we consider only the metaphors by themselves, as closest to the underlying, unconscious context. It is emotionally draining to read the above list, because it feels so overwhelming. There is nowhere to hide. There is no protection from total vulnerability. Perhaps that is what it feels like to work at this hospital.

Vignette 3

At one large urban, academic health sciences center that consisted of a confederation of a dozen specialty hospitals, it was widely rumored in late 1994 that some 400 people would soon be fired from the hospital system, and 400 additional unfilled hospital staff positions (clinical and administrative) would be eliminated. One entire hospital building was to be closed, and position transfers to other hospitals would not be permitted. The campus learned of this decision and of its imminence through the local newspaper in mid-January 1995. I was invited by upper management to work with the department of human relations, the personnel department, and nursing administration of the hospital system to assist a task force in preparing the campus for this process and to help them deal with the extended aftermath. My consulting role continues through the present.

During an initial 2-hour meeting in late January, members of one planning committee said many things that resonate with what was said and felt at the hospital I discussed in Vignette 2 above. The comparative study of accounts of organizational disaster such as downsizings will help consultants and theorists alike to identify and distinguish between local and universal themes, and to learn how to be helpful. Among my field notes from the meeting appear a number of poignant phrases spoken by staff members:

> I'm planning a funeral for somebody who's going to die but doesn't know they're going to die. … As a manager I feel it's like World War II. The Nazis have come in and tell us "Point out all the Jewish people" so we can get rid of them. Then tell us the Gypsies, then the Poles. … That's what it feels like. … We're asked to plan a funeral and we don't know who's going to be attending. … This is my home (the hospitals; spoken with tears in her eyes)! They are my family! … Nursing is nurturing and difficult to let people go. So how does a nurse tell another nurse she's fired? I'm a manager. How do I work with a shorter staff (and still be nurturing)? If I survive this time around, how do I know I'll be here the next cutback? … I have vast concerns that I will not be employed here long, and I'm one of the people in charge of the program for the people who are being fired now.

Vignette 4

The material in this example is taken from field notes that I made during and after a postdownsizing meeting of a large hospital's middle adminis-tration in April 1995. Although hospital administrators did not question the need for large-scale layoffs, they invited my partici-pation as consultant to try to minimize the human suffering from the outset, to try to help the immediate and long-term process to be more humane. The meeting took place after participants had con-ducted four 2-week "displacement training workshops" for groups of people who had been laid off. Holocaust imagery pervaded the discussion:

> People [at the hospital] are just waiting for the Nazis to come and demand the next trainload of Jews to ship to the camps. We've been through three downsizing displacement training workshops now. What will hospital restructuring do to us?

No one tells us. Decisions come down from the top, and we're supposed to carry them out. We might be the next to go, no matter how well we do our jobs.

During the four downsizing workshops at St. Gregory's Church, we held a job fair, helped people to prepare resumes, to fill out forms to collect unemployment compensation. We had consultants give excellent career counseling; it wasn't just touchy-feely. We were totally ignored by everyone in the hospital. It was as if we weren't there, as if the RIF hadn't taken place. Nobody talked about it; nobody talked to us. It's like they didn't want to know, even though people in our departments knew full well what we were doing all those weeks. Couldn't a doctor have offered to buy or bring the *pizza* (emphatic, anguished) for a lunch, for the staff or for displaced people? We go around here [the hospitals], and they [other employees] act like they don't even know us. Nobody else sees what we do. They don't want to know.

Vignette 5

The data in this vignette are taken from field notes I took during a middle management hospital postdownsizing meeting about 7 months after 500 people had been laid off from a workforce of 3,500. Here, a veteran nurse, now in nursing administration, speaks about the atmosphere in personnel [the unit where we were meeting]. She had had to walk through the department to get to our conference room:

Personnel used to be upbeat, where you could go in the hospital to feel good. Not upbeat now. It is worse in personnel than in other hospital departments. There is a feeling of helplessness, hopelessness, powerlessness. You want to scream and say: "I'm affected, too! Not only the people who are no longer here. … There were no raises in personnel except the *internal auditor* who showed [to the upper hospital management council in charge of the layoffs] what could be done on the computer. *He* got a raise. "Just get them out [the ones being laid off]" was the message we got. "And we don't want to hear about it." No one got any pay or even a compliment for the

kind of work we did [2-weeklong "work fairs" in which they
provided support and information for each group whose jobs
had been eliminated].

Interpretation, implications, and conclusions

What do we—as leaders, managers, consultants, social scientists,
vulnerable mortals—make of these vignettes, and of the meanings
of downsizing in whose shadow they stand? Do they help illumine
the effects, the process, the meaning, the symbolism, and the catastrophic emotions brought to, and evoked by, downsizing? Do
they convey something vital about American culture, about human
nature, and about what we ought to do with their message? Do
we—as scientists, clinical practitioners, managers—shrink from
responsibility for cultural change by taking a schizoid flight to the
moon to find refuge and revenge? Do we secretly obtain vicari-
ous pleasure from the destruction of human lives? Is downsizing
a modern, highly abstracted form of human sacrifice: That is, if
one lives, must another die? Is downsizing or RIFing our equivalent form of, say, Aztec bloody rites to assure the return of the
sun? In downsizing, do we literally try to "buy time" for ourselves
and our organization's "survival" through the symbolic death of
others? (The notion of workplace or other organizational survival
is itself a reification, projection, and anthropomorphization [see
Alford, 1990], an example of the logical "fallacy of misplaced concreteness," for no workplace organization is a literal biological
organism that goes from birth to death.)

The ethnographic data here suggest the answer is a grim yes to
all of these questions, and no amount of death suffices to assure
and regenerate life. The corporate immortality project (Becker, 1973,
1975) of downsizing must fail, but it cannot be interrupted. There is
always some "fat" and "dead meat" that can be cut or trimmed (con-
densing numerous primitive anxieties from annihilation, to separation, to castration).

Can we acknowledge the enormous loss and grief—the emotional
price and cost—this specific form of induced social change has
caused? Can we not retreat into psychology as smoke screen, but
use psychology as lighthouse to show us where we have done evil
and where we can repent, console, and make amends?

The five vignettes in this article constitute frequently encountered narrative accounts and metaphors offered by people involved in downsize-ing. As images and story lines, they are *thematically* representative of lived worlds, although not necessarily *statistically* so. That is, they serve as cultural exemplars of events and processes that extend far beyond them-selves. They tell the story of modern America as refracted through dominant business language and practice.

In this article, I have tried to keep to the phenomenological level, that is, the world as experienced and articulated by the interviewee and client rather than the one mostly interpreted by the participant observer. I have tried to let the vignettes mostly speak for themselves rather than to force an interpretation on them, or attempt to dissect them in terms of a preferred psychoanalytic and anthropological theory (e.g., classical topographic or structural theory, object relations theory, self-psychology, textual decon-struction). Still, as Freud and Oppenheim (1911/1958), Koenigsberg (1975), Dundes (1984), Paul (1987), and Stein (1994a) have argued, myth, folklore, fairy tales, political ideology, and legend all contain the outlines of their own interpretation. From folklore we could reinvent everything we have learned from clinical psychoanalysis via the couch, free association, and the dream.

In a sense, although Freud's topographical model of mental functioning—that of the vertically organized dynamic process involving the triad of unconscious, preconscious, and conscious thought—is immensely useful, it is also at times a misleading fiction. For "the depth" can often be readily seen and heard at the cultural surface. Those whom in business and other organizations we observe and with whom we consult are telling us the secrets of their hearts even as they are disguising them.

Experience and interpretation or analysis (explanation) are inseparable. Why, for instance, do people liken downsizing to a Holocaust rather than to other cataclysms? Why are we making everyone into Jews to be gassed, or to Nazis? What makes managers blind (or self-blinded) to real economic costs, in rational terms, of downsizing—not to speak of the human costs? Why is sacrifice invoked and implemented as the obligatory mode of problem solving? At least the beginning and direction (content) of answers to these linked questions—"Why sacrifice?" (solution) "But why *these* symbol choices (metaphorical Holocaust, Jews, Nazis)?" and "Why now?" (timing)—come from the downsizing interview and work group narratives themselves and from their wider cultural reverberations. *The subject of the Holocaust drama is sacrifice, the wish to purify and magically restore one national "body" by purging it of another (indeed, of all others) felt to threaten and defile it.*

In the West, Jews have been history's perennial scapegoat or victim, an always-available "other" or foil through whom other ethnic, national, and religious groups attempt to solve their group identity panics (Erikson, 1963). When "we" become threatened with dissolving boundaries, we are, in turn, menaced by what those boundaries contained and kept safely from us: for instance, the hitherto repressed and dissociated "bad" parts of ourselves such as unacceptable sexual and aggressive wishes, death, and separation/dependency conflicts. At the level of social interaction, Jews as real people and as image (internal representation) become the *them* through which *we* can redefine, revitalize, and restore ourselves as "good" once again—an identity struggle likewise played out throughout Jewish history in conflicts over assimilation, separatism, accommodation, and other temporary adaptations.

> In *The War Against the Jews, 1933–1945*, Lucy S. Dawidowicz (1975) writes that "The Holocaust" is the term that the Jews themselves have chosen to describe their fate during World War II. ... The word derives from the Greek *holocauston*, the Septuagint's translation for the Hebrew *olah*, literally "what is brought up," rendered in English as "an offering made by fire unto the Lord," "burnt offering," or "whole burnt offering." The implication is unmistakable: Once again in their history the Jews are victims, sacrifices (p. xxiv).

Since World War II, many religious and ethnic groups have adapted the term *Holocaust* to depict the cataclysmal destruction visited upon them-selves as sacrificial victims in their histories as well. For one to live, another must die, is the magical formula through which a person or group offers another person or group up to a savagely demanding deity and conscience in order to purchase immortality, or at least some more time on this side of death's divide.

A culturally clinical formula comes into play: "We are dying," is the diagnosis; "sacrifice" is the treatment. If "we" feel we are dying, "infected" with death (as introject), then, under the pull of regression and the catastrophic dread of annihilation (Devereux, 1955), "we" initiate the sacrifice of "them" as a sacred ritual of purification to restore "us" to life, to enable "us" to be reborn as a group, by expelling and "killing" death. Through sacrifice, "we" bring order (life) out of the chaos (death). Sacrifice is the designated means toward this end. The identification, segregation, and elimination of metaphoric Jews from the workplace is the symbolic action by which organizations expect to be magically renewed, cleansed, and born again by the casting out of death (i.e., symbolically putting one's own death into another, and then eliminating them, as in scapegoating).

What *now* invokes the archetypes (Jung) or unconscious fantasies (Freud) of sacrifice? What creates the need for metaphoric Nazis and Jews in the workplace and beyond?—the collapse of previously internally and intersubjectively stabilizing boundaries, the conflation of "good" (inside) with "evil" (outside), the regression in the face of overwhelming anxiety, and the desperate effort to reorganize the inner world by radically segre-gating "good" from "evil" to contain evil once again outside oneself and one's social units ranging from workplace to nation (see Klein, 1946).

At least in part because of the end of the cold war, the clear-cut polarity of good and evil, of victim and aggressor as inner representations (Meissner, 1978), and of sacrificer and sacrificed has been denied not only to Americans but to the rest of the world as well. The boundary between oppressor and oppressed is unclear. It fluctuates from one moment to the next. Distinctions blur, and with it free-floating anxiety and the search for enemies erupts. Jews and Nazis, as conscious images of the oppressed and oppressor, boomerang to become uncomfortably a part of us (introjects or internal objects, that is, indigestible, unassimilatable, haunting presences, in psychoanalytic terms). If the sacrifice of Jews has been a historical solution to restore the purity of the social body, to restore magically the symbiotic fusion of infant with "good" mother (Koenigsberg, 1975), this same solution is fraught now with anxiety, shame, guilt, and even identification. In World War II, Americans waged "the good war" against the Nazis, and (together with other Allied armies) liberated the Jews from the death camps—only to have now internalized the war against the Jews and the fear of victimization within the boundaries of the United States. We want to sacrifice; we are the sacrifice. We wish to be and to do good; no matter what we do, we are evil; we carry out our own or others' evil. Even to be a loyal Nazi or bureaucratic servant is no assurance of personal or corporate survival. As the above vignettes poignantly attest, we oscillate between both extremes, even as we contain both and further consciously identify with Jews and counteridentify against Nazis. But we are inescapably both: innocent sacrifice (victim) and guilty tormentor. We are Nazis or zealous bureaucrats one day, Jews the next.

In business and other organizational contexts, *we strive to buy time, if not survival and immortality, through continuous sacrifice* (a sacrifice that attempts to get rid of the "bad" all at once and at all developmental levels: both preoedipal and oedipal, from ridding ourselves of disavowed primitive parts of the self, to killing off the competitive parent of the same sex and the rebellious child who wished to kill). The idiom or language of this sacrifice is that of economics or business: We wage continuous, relentless economic competition to save and revive our institutions. Through sacrifice, we believe that if—by endless cycles of cuts and belt-tightenings—we trade enough death for life, we will survive and gain in profit, morale, and productivity. That is the magical wish and deed. But the miracle never happens, or it only happens over a brief short term. The organization and the nation are consumed by dread and hate. Psychodynamically, "bad objects" are not clearly put and kept "out there"; we are virtually possessed by them, in here, everywhere. We act such that all "good objects," all decency, all love, all kindness, all generosity, and all civility have been or should be destroyed, because there is no way we can live up to them (and be loved by them) as ego ideals, as sources of love, as culturally shared symbolic "objects" of value. We cannot be rid of our Jews fast enough, and there never are enough Jews to be rid of. Like World War II Germany, we consume ourselves in our frenzy to rid ourselves of Jews. But even the choice of what Erikson (1968) called the "negative identity," the negative ideal, is insufficient, because we both wish to be and not to be Nazis, and we both wish not to be yet become Jews. No symbolic solution is "final," unambivalent, or secure.

From the historical fear of being Jews (even Jews struggle with their cultural identities), we have come to the point that we are all Jews potentially, imminently. "We" don't sacrifice "them"—or if we do, it is only for a time; "we" are "them," as everyone becomes a sacrifice. We cannot be rid of the bad whether we are Nazis or Jews; and there is no way, or even hope, of restoring the good. Put differently, the false self-triumphs with the utter exile and despondency of the true self. Nothing we—as imagined Jews or Nazis—do will save us, although we act as if we can and must save ourselves, or at least our institutions. We condemn ourselves to be the condemned.

We cannot, and may not, stop ourselves. In this Schindler-less world, there is no goodness or benevolence; there is no longer any long-term social contract; everyone is a "temp" (temporary worker). In short, the Holocaust, Jews, and Nazis all condense-as in groups' dreams dreamt in wakeful hours—into a single image and epic story line where wish, motivation, fantasy, defense, relationship, and real world all define what downsizing is about and why it is obligatory.

If by listening carefully enough to individual patients and clients (both individuals and groups), therapists and counselors learn how to treat them and how to consult, when to speak (e.g., interpret) and when to remain a silent presence, the same ought to apply to our work as researchers and consultants with organizations, especially those where images of disaster prevail. By attending carefully to people's expressed and lived-in worlds, we will learn what to do. This is not to repeat the old and wrongheaded anthropological dictum that "the native [of the group under study] is always right"; rather, the more carefully one listens, the more clearly will the complex texture of the story emerge. Conversely, it is precisely the *neglect* of the inner and intersubjective experience of downsizing that has us as a nation in the difficulty in which we find ourselves. Our slaughter of innocents comes from *not* attending to meanings and feelings—those of others and of our own. Downsizing, which has long looked so appealing as a *solution,* is emerging instead as an enormous emotional as well as economic *cost* and *casualty* of our war with ourselves.

We have made certain that no one is safe for very long, if at all. In *Schindler's List* lies our contemporary wished-for and dreaded biography of a few good and lucky women who make it as "essential workers"—and even they come to know how precarious their safety is. Ours is no American triumphant self-creation through hard work.

The relentlessness with which downsizing is often executed tells us that fathomless rage, sadism, envy, greed, and revenge—among other emotions and motives—are the "bottom line" designated to eradicate every previously espoused element of American culture, a kind of cultural scorched-earth policy we practice on ourselves. Downsizing is part of a social aesthetic that has no place for dandy-capitalist-turned-wily-rescuer Oskar Schindler, his protective list, or a protected cadre of essential workers. In this ethos devoid of the sentiment of mercy, there are, mercifully, signs of increasing *resistance*—not in the Freudian sense but in the sense of "underground," on the part of Americans who are coming to have a healthy disgust and even healthier regret for the nightmare we have created in the name of good business, efficiency, and streamlining, without so much as spilling a single drop of blood.

In the West, since the Calvinist days of the Protestant ethic and the spirit of capitalism (Weber, 1930), we have single-mindedly believed that success from one's work was a sign of God's smile in this world, that personal effort would result in upward social mobility, and that ultimately, hard work would set us free of our past and present station. It was the sinister achievement of the Nazi era to transvalue this work ethic, to welcome its condemned slave labor to their labor-to-death camps with the large-lettered sign, *"Arbeit macht frei,"* ("Work will make you free"). It was the special despair—joined with identification with the aggressor—of the doomed inmates to believe their captors' lies.

It is the special horror of our time in America to have created a latchkey world for ourselves and our descendants, in which no one can make it onto Schindler's List, even if a benevolent CEO or chairman promises that some elect will be spared. The relentlessness of downsizing, RIFing, and its lengthy train of euphemisms, bears the same message as presided over the gates of Bergen-Belsen and other Nazi slave labor camps, *Arbeit macht frei,* and one dare not question its sincerity. In this world of computerized, stylized, bureaucratized, and economically rationalized hate, *work is only good for the production of death.* One could not be further from the work ethic by which every aspiring Horatio Alger believed he or she could pull him- or herself up by the individualistic bootstraps.

In the workplace and larger society governed by downsizing and the constant threat of further disruption, the turn toward frenetic work and productivity as "freeing" represents not only an identification with the aggressor but a short-term adaptive denial of reality. It is a denial that diminishes paralyzing psychotic anxiety. It fuses omnipotence of thought with omnipotence of deed: "If I work hard enough, if I am productive enough, it won't happen to me"; one tries to persuade oneself to resolve the cognitive and affective dissonance. One desperately tries to unknow what one already knows. These work beliefs serve regressively as magical thinking that bribes the ego into thinking that through hard work one will be spared one's destiny, despite the overwhelming evidence to the contrary that virtually everyone is disposable, expendable. A text more parallel with the beliefs held by many doomed Jews in the labor camps in Europe during the Nazi era could not be found. There is, of course, sad irony to this adaptation. A defense that works for the short term is powerless to influence the long term to which it submits and, more ironically, is complicit in bringing about.

Personnel departments and outplacement organizations are especially saddled with (i.e., psychologically speaking: delegated, projected onto) this task: how to dispose of people, and only secondarily how to find work for disposable people. Those who perform the selections must somehow emotionally adapt to doing their odious task, rationalizing the very nature of their work (including their own aggressive impulses). They know full well they are performing on behalf of upper management and "the organization" the symbolic equivalent of digging mass graves for the soon-to-be-dead. Both love and the quiet voice of reason are banished, exiled from this promised land. Short-lived organizational rebirth and profit draw their nourishment from death, even if "only" symbolically.

Despite the screen of rationality, of dispassionate objectivity, of neces-sity, and of computerized impersonality, the selection of who is to be kept and who is to be fired is always personal choice and never mere number. Stylized apologies such as "don't take it personally" and "nothing personal," offered to those being laid off are self-deceptions to distance oneself from one's deeds. Senior executives, midlevel management, and consulting firms all appoint or recommend certain people, and not others, to serve on employee selection committees. The process is not entirely alien to that employed by death camp physicians who decided who, in the long lines of people just disembarked from the trains, should go to the left and who to the right, who would live and who would die.

Despairing since the 1960s that the American dream, the national ideal as embodied in the martyred Kennedys and Martin Luther King, Jr., was forever unreachable, even approximately, most Americans have all but thrown it away. The land of opportunity has now long become replaced by a land of frantic opportunism (Stein & Hill, 1977). We have no Zyklon B cyanide gas chambers, no crematoria and tall smokestacks to belch human flesh's ashes upward, no barbed wire and tall watchtowers around our death camps. But make no mistake about it: Downsizing is not primarily about economic competition and survival. Its hardened heart is about death, the dominion and triumph of death (Lifton, 1979; Wangh, 1986). It is about endless cycles of sacrifice to keep "the organization" alive, cleansed, profitable, and competitive, while consuming, one way or another, everyone in its midst. There is the unmistakable stench of burning human flesh in the air.

References

Alford, C.F. (1990). The organization of evil. *Political Psychology*, 11(1):5–27.

Allcorn, S., Baum, H., Diamond, M.A. & Stein, H.F. (1996). *The HUMAN cost of a management failure: Organizational downsizing at General Hospital*. Westport, CT: Quorum Books.

Becker, E. (1973). *The denial of death*. New York: Free Press.

Becker, E. (1975). *Escape from evil*. New York: Free Press.

Dawidowicz, L. (1975). *The war against the Jews*. New York: Holt, Rinehart & Winston.

Department of Health and Human Services, Public Health Service, Centers for Disease Control, National Institute for Occupational Health. (1995). *Prevention of stress and health consequences of workplace downsizing and reorganization* (Announcement No. 572). Atlanta, GA: Author.

Devereux, G. (1955). Charismatic leadership and crisis. *Psychoanalysis and the Social Sciences*, 4:145–157.

Diamond, M.A. (1984). Bureaucracy as externalized self-system: A view from the psychological interior. *Administration & Society,* 16(2):195–214.

Diamond, M.A. (1985). The social character of bureaucracy: Anxiety and ritualistic defense. *Political Psychology,* 6(4):663–679.

Diamond, M.A. (1988). Organizational identity: A psychoanalytic exploration of organizational meaning. *Administration & Society,* 20(2):166–190.

Diamond, M.A. (1993). *The unconscious life of organizations: Interpreting organizational identity.* Westport, CT: Quorum Books.

Diamond, M.A. & Allcorn, S. (1985). Psychological responses to stress in complex organizations. *Administration & Society,* 17(2):217–239.

Dundes, A. (1984). *Life is like a chicken coop ladder: A portrait of German culture through folklore.* New York: Columbia University Press.

Edgerton, R. (1992). *Sick societies: Challenging the myth of primitive harmony.* New York: Free Press.

Endleman, R. (1995). *Relativism under fire: The psychoanalytic challenge.* New York: Psyche Press.

Erikson, E.H. (1963). *Childhood and society* (Rev. ed.). New York: Norton.

Erikson, E.H. (1968). *Identity, youth and crisis.* New York: Norton.

Freud, S. & Oppenheim, D.E. (1958). *Dreams in folklore.* New York: International Universities Press. (Original work published 1911)

Grimsley, K.D. (1995, November, 13–19). The downside of downsizing: What's good for the bottom line isn't necessarily good for business. *The Washington Post National Weekly Edition,* pp. 16–17.

Hilberg, R. (1992). *Perpetrators, victims, bystanders: The Jewish catastrophe 1933–1945.* New York: HarperCollins.

Klein, M. (1946). Notes on some schizoid mechanisms. *International Journal of Psycho-Analysis,* 27:99–110.

Koenigsberg, R. (1975). *Hitler's ideology: A study in psychoanalytic sociology.* New York: The Library of Social Science.

La Barre, W. (1972). *The Ghost Dance: The origins of religion.* New York: Dell.

Lifton, R.J. (1979). *The broken connection: On death and the continuity of life.* New York: Simon & Schuster.

Lifton, R.J. (1986). *The Nazi doctors.* New York: Basic Books.

Meissner, W.W. (1978). *The paranoid process.* New York: Aronson.

Mitscherlich, A. & Mitscherlich, M. (1975). *The inability to mourn: Principles of collective behavior.* New York: Grove.

Noer, D.M. (1993). *Healing the wounds: Overcoming and revitalizing downsized organizations*. New York: Jossey-Bass.

Paul, R.A. (1987). The question of applied psychoanalysis and the interpretation of cultural symbolism. *Ethos, 15*(1):82–103.

Richards, A.I. (1956). *Chisungu*. London: Faber & Faber.

Rosenfeld, S.S. (1995, November 17). Where to cut defense. *Washington Post*, p. A25.

Spielberg, S., Molen, G. R, Lustig, B. (Producers) & Spielberg, S. (Director). (1993). *Schindler's list* [Film]. (Available from Universal Pictures, 100 Universal City Plaza, Universal City, CA 91608)

Stein, H.F. (1990a). *American medicine as culture*. Boulder, CO: Westview.

Stein, H.F. (1990b). In what systems do alcohol/chemical addictions make sense? Clinical ideologies and practices as cultural metaphors. *Social Science and Medicine, 30*(9):987–1000.

Stein, H.F. (1993). Organizational psychohistory. *The Journal of Psychohistory, 21*(1):97–114.

Stein, H.F. (1994a). *The dream of culture*. New York: Psyche Press.

Stein, H.F. (1994b). *Listening deeply: An approach to understanding and consulting in organizational culture*. Boulder, CO: Westview.

Stein, H.F. (1995a). Domestic wars and the militarization of biomedicine. *The Journal of Psychohistory, 22*(4):406–415.

Stein, H.F. (1995b). The rupture of innocence: Oklahoma City, April 19, 1995. *Clio's Psyche* (A Quarterly of the Psychohistory Forum), 2(1):1, 12–15.

Stein, H.F. (1995c, Spring). When the heartland is no longer immune: The April 19, 1995 bombing of the Oklahoma City Federal Building. *Psychohistory News: Newsletter of the International Psychohistorical Association, 14*(3):2–4.

Stein, H.F. & Apprey, M. (1987). *From metaphor to meaning: Papers in psychoanalytic anthropology*. Charlottesville: University Press of Virginia.

Stein, H.F. & Hill, R.F. (1977). *The ethnic imperative: Exploring the new White ethnic movement*. University Park: Pennsylvania State University Press.

't Hart, P. (1991). Irving L. Janis' victims of groupthink. *Political Psychology, 12*(2):247–278.

Volkan, V.D. (1988). *The need to have enemies and allies*. Northvale, NJ: Jason Aronson.

Wangh, M. (1986). The nuclear threat: Its impact on psychoanalytic conceptualizations. *Psychoanalytic Inquiry, 6*(2):251–266.

Weber, M. (1930). *The Protestant ethic and the spirit of capitalism* (T. Parsons, Trans.). London: Allen & Unwin.

The primary risk

Larry Hirschhorn

In the Tavistock tradition, we understand an organization by first iden-tifying its primary task. We ask, what is this organization set up to do, how is it organized to accomplish this objective, and what unconscious dynamics limit or distort it members' ability to do their work? This approach, while powerful, does not help us understand organizations that live at strategic junctures in their life cycles. In these situations, the task is to choose a task. We need a conceptual framework to help us understand the psychodynamics of organizing and deciding in these situations. The following article develops the concept of the "primary risk" to explain how organizations behave in these situations. It links the primary risk to the psychoanalytic idea of ambivalence and the Gestalt idea of the figure/ground relationship. It draws on case material to illu-minate its concepts.

Introduction

Organizations increasingly face significant strategic dilemmas; yet thinkers and practitioners in the psychoanalytic theory of organiza-tions, particularly those like myself who have been deeply influenced

153

by the Tavistock tradition, have not kept apace. The Tavistock tradition, of organizational diagnosis and consulting particularly as it was articulated by A. Kenneth Rice and Eric Miller (Miller & Rice, 1990), was developed in response to problems of organizational design, functioning and relationships of authority, rather than to issues of strategy. The consultant working within this tradition would typically ask the following set of questions.

> Is this organization appropriately designed to accomplish this work? Where are the relevant boundaries that determine where one unit ends and another begin? Are there indications that these boundaries exist primarily as social defenses, to contain anxiety, rather than to accomplish work? If so, can we trace the organization's failure to perform to these social defenses? What is the source of this anxiety—in the task itself, and/or in the way leaders contain this anxiety?

Note, however, that these questions presume that we can locate and define the organization's primary task. The primary task we presume, should be evident from what the enterprise does day-to-day to garner resources from its environment. The restaurant serves food to customers, the architect's office prepares building plans, the bakery makes donuts, etc. With this knowledge of the task in hand we can then ask if the anxiety it stimulates is optimally bounded by the organizational design. Thus, William Whyte (Galbraith, 1977, p. 58) in his famous study of restaurants noted that the boundary between the waitresses and the cooks provoked conflict because there was no system in place to insure that waitress's orders were fulfilled in the order received. Waitresses felt unduly dependent on the particular chef's largess and so could not estimate how long it would take before their patrons got food. (Whyte showed how a spindle for holding orders, placed on the ledge between the kitchen and restaurant proper solved this problem.)

However, these questions may not help us understand the organization whose primary task is up for grabs. Executives, managers, and workers in such a setting face situations in which their conception of the task, and its concomitant expression in the organization's design, no longer meets the needs of clients or customers. Thus, for example, a restaurant may find that its patrons have much less time to linger over food, and that it can better serve its market by redefining its task as "preparing food to take home." In making this shift, in redefining its primary task, the restaurant owners have changed the strategy of the enterprise. They have made a strategic choice.

Organizations often have difficulty making such choices. Changing strategy entails significant risks, though if the market is evaporating, not changing strategy creates great risks as well. In observing or helping such organizations, we are more likely to ask:

> Why does this organization appear to be drifting? Why is it that leaders cannot seem to articulate its primary task? Why does their mission statement appear so abstract? Why can't certain thoughts or words be expressed here? What prevents the leadership from focusing on a few priorities?

In this paper I outline a framework of analysis that helps answer these second questions. It is based on the concept of the "primary risk." In the first section, I explicate the meaning of the "primary task"; in the second I contrast this concept with the notion of the "primary risk"; in the third I provide a case study of the psychodynamics of the primary risk; and in the fourth, I provide some guidelines for consulting with the primary risk in mind.

The primary task

The concept of the primary task plays a central role in the Tavistock theory: It helps posit an arena in which nonpsychological forces, deriving from the characteristics of the work itself, create a demand for action or responsiveness on the part of the enterprise. This concept has proven important to organizational diagnosis for three reasons. First, by focusing our attention on the organization's work, it simplifies the difficulty we face in describing the organization's environment. We start our diagnosis not by looking at all features of the environment, e.g., the structure of competition, the sources of revenue, but rather on what the enterprise is called primarily to do.

Second, by virtue of our focus on the concept of anxiety and its roots in Kleinian theory, we might over-focus on people's fantasies or subjective assessment of the enterprise and its purposes. In doing so, we would fail to take account of the enterprise as a system with characteristics that transcend the subjective experiences of its members. After all, the enterprise must satisfy customers, generate revenue, pay employees, etc. If we focus primarily, as psychoanalysis does, on the fantasies people use to construct their view of the world, we are at risk of ignoring the actual pressures organizations face. In this sense, the Tavistock concept of the primary risk blends a psychological and structural view of work. We respond to the task with our psychic resources but the task itself represents realities over which the enterprise has influence but only limited control. As such, the primary task is analogous to what Freud called the reality principle (Freud, 1911).

Third, the primary task makes concrete the institution's actual or operating goals. It uncovers people's *practices*, rather than their beliefs. A college president may state or believe that the goal of the college is to preserve Western civilization or create the well-rounded student. But studying the college, we may discover that day-to-day students and faculty act as if the college's primary task were to prepare students for professional schools. In other words, actual practices show that the college *trains* students rather than *develops* them. As Gordon Lawrence has emphasized (Lawrence, 1977), we must distinguish between the stated and actual task. Indeed, it is useful to define the primary task as the ensemble of its primary practices, that is, those practices that make manifest its actual goals.

The limits to the primary task concept

Though fundamental, the concept of the primary task may limit our thinking and understanding. It fails to explicate the process through which people and organizations make choices about which primary task to focus on and why. It helps us understand the organization's operations but not the process through which it shapes a strategy.

Consider the following example. I was consulting to two architects, Jack and Phil, who had formed but had to yet to activate a partnership with a third architect, Henry, well known throughout the country for his design talent. Henry had a small practice of his own, but spent the bulk of his time teaching architecture at a prestigious university. In my initial conversations with Jack, the partner most eager to push the partnership forward, he emphasized the dispute he and Phil were having with Henry around marketing. Henry wanted to invest little, suggesting that clients would come to him because of his reputation, while Jack and Phil felt that they had to mount a significant marketing effort. They felt that while Henry was indeed a famous designer, he had no track record for landing big projects.

I initially thought and suggested to Jack that perhaps they were interpreting Henry's stance as one sign that he wished to limit his financial exposure to the vicissitudes of the new enterprise. He did not, I suggested, want to put much "skin in the game." Jack replied forcefully that indeed, he believed that in a true partnership every partner had to feel financially at risk. He agreed that Henry's anxiety about marketing expenses was actually a sign that he did not want to invest much money at all. Unless they could resolve this, Jack thought, they could not really make this partnership come alive.

As we spoke further, Jack revealed a more fundamental concern. Because Jack and Phil wished to capitalize on Henry's reputation they had decided to make Henry the named partner of the firm. What if Henry then withdrew from the partnership? Jack and Phil would have invested substantial time and money in building up Henry's reputation in the market, only to lose his name. I revised my hypothesis. I suggested to Jack that the issue he and Phil faced was not Henry's willingness to take a risk, but rather *their* willingness to take a risk. Was Henry's design talent good enough for them to risk marketing his name, knowing there was always a chance they could lose him?

Jack, sounding more tentative than usual, replied that he thought Phil was less willing to take this risk than he was. I then suggested that he and Phil had described their task incorrectly. It was less to build a partnership of equals than to build a firm where one partner was a star and, therefore, could demand special treatment.

Let us look at this vignette in light of the argument we have developed thus far. Jack and Phil could construct or envision the task they faced in two different ways: to "build a partnership of equals" or "to rope in a star performer." These tasks pulled them both in opposite directions: to either treat Henry the same as themselves or to treat him differently. Jack and Phil had consciously chosen the former, but the latter, though suppressed, continued to exert its pull. It created a subtle divide between Jack and Phil. This suggests in turn that Jack's early forcefulness, "all partners should put up equal stakes," but his later tentativeness, meant that in choosing the first task he was defending against the anxiety associated with the second. Moreover, as Jack suggests, by choosing the first, he and Phil were less likely to create a conflict amongst themselves—better to fight Henry than each other.

This vignette highlights the limitations of the concept of the primary task. Jack was caught in the ambiguous space between two alternative conceptions of his task, "rope in a star" or "build a partnership." These two tasks were in fact mutually exclusive since in taking up the former, Henry would have to be treated differently, while in taking up the latter, Henry would have to be treated the same. Attempts to do both at the same time could only undermine each. Jack faced difficulty in deciding because each posed a risk that he found unpalatable. If he and Phil insisted that Henry be an equal, they risked losing the partnership; if they let him be a star, they risked losing a lot of marketing money.

Jack's dilemma points to the psychodynamics of this "zone of task ambiguity." The ambiguity itself creates anxiety and, consequently, the person fails to grasp the choice and risks he must take. Instead, to manage the anxiety he develops a defensive fantasy of the situation such as, "Henry is arrogant. He thinks clients will come to him just by sitting there." The fantasy precludes Jack from understanding his own situation and therefore emerging from the zone of task ambiguity. In this case, he and Phil could not *acknowledge the risk they felt*, what I call the *primary risk*. They could not make the bet they felt most comfortable with, and then manage themselves according to the primary task they selected. They were stuck insofar as they could not choose.

The Tavistock concept of the primary task is not helpful here, because at a moment of strategic choice, it simply does not exist. What exists is the choice between tasks. The resulting anxiety is stimulated not by a task but by the ambiguity surrounding the choice.

The primary risk

What frightened Jack? Clearly he was preoccupied with the danger (though not necessarily consciously) that he might choose a primary task that he could not execute. *The primary risk is the felt risk of choosing the wrong primary task, that is, a task that ultimately cannot be managed.* This risk, however, is not based on some arbitrary conception of the organization's environment. I do not argue here that if a group of senior executives decides in a moment of brainstorming that their enterprise could choose among one of eight different tasks, ranging from its current one to one that implies a wholescale reinvention of the organization, it is assessing its primary risk. Instead, the risk is an emergent property of the enterprise's existing relationship to its environment. In the above example, Jack did not "invent" the risk he faced; it was embedded in the situation he was grappling with. Indeed, as the example suggests, he understood the risk, but the resulting anxiety suppressed his awareness of his own understanding. That is why he blamed Henry for his own indecision. In other words, the primary risk is embedded in the situation shaping both actual choices as well as the psychological response to them. Though overtly, Jack had defined his task "building a partnership of equals," the task not chosen—bringing a prima donna on board—was nonetheless part of the force field shaping his consciousness. Indeed, this is why he felt stuck and sought help.

Figure and ground

There is a tendency when assessing a situation such as Jack's to wonder why Jack and Phil must choose between one or another task. In the face of this complexity, why can't they choose to do both? Indeed, if they define their task as "roping in a star" won't they still face tensions and choices around how unequal they will allow Henry to be?

I suggest that we see the kind of choice they faced through the Gestalt psychological concept of figure/ground relationships. In choosing one task over the other, they must choose to make one task the figure, the focal point for their thinking and planning, and the other the ground or context for the chosen task. The effects of the task placed in the ground do not disappear, there are, for example, limits to the special privileges they could give Henry. Rather these effects are managed in relationship to the chosen primary task: how to treat Henry as a star.

Figure/ground relationships differ from relationships of compromise. In the latter, we blend two choices together, trying to find the optimal point. In the former, we continue to differentiate between the two choices, but define a particular relationship between them. (This is one feature of the general distinction between qualitative and quantitative relationships.) Classical Gestalt psychology suggests that when we cannot differentiate between figure and ground our perception is chronically unstable. This is the basis for the famous picture in which, depending how we look at it, we see either a beautiful young lady or an ugly old woman.

When people cannot make one task the figure and the other ground, they are likely to fall into two kinds of errors. First, they may deny that they must make a choice, hoping to in fact strike a compromise between the two tasks therefore satisfying neither. This creates the confusion associated with an unstable figure/ground relationship. Second, and this was the case for Henry, they may focus only on the figure, "we want a partnership of equals" denying the other task, however displaced from consciousness, still demands attention. To use a psychoanalytic metaphor, they "repress" the ground.

The psychodynamics of the primary risk

Vacillation and ambivalence

I want to argue that ambivalence plays a critical role in shaping how people cope with the challenge of taking a primary risk. Consider, for example, the well-publicized case of Apple computer. It has vacillated for some time between two definitions of its primary task; will it continue to be the great "innovator," or should it become a mainstream computer company competing on price while operating efficiently. Each task creates in its wake different business decisions. If Apple is to compete on price, it should clone the Mac and relinquish the high profit margins it once needed to fund innovation. It would make money on volume, and by increasing its market share make its operating system an industry standard. If it should continue to be the innovator, then it needs high profit margins to fund its research and development, and should not clone the Mac. Throughout much of its recent history, Apple executives have been pulled between these two visions of the company. Indeed, in 1993,

John Sculley, then the CEO of Apple, actually developed a plan, never implemented, to split the company into a hardware and software company, the former producing "boxes," and the latter innovative software projects (Carlton, 1997, ch. 8). Moreover, as recent history shows, Apple executives still cannot make this business decision, since in 1996, they licensed the Mac to two clone manufacturers only to withdraw these licenses a year later! Facing a primary risk, they are pulled between two conceptions of their task and therefore cannot make a pragmatic business decision cleanly. Indeed, Steve Jobs' recent re-entry into Apple accompanied by an ad campaign that emphasizes Apple's creativity, suggest that Apple is still the "outsider" with an ability to revolutionize computing.

While we do not have access to the psychodynamic meanings of these choices to particular Apple executives (that is, we must avoid glibly concluding that "Jobs is grandiose" or "Sculley felt unworthy outside the mainstream"), we can with greater certainty try to understand people's experiences at the group level, that is, experiences that are reflected in the culture and practices of the company. We have data about the latter, from numerous histories and reports about the company (Carlton, 1997). Our most important indicator here is that by 1990, a moral discourse emerged within Apple in which the Macintosh operating system took on totemic qualities within Apple's culture. As one industry analyst noted, "It got to the point at Apple where anybody proposing to change the famous Macintosh user interface and improve it, even in small ways, was regarded as a heretic. There became a term "Maclike," as in "it isn't Maclike" (Mossberg, 1996).

It is interesting to contrast this rigidity, which only grew stronger over the course of this decade, with the consequent vacillation in business decisions. How can vacillation and rigidity go hand in hand? We are familiar with this process at an individual level. Rigidity in behavior, belief, or character may mask an underlying experience of chaos or at least confusion. The chaos in turn is linked to impulses or wishes which cannot be acknowledged consciously but which continue to exert a force on one's psyche. But why we may ask should the impulse to innovate, the key to Apple's success, now be considered dangerous? The development of the Macintosh itself provides one clue. By all accounts, it was both an enormously exciting but also a destructive process. Steve Jobs divided the company by supporting the Macintosh team as an elite group unbeholden to the "laws" and regulations of the company. He flew a pirate flag from the Macintosh building, freed Macintosh developers from travel expense strictures, pampered them with resources (freshly squeezed orange juice) and alternatively praised and terrorized them. His goal moreover was to render obsolete, to destroy the products non-Mac people were supporting and selling. One hypothesis, supported by Guy Kawaski, a key executive at the time, is that Apple could simply not sustain another such "revolution" (Kawaski, 1990, p. 25). (Indeed, we know from many accounts of the process of technological development that such massive development efforts create significant strains between husbands and wives and can lead to divorces.) This may in fact be why its later attempts to innovate, particularly in developing the Newton, failed. These later efforts were perhaps insufficiently destructive. Indeed, Apple executives, while supporting the Newton project with significant resources, failed to provide it with consistent executive leadership. It was allowed to drift and therefore lacked focus and presence (Carlton, 1997, p. 232).

But why then did Apple later find itself vacillating between two conceptions of its primary task? The rigidity we described provides a clue. They were unprepared to relinquish their history of innovation to call an end to their story. There was too much pleasure, excitement, and indeed identity invested in it. They felt, in short, ambivalent about the Macintosh experience, and to manage this ambivalence they constructed a rigid code of conduct, in which innovation was suppressed not, at least consciously, out of fear, but because the Macintosh was in fact perfect! If we look upon ambivalence classically, we can say that they could not acknowledge the hate as well as the love they felt for the Macintosh, and that ultimately this unacknowledged hate was the source of their vacillation.

Jack and ambivalence

We can apply a similar analysis to Jack and Phil's situations. I want to suggest that, in forcefully telling me, as if it were a dictum or moral law, that every partner had to be at financial risk, Jack was deploying a rigid code of conduct. As in the Apple case, this rigidity masked chaotic feelings linked to unacknowledged impulses or desires. Here we have some data about Jack's inner life.

To help me understand his own desires, I asked him to tell me what he loved doing. After some meandering he told me that what he loved most was managing projects, negotiating with contractors, and managing the client's expectations and hopes. He liked the building process and was less interested in the building design. I asked him why he needed to work with Henry to create this kind of work, since Henry after all was a designer. He noted that nonetheless he felt uneasy practicing at some distant from the world of "high design." He then quite spontaneously noted that, as a child, he spent considerable time supporting and helping a disabled brother, which his parents appreciated.

This sequence is suggestive. While I did not ask Jack further questions about his early family life, it is plausible to assume, in light of his free association to his family, that his feelings about Henry were linked to conflicts he felt in relationship to his brother. One might imagine that on the one side he won his parents' praise for being so helpful but on the other, he sacrificed some of his own pleasures. If, as this sequence suggests, he has projected an internalized image of his family life (as a set of object relations) onto the current situation, we can conclude that he felt ambivalent about taking up a role in which he primarily supported Henry. But failing to work through this ambivalence, he was likely to repress it, particularly when facing stressful situations or difficult decisions. This was why he could maintain with some rigidity that all partners in the firm should be treated equally. He could not tolerate the complexity of feelings he experienced upon remembering the praise he garnered in supporting his brother. This also suggests that insofar as he could not work on or through his ambivalence he was not able to fully explore the benefits and liabilities of pursuing his own desires.

This vignette suggests finally, that the "ground" in the domain of perception can play the same role as the repressed unconscious in the domain of awareness. Jack *suppressed* the primary task, "rope in Henry as a star" as the ground for his perception of his situation because he had already *repressed* his ambivalent feelings about his role in his family of origin.

This link gives us a better understanding of the psychodynamics of figure/ground relationships. We cannot say that Jack and Phil simply presumed that Henry should be a partner among equals. Rather they repressed the idea, that in structuring the partnership in this way they would have to continue to manage the consequences of Henry's *not* being the star. In other words, the question of Henry's stardom would never disappear, it would always have to be managed. Figure/ground relationships express psychodynamic conflicts, when this process of "negation," expressed in relegating one task to the ground, is itself denied.

The case of Brad

Consider for example the case of Brad, a government executive who directed the human resources division for large multi-agency system. Responding to a mandate to reduce expenditures, Brad had envisioned a human resources function in which his division personnel acted as consultants to the executives and human resources staff of the different agencies. Instead of simply monitoring the human resources policies in the agencies and providing them with some direct services, e.g., the management of some of the benefits programs, his division personnel would help agencies customize their own HR system to fit the needs of the agency's core professional group (e.g., engineering, health care workers etc.). This was a grand vision and a challenging one. Division personnel would have to be more insightful and creative than they had been in the past if agency executives were to seek their advice.

Brad developed what he called a multistage "transition plan" for helping his employees change the focus of their activities and acquire new skills. It sounded thoughtful, replete with new committees, task forces, temporary teams, etc., but upon reading his strategy document I was struck by its seemingly abstract quality. It hovered above any concrete description of the new tasks. Instead, he spoke loosely of a new culture of work and the new empowered employee. Reading the document you could not tell what work employees would relinquish and what work they would take up. I wondered what accounted for its fuzziness?

Later in the consultation, Brad told me something that helped to explain why his plan was so vague. Reflecting on his superiors, the president and vice president of the agency, he noted with some contempt how "they had to put in place a new organization design but have given no thought to a transition plan." They did not understand, he noted, how you needed the latter if you were going to achieve any objective. As sensible as his statement sounded, his expressed contempt was a tipoff. After all, his strategy document and his own method of deliberation revealed the opposite bias: he paid a great deal of attention to transitions but failed to define his objectives or destination.

His condemnation of this superior, like Jack's condemnation of Henry and Apple's executives' condemnation of those who would change the Mac interface, points to some dynamic conflict he felt in selecting one primary task as figure, in this case making a transition, while acknowledging the continuing pull of the other as ground, in this case reaching a destination. In making the first the figure, he suppressed his awareness of the way in which the second as ground, continued to exercise a claim on his attention. He denied his negation.

Following the model of the primary risk we have developed thus far, we must also ask how ambivalence shaped his awareness. Here I have no personal data, but I can draw on my experience of him as well as interviews my colleague and I conducted with his subordinates. As we continued to work with Brad, it became apparent that Brad relished open-ended discussion and resisted making decisions. In working with this top team he seemed to relish taking the role of the provocateur, opening up a question or issue just as it seemed the group was coming to a consensus. Yet, in a manner that was puzzling, he did so in what appeared to be a gentle way, as if he were being an honest executive open to new ideas and thoughts. We also knew, based on individual interviews with the members of his top team, that his style made them uncomfortable and anxious.

In addition, I often felt uneasy working with Brad, worrying that directness on my part would somehow upset his self-esteem. This was confirmed when my co-consultant told me that Brad was afraid of me. During meetings and retreats he and his assistant Joe whispered frequently to each other, seemingly evaluating what was being said. They seemed to form a tight pair. My fantasy was that they were reassuring themselves, that they helped quell one another's puzzlement over what had been said or noted.

These two data points suggest that he gained pleasure from being "leader" but was frightened by the intimacy and directness leadership required. He wanted to provoke rather than direct, partly because he worried about stimulating resistance or negativity. By suppressing the ground, that is, by giving insufficient attention to objectives or goals, he avoided making commitments that his subordinates might object to.

The case of the Poverty Research Institute

An organization faces strategic challenges when changes in its environment complicate its ability to accomplish its inherited primary task. At such a point in its history, it faces the prospect of taking a primary risk. But since, often, organizational environments change incrementally the organization can postpone taking a primary risk. As a result, it appears to "drift"; while certain managers, responding opportunistically to these changes can take up parts of a new primary task on behalf of the organization. At some point, a gap emerges between what the organization believes to be its primary task, based on its history and what in fact people are increasingly doing. In this gap, we can experience the organizational psychodynamics associated with the primary risk.

Consider the following case. A policy research institute (PRI) committed to funding and disseminating research on poverty had over the years been successful in attracting funds and producing well-regarded research reports. I was a shadow consultant to a team of consultants who were asked to help the institute plan for its future. The senior staff had produced a strategic plan a few years before the consultation, but major difficulties remained. Most important, fundraising was falling off, while other institutes around the country were competing successfully for the money and visibility the PRI had once garnered. The executive director, Charles, a man in his late 50 s, with considerable charisma and connections to the rich and powerful, could still command attention and raise money from his personal network, but he was working harder and clearly near the end of his career. Additionally, there was a chronic conflict between the fundraising and research divisions. The latter felt that the former tried to dictate research priorities based on their reading of donor interests. They complained that the integrity of the research process was being compromised. The fundraising department felt in turn that the research division was unreliable, did not meet promised deadlines, and sometimes embarrassed the institute with incomplete work.

There are many ways of viewing this presenting situation. We could take a life-cycle perspective and infer that people were aware of their dependency on Charles; they worried that the Institute would fail if he were not its director. We could interpret the presenting issues as a dilemma of organizational design. We might inquire as to the nature of the boundary between the research and fundraising divisions: How did they collaborate in planning the portfolio of research? Perhaps it would be better to have the fundraising group raise unrestricted funds while the research group would be responsible for raising money in its own domain? Finally, we could interpret the situation as reflecting problems in implementation. The senior group had produced a reasonable strategic plan, but they neither trusted one another sufficiently nor were very skilled to steer this process of organizational change.

These frames of reference are sensible, but when revenue is falling, competition is growing and worries about the future surface, it is more useful to interpret the problem as a strategic one. Taking a rational view, we might work with the client to develop a marketing plan, to create new research products, to create a web site, etc. However, such an approach fails to take account the psychodynamics of the primary risk. We should presume instead that the client is quite capable of devising such practical plans. Indeed, the strategic plan displayed considerable technical virtuosity in using modern management concepts such as market share, audience segments, and distribution channels. Rather they cannot begin this work because the unacknowledged experiences and fantasies, related to the primary risk, obstruct their ability to think together.

To explore hypotheses about the primary risk of an enterprise we first examine its institutional history. PRI was founded in the early seventies when a strong liberal consensus existed and felt that the richest society on the earth should not tolerate poverty among its citizens. There was considerable faith that government programs could help poor people, and that cities could develop and renew their communities. In addition, scholars were creating a new "policy science" based on methods of evaluating social programs and assessing how social programs were and could be implemented. PRI was a creature of its time. Under these conditions, its research program emerged from its setting. PRI leaders did not have to invent it nor convince donors of its legitimacy.

How could we characterize its primary risk at that point of time? A organization dependent on donors faces a fundamental choice:

Do they raise money by doing what potential donors are interested in, or do they decide what they want to do and then find potential donors? In the first option, the primary task is to satisfy donors, in the second, to satisfy themselves or, in this case, to follow their own values. Organizations with deep roots in a donor community, such as a religious organization or a hospital, often face no risk here since the values that link the organization and the donors are held sacred by both. Organizations like PRI, however, which must compete with other institutions for funds and whose history is linked to a particular constellation of social forces, confront this risk more directly. Because of the liberal consensus, in its earlier years PRI could decide what research to do and then find money to support the research. It managed the uncertainty this choice imposed by relying on Charles to raise money from his own network of donors who shared PRI's values, when gaps in funding emerged. In our terms, the "figure" was "fund our own research interests/values" and the "ground" was "fund the research interests/values of our donors."

I need not repeat the oft-told tale of the decline in the liberal consensus. PRI responded to this decline incrementally and its members' imperceptibly by refashioning its strategy. Instead of establishing research and then raising funds, it found increasingly that it had to create research categories that would stimulate contributions and grants. This development evoked a new primary task. Instead of doing research, its first primary task could be the business of providing services to donors. Potential donors became customers and without violating basic values (e.g., PRI would not get funding from the NRA), PRI began to express donor values rather than simply expressing their own.

However, this shift was not acknowledged. Instead, at a major planning retreat, Charles, assuring his staff that the institution faced no crisis, that it faced no remaking, noted that "its role was as a research institution." This equanimity stimulated certain consequences. Since in fact PRI had begun to act like a service institution, it could only back into its new primary task. Thus, for example, PRI sought funds to pay for staff members' uncovered time, and it fell into some consulting work. Increasingly, the fundraising division appeared to be in charge, so that completing a research project seemed less important than securing its funding. Tensions between the research and fundraising departments grew and some talented researchers left. By drifting from one primary task to the other, by not taking a primary risk, PRI appeared to losing its vitality. Indeed, interviews with the staff conveyed a sense of malaise.

As we saw in the case of Apple, when facing strategic shifts, people can reify the original primary task; they begin to treat it as an icon or mantra. At PRI, executives developed such a discourse. Their strategic planning document is revealing in this way. First, their budget was constructed around research programs or areas, with each area costed out to the penny. Yet the plans showed that many of these programs lacked funding. With no dollars to spend, the budget numbers appeared to be too precise. This precision created a false sense of reality as if the research plan in the mind and on a piece of paper was a research plan with real resources.

Second, in a forceful statement the plan asserted the Institute's uniqueness, noting that unlike other institutions it did not focus narrowly on this or that economic issue but took into account the whole community. Indeed, one consultant on the team noted that when first encountering Charles, he was struck by Charles' insistence that the Institute would not specialize in particular areas. This statement in the document can be usefully interpreted in a few ways: in stressing the Institute's uniqueness it helps deny its growing dependence on donor tastes and preferences; in resisting specialization, it masks the inevitable opportunism associated with chasing money by cloaking it in principles; and in focusing on the whole community it sustains the fantasy that the Institute can fund its own values.

Third, as I have already noted, in discussing marketing, the tone of the document becomes resolutely technical, referring to audiences and segments. The terms convey a sense of mastery, of efficacy, which is belied by acknowledgment of the growing difficulty the Institute faced in raising money for its activities.

Moral condemnation

As we saw in the case of Jack, when the primary risk is denied, people may find others to condemn to contain their own anxiety. At PRI, this process of moral condemnation emerged with a twist. Many people believed that chronic conflicts between fundraising and research explained the institution's difficulty. Increasingly, fundraising shaped what research was funded, yet the head of research noted she did not require her professionals to write proposals. Fundraising was in charge of this "lower" function. Indeed, some researchers saw themselves as academics, people who generated ideas that were valuable in their own right. Fundraisers in turn worried about the researcher's detachment from the politics of financing research. Research projects remained unfinished, they thought because researchers themselves did not feel accountable to donors. Each represented a potential moral compass, the integrity of ideas on the one hand and the accountability to donors on the other. However, insofar as these two groups were experienced to be in conflict, people could use these moral ideas as tools for condemning one or the other group. Fundraising was opportunistic and money-oriented, and research was irresponsible and out of touch. In effect, in contrast to the case of Jack or Brad, moral condemnation was internalized. Not others, but parts of themselves were sinners. This may account for the malaise staff projected as well as PRI's protracted stalemate.

I do not make these observations critically as if Institute leadership had somehow failed. While holding leaders accountable it is also sensible to see the Institute's history as part of calamity that befell the liberal community in the 1980 s. Very few liberal institutions have known how to respond. Rather, what I mean to emphasize here are the defenses people develop to ward off the demands of the primary risk.

Consulting to the primary risk

Interpreting figure and ground

This analysis of the primary risk provides us with some guidance on consulting to organizations facing strategic questions. When managers and executives seem stuck or unable to choose a direction for the enterprise, when there appears to be a gap between the stated primary task and what people actually do, when executives are unable to make seemingly pragmatic decisions, when people in the organization describe their experience as "drifting," it is useful to assume that the organization has been unable to take a primary risk.

To understand what is inhibiting choice, and how this inhibition is linked to symptoms of organizational dysfunction (e.g., conflicts between departments, the failure to execute plans, etc.) we should help our client articulate the choices they face among potential tasks in figure/ground terms. Based on my experience thus far, I would suggest the following guidelines.

- Ask people the following questions: "Right now, what are you trying to do?" "If you failed at 'something' right now for which you would hold yourself deeply accountable, what would that 'something' be?" "In trying to do 'something' right now what have you decided *not* to do? And why?" "What risks are you taking in *not* doing it?" (I recommend using the term "right now" to prevent people from providing you with answers that sound like mission statements or vague goals.)
- Help the client verbalize a figure/ground relationship that has the feel of a duality, a contrast, such as in the case of Brad, "making transitions or reaching destinations." The duality insures that each side of the coin is structurally or thematically related to the other. (An example of a nonduality would be "sell products or hire good people.") The duality assures us that indeed we have discovered or interpreted a figure/ground relationship and that if figure and ground were switched we would be describing a meaningful choice.
- See if you can uncover feelings of ambivalence linked to the task not chosen, rejected, or perhaps morally condemned. If you do this well, you should also understand how and why the chosen task as well is held ambivalently. (If it were not, then the client is less likely to be facing a strategic dilemma.) The roots of the ambivalence may lie in the personal character of the leader, or in the culture and history of the institution.

If you have identified or usefully "interpreted" the figure/ground relationship and the roots of the ambivalence, you should be able to give an account of the symptoms comprising the organization's dysfunction. For example, Brad's provocative style of leading and its impact on his subordinates is linked to the anxiety he would feel if he focused on a "destination" for his group.

Mourning and melancholia

It is useful to apply Freud's model of "mourning and melancholia" to the process of taking a primary risk (Freud, 1917). Recall that Freud argued that a person cannot complete the mourning process, and becomes in Freud's terms "melancholic," insofar as she does not acknowledge her hateful feelings toward the "other" who has died. The hate instead is introjected ("the shadow of the object falls on the ego") so that she berates herself ceaselessly, as if she had caused the other's death. In contrast to normal grieving in which we come to terms with relinquishing that which we loved, in aborted mourning we have failed to come to terms with that aspect of the object we hate as well as love.

We can apply this model to the situation Jack faced in the following way. In repressing the primary task "rope in a star" he was denying the hatred he felt for the supportive role he took in his family of origin. (Though we should not forget that he also felt love for this role, he gained pleasure from it, due to his parents' approval.) This hatred however is introjected and "casts a shadow" on the primary task chosen as the figure "all partners are equal" which then gives this task its rigid quality, and why Jack cannot choose either.

Working through this ambivalence, he might then be able to support Henry freely, as a matter of choice, if he judged that this were in fact the best business decision he could take. Then the figure would become "rope in star" and the ground would be "all partners are equal." No longer ambivalent about this choice he could attend fruitfully to the task in the background, and find ways to engage in the management of the building process, to satisfy his own desires, within the context of selling Henry's design talent to clients.

Similarly in Brad's case the hatred he feels for the intimacy and directness leadership requires leads him to suppress the task "reach a destination." Yet his ambition and position suggest that he loves the leadership role as well. The "hating side" of his ambivalence then casts a shadow on the primary task chosen as the figure, "manage transitions." He consequently holds on to this task rigidly, producing as a result vague plans. Working through this ambivalence he might still decide to focus on building a transition plan, but he would pay greater attention to the question of goals and objectives. He may decide, for example, that it is too early to nail down a specific goal, or a particular concept of how his division should provide services. But he could, for example, ask his subordinates to develop several alternative designs in specific and concrete terms.

Finally, in the case of PRI, the task "satisfy donor values" is not so much suppressed, but enacted without acknowledgement. It is hated in part because it represents a loss of autonomy and signifies that its golden age, when the liberal consensus allowed PRI researchers to pursue their own interests, is now over. Yet it is also loved because it increasingly provides PRI with resources and might release PRI from its excessive dependence on Charles. Working through this ambivalence, PRI staff would be better able to support "serving donor values" as the primary task, while learning to work with donors in ways that narrowed the gap between donor values and their own values. This would lead to much better relationships between the research and marketing departments.

Consulting to the problem of the primary risk thus involves five steps:

1. Verbalizing and interpreting the figure/ground relationship in play.
2. Interpreting the abivalent feelings stimulated by the task in the background.
3. Clarifying how this ambivalence undermines the performance of the task in the foreground.
4. Helping the client let go of the hate or antipathy she feels toward the background task.
5. Constructing a more vital figure/ground relationship among the tasks which make business sense and allow the client to attend to both tasks appropriately.

Acknowledgement

I would like to thank Barbara Feinberg for her very thoughtful critique of earlier drafts of this article.

References

Carlton, J. (1997). Apple: *The inside story of intrigue, egomania, and business blunders*, New York: Random House.

Freud, S. (1911). *Formulations on the two principles of mental functioning* (standard ed., Vol. 12), pp. 218–226.

Freud, S. (1917). *Mourning and melancholia* (standard ed., Vol. 14), pp. 243–258.

Galbraith, J.R. (1977). *Organization design*, Reading: Addison-Wesley.

Kawasaki, G. (1990). *The Macintosh way: The art of guerrilla management*. New York: Harper Perennial.

Lawrence, G. (1985). Management development: Some ideals, images and realities. In A.D. Colman and M.H. Geller (Eds.), *Group relations reader 2*, Washington, DC: A.K. Rice Institute.

Miller, E.J. & Rice, A.K. (1990). Task and sentient systems and their boundary controls, In E. Trist, and H. Murray (Eds.), *The social engagement of social science* (Vol. 1), Philadelphia: University of Pennsylvania.

Mossberg, W. (1996). Apple May be Ripe for a Takeover. *All Things Considered*, National Public Radio Transcript, 01–27–1996, Washington, DC.

'Psychic retreats': The organisational relevance of a psychoanalytic formulation

David Armstrong

'Psychic retreats' was first presented at the 1998 Symposium of ISPSO, in Jerusalem. The theme of the Symposium was: 'Drawing Boundaries and Crossing Bridges—Psychoanalytic Perspectives on Alliances, Relationships and Relatedness between Groups, Organisations and Cultures'.

The paper was based on a reading of John Steiner's psychoanalytic formulation of 'psychic retreats', as these may emerge in clinical work with patients. It traces the ways in which Steiner's concept of the 'internal organisation' and its genesis can be echoed within experiences of organisational life and the conditions which inform this. A provisional distinction is drawn between the <u>en</u>actment and the <u>in</u>-actment of internal mental states, which I now see as central to the distinction between individual and social 'pathology'.

In a postscript to the paper, written but not presented at the time, I speculate on the idea of a 'psychic retreat in reverse', in which organisational meaning is both denied and evaded through a 'privileging of the self'.

The idea of this paper dates back eighteen months, when I first read John Steiner's book, *Psychic Retreats: Pathological Organizations in Psychotic, Neurotic and Borderline Patients* (Steiner, 1993). [Unless otherwise indicated, all citations from Steiner are from his first chapter, 'A theory of psychic retreats'.]

John Steiner is a Kleinian analyst who works in private practice and was also, until recently, a consultant psychiatrist at the Tavistock Clinic. His book sets out to describe and understand clinical experiences with groups of patients who are 'difficult-to-treat' and make 'meaningful contact' with. The term 'psychic retreat' is introduced to refer to ways in which the patient can withdraw from such contact into states which are 'often experienced spatially as if they were places in which the patient could hide' (Steiner, 1993, p. xi).

Such states may appear, consciously or in unconscious phantasy, as literal spaces: a house, cave, fortress, desert. But they may also 'take an inter-personal form, usually as an organisation of objects or part-objects which offer to provide security [and which] may be represented as a business organization, as a boarding school, as a religious sect, as a totalitarian government or a Mafia-like gang'. The patient appears, as it were, to be in liege to this organisation, which may be simultaneously feared and idealised.

In his book, Steiner seeks to trace the origin of such states of mind in the patient's attempts to ward off or gain relief from intense anxieties and dread associated with either the paranoid-schizoid or depressive positions, driven by powerful innate destructiveness, or the impact of external trauma, or the intolerance of separation, loss, and an inability to mourn. In more severely disturbed patients such anxieties may lead to a more or less permanent residence in the retreat, where all contact with the analyst or with external reality appears to be lost. But a retreat may also emerge in the treatment of less disturbed patients, at times when external or internal situations threaten the limits of their capacity to contain mental pain.

Steiner examines and explores with great sensitivity the particular challenges which patients inhabiting or inhabited by such states of mind present to analytic work and the various ways in which one can get drawn into enacting a role within the pathological organisation in which the patient is living. For example:

> the analyst may be tolerated only if he submits to the rules imposed by the organization. Pressure is put on him to agree to the limits which the patient sets on what is tolerable and this

may mean that certain types of interpretation are either not permitted or not listened to. If the analyst becomes too insistent that his task is to help the patient gain insight and develop, an even more obstinate withdrawal to the retreat may result and an impasse can materialise which is extremely difficult to negotiate. If, on the other hand, the analyst takes too passive a stance, the patient may feel he has given up, and may see the analyst as defeated or dishonestly caught up in a collusion with a perverse organization.

This quotation can serve to illustrate the impact of Steiner's writing on someone coming to his book from a very different experience of emotional work with clients. For it is hard not to read this statement without hearing echoes from one's own struggle, on occasion, to make contact with the world presented, either by individuals or by groups, within organisational consultancy. In fact, I think this metaphor of 'echoing' captures a good deal of what passes between psychoanalytic and group or organisational work. But it also has risks. Is it just one's own voice one is hearing back, or is it another's that can help one locate one's own?

I am not qualified to comment in detail on Steiner's clinical argument. My interest is rather first, in what that argument suggests about the flow of interaction between, or the interpenetration of, individual and organisational worlds; second, in what the idea of 'psychic retreats' may add to our understanding of organisational dynamics in the face of radical environmental or contextual change. Having said that, I need at least to try and capture something of what Steiner means by 'pathological organisation'. For it is this phrase which both gives depth and substance to the concept of the psychic retreat and which, in Steiner's usage, evokes the most direct echoes to experiences with groups and organisations.

The 'pathological organisation' in the inner world

Steiner introduces and deploys this term in two linked senses. On the one hand, it refers to 'the organized nature of the process' through which the particular system of defences characteristic of the psychic retreat is constructed. On the other hand, as indicated in the quotation cited earlier, it refers to a concrete and personalised phantasy of an internal organisation, made up of objects and part objects in relation to each other.

In Steiner's account, the origin of these states of mind lies in 'the universal problem of dealing with primitive destructiveness', which threatens the integrity of the individual 'unless it is adequately contained'. Defensive organisations in general 'serve to bind, to neutralise and to contain primitive destructiveness whatever its source and are a universal feature of the defensive make-up of all individuals'. Where problems relating to such destructiveness are particularly prominent, the defensive organisation comes to dominate the psyche. Less disturbing versions, however, can also be identified in neurotic and normal individuals.

Such organisations, Steiner maintains,

> function as a kind of compromise and are as much an expression of the destructiveness as a defence against it. Because of this compromise they are always pathological, even though they may serve an adaptive purpose and provide an area of relief and transient protection. ... In normal individuals they are brought into play when anxiety exceeds tolerable limits and are relinquished once more when the crisis is over. Nevertheless, they remain potentially available and can serve to take the patient out of contact and give rise to a stuck period of analysis if the analytic work touches on issues at the edge of what is tolerable.

Steiner sees the structure of the defensive organisation as linked to the operation of 'projective identification'. This mechanism of defence was first identified by Melanie Klein in a famous and hugely influential paper (Klein, 1946) and further elaborated by her colleagues and most notably Wilfred Bion (1962). At the simplest level, it refers to the splitting off and projection of a part of the self into an object. 'The object relationship which results is then not with a person truly seen as separate, but with the self projected into another person and related to as if it were someone else'.

In itself projective identification is not a pathological mechanism. It forms the basis of 'all empathic communication. We project into others to understand better what it feels like to be in their shoes and an inability or reluctance to do this profoundly affects object relations'. This ego-syntonic aspect of projective identification, how-ever, depends on 'being able to use it in a flexible and reversible way and thus be able to withdraw projections and to observe and interact with others from a position firmly based in our own identity'.

Under internal or external pressure, however, 'such reversibility is obstructed and the patient is unable to regain parts of the self lost through projective identification, and consequently loses touch with aspects of his personality, which permanently reside in objects with whom they become identified. Any attribute such as intelligence, warmth, masculinity, aggression, and so on, can be projected and disowned in this way and when reversibility is blocked, results in a depletion of the ego, which has no access to the lost parts of the self. At the same time, the object is distorted by having attributed to it the split-off and denied parts of the self'. The outcome can be confusional states where the differentiation between the self and the other is lost or unstable.

Steiner suggests that this can happen when normal processes of splitting break down. In referring to 'normal processes of splitting', Steiner is drawing on Klein's view that development in earliest life depends on processes whereby the infant splits its object into good and bad, each associated with different constellations of experience and feeling. This splitting of the object is accompanied by a corre-sponding split in the ego. A 'good' part of the self in relationship with a good object is kept separate in this way from a 'bad' part of the self in relation to a bad object. If this split is successfully maintained, good and bad 'are kept so separate that no interaction between them takes place'. But if it threatens to break down, the individual may try to preserve his equilibrium by turning to the protection of the good object and good parts of the self against the bad object and bad parts of the self. If such measures also fail to maintain an equilibrium, 'even more drastic means may be resorted to'.

It is important in reading the above to keep in mind, firstly, that what is being described is part of a more extended process; that is, splitting as described here is not the end but the beginning of a story, the prel-ude to the challenges of the 'depressive position', in which split-off parts of the object and the self can be brought together and acknowl-edged in a more integrated way. Secondly, one needs to remember that this developmental trajectory is not simply time-related, that it is not ever achieved or passed through once for all. Rather it recurs

wherever and whenever we confront new internal or external disturbances or challenges for which we are mentally unprepared. What is
being described is a dynamic that runs throughout our mental life,
though, hopefully, earlier experiences, if adequately negotiated, may
help us better to sustain the shock of the new.

It is at this point in Steiner's account that the richness and sub-
tlety of his conception of the pathological organisation begins to
come more clearly into view. In 1957, Wilfred Bion, in a paper on the
differentiation of psychotic and non-psychotic personalities, drew
attention to a form of pathological splitting which may occur when,
for internal or external reasons, other defences against paranoid/
schizoid anxiety break down. In this situation, both object and self,
including the individual's mental apparatus are subjected to fragmentation and forcibly expelled 'in a more violent and primitive
form of projective identification'. To put this another way, it is as if
the self and its object are dismantled and spread across the whole
psychic field in innumerable bits, each of which contains one not
easily identifiable element: a world of what Bion (1957) referred to as
'bizarre objects' and later as Beta elements (Bion, 1963).

> Pathological organizations may then evolve to collect the frag-
> ments, and the result may once again give the impression of a
> protective good object kept separate from bad ones. Now, how-
> ever, what appears as a relatively straightforward split between
> good and bad is in fact the result of a splitting of the personality
> into several elements, each projected into objects and reassem-
> bled in a manner which simulates the containing function of
> an object. The organization may present itself as a good object
> protecting the individual from destructive attacks, but in fact
> its structure is made up of good and bad elements derived
> from the self and the objects which have been projected into
> and used as building blocks for the resultant extremely complex
> organization (Steiner, 1993).

One aspect of this complexity is the ensuing relation between what
Steiner refers to as the 'dependent self' and this internal organisational structure. For although at times the self may appear as
dominated by or a victim of this organisation, he or she is also in
identification with and a participant within it.

It is not clear to me how far Steiner's account is bound to the more extreme forms of psychotic processes that Bion and others have described. Certainly in his book he describes how pathological organisations may surface from time to time in less gravely disturbed patients. For the present I am inclined to the view, or at least wish to entertain the view, that what he is describing is a process latent and as it were realisable in any and everyone.

To return to Steiner's text, the pathological organisation can be seen as the resultant of a process through which 'projective identification is not confined to a single object, but, instead, groups of objects are used which are themselves in a relationship'. These objects, or part objects, are constructed out of experiences with people found in the patients' early environment. The resulting fantastic figures of the patients' inner world are sometimes based on actual experiences with bad objects and sometimes represent distortions and misrepresentations of early experience. 'What becomes apparent in the here and now of the analysis is that these objects, whether they are chosen from those which pre-exist in the environment or created by the individual, are used for specific defensive purposes to bind destructive elements in the personality'.

I suggest that this formulation significantly adds to our understanding of what might be termed the social construction of the internal world, although it is not a particularly comforting perspective. I will suggest later that it may equally illuminate aspects of our engagements and enactments in the actual social worlds we live and work in.

But Steiner goes on to make another move, which opens up a more specifically organisational domain. And this is where the second sense of 'pathological organisation' I referred to earlier comes into its own. Drawing on previous studies by Herbert Rosenfeld (1971) and Donald Meltzer (1968), Steiner describes how the collection or groups of objects into which destructive impulses have been projected

> are often assembled into a 'gang' which is held together by cruel and violent means. These powerfully structured groups of individuals are represented unconsciously in the patient's inner world [for example, as an internal Mafia] and appear in dreams as an inter-personal version of the retreat. The place of

safety is provided by the group who offer protection from both persecution and guilt as long as the patient does not threaten the domination of the gang. The result of these operations is to create a complex network of object relations, each object containing *split-off parts of the self and the group held together in complex ways characteristic of a particular organization.* The organization 'contains' the anxiety by offering itself as a protector, and it does so in a perverse way very different from that seen in the case of normal containment (italics added).

The organisation becomes 'personified': controlling, sanctioning, and protecting as long as it remains unchallenged. Correspondingly, the individual becomes locked into the organisation and in a way that makes it difficult to regain, reassemble, and move beyond the fragmentation of the self. 'It is not possible to let any single object go, mourn it, and, in the process, withdraw projections from it, because it does not operate in isolation but has powerful links which bind it to other members of the organisation. These links are often ruthlessly maintained, with the primary aim of keeping the organisation intact. *In fact, the individuals are often experienced as bound inextricably to each other and the containment is felt to be provided by a group of objects treated as if it were a single object; namely, the organisation'* (p. 9; italics added).

Steiner argues that where a patient is living in this state of mind it is not possible or helpful for the analyst 'to try to confront or combat the organization head-on. … [But] if it can be recognised as one of the facts of life making up the reality of the patient's inner world, then gradually it may become possible to understand it better and as a result to reduce the hold it has on the personality'. Later, Steiner adds that 'it is important not only to describe the mental mechanisms which operate at any particular moment but also to discuss their function: that is, not only what is happening but why it is happening—in this instance to try to understand what it is that the patient fears would result if he emerged from the retreat'. But he also notes how precarious this move can be. 'Some patients depend on the organization to protect them from primitive states of fragmentation and persecution, and they fear that extreme anxiety would overwhelm them if they were to emerge from the retreat. Others have been able to develop a greater degree of integration but are unable to face the depressive pain and guilt which arise as contact with internal and external reality increases. In either case, emergence to make contact with the analyst may lead to a rapid withdrawal to the retreat and an attempt to regain the previously held equilibrium'.

Shifting focus: From the 'personalised' organisation to the 'organisation-in-the-mind'

In Steiner's account, the pathological organisation emerges as an unconscious personal construct, evolved to offer illusory containment in the face of intense anxiety or mental pain. Suppose, though, one shifts the focus, from the emotional world of the individual to those of the group and/or organisation understood as a *social* and not simply a personal referent. What is it then that Steiner's work may illuminate and contribute to across this bridge?

First of all, in reading this book I sometimes experienced an uncanny feeling of listening to myself as a member of or in the presence of a group. I am referring partly to the experience of anonymity or of being unable either to locate oneself or others in a way that confirms integrity. Also, to the great difficulty one has at times as a consultant in making contact with 'the group', which links in my mind to what Steiner has to say about the position of the analyst facing the patient's group or organisation in the mind.

This, of course, is territory which Bion described in *Experiences in Groups*, and led him to his formulations of group mentality and the differentiation of work group and basic assumption functioning. But I think Steiner's descriptions of the role the group plays in the inner world of the individual and what drives this role may add significantly to these formulations. In particular, it suggests that we may need to pay more attention than in my experience is customary to the fine grain of basic assumptions as these are mobilised in groups and what is driving them; to seek ways of gaining access to the underlying phantasies and the ways in which roles are distributed and interlocked in the service of non-development.

All groups can function, if not exclusively, as 'psychic retreats'. This is implicit in Steiner's account of groups in the internal world. But one can also see evidence that every external 'group' potentially constitutes an arena which our latent groupishness, in Steiner's sense, can 'cathect', occupy, as it were collectively.

You may recall that in the introduction to *Experiences in Groups*, Bion states that his 'present work' (by which I take it he is referring to his individual analytic practice), 'convinces me of the central importance of the Kleinian theories of projective identification and the interplay between the paranoid-schizoid and depressive positions. ... Without the aid of these two sets of theories I doubt the possibility of any advance in the study of group phenomena.' (Bion, 1961, p. 8.) I think Steiner's and other Kleinian contributions take this project some way forward, as indeed did Bion's later work. But they have not as far as I know been extensively drawn on even by many Group Relations practitioners, perhaps because the number of those with direct experience of analytic *and* group work is relatively small. One signal exception to this is a paper on 'The fifth basic assumption' (Lawrence, Bain, & Gould, 1996), which I refer to later. It is worth noting however that much of the response to this paper has been driven by a rather sterile debate along the lines of 'how basic is this basic assumption?', as if somehow Bion's triad were set in tablets of stone.

A second implication of Steiner's thinking for our understanding of group and organisational processes is his characterisation of the 'personalised' organisation in the patient's inner world and the way in which this functions as an illusory container of anxiety, offering protection but at the expense of development and the evolution of meaning. This seems to me a very powerful contribution to our understanding of the 'organisation-in-the-mind'. I think this phrase was first used by Pierre Turquet with reference to experience in the Institutional Event in Group Relations conferences. I have drawn on it myself as, in slightly different ways, have colleagues at The Grubb Institute to refer either to peoples' conscious or unconscious mental constructs of the external organisation they are members of, or to the resonance in individual role holders, especially those operating on the boundary of the organisation as a whole, of emotional currents which are a property of the organisation as a whole and may relate either to the emotional demands of its task, or its structuring, or its relation to the external context—or to all three.

Steiner's formulation of the 'organisation', and its formation and function in the internal world, has strong echoes with independently arrived at formulations of the ways in which real life organisations can function as defences against anxiety. Consider, for example,

Isabel Menzies Lyth's account of work in this tradition, offered in a review of psychoanalytic perspectives on social institutions first published some ten years ago (Menzies Lyth, 1989). She is writing of the ways in which the presenting symptoms in an assignment may appear discrepant with the emotional charge that accompanies them and that has led the organisation to seek consultancy in the first place.

> I think what may be happening is something like this. There is within the job situation a focus of deep anxiety and distress. Associated with this there is despair about being able to improve matters. The defensive system collusively set up against these feelings consists, first, in fragmentation of the core problem so that it no longer exists in an integrated and recognizable form consciously and openly among those concerned. Secondly, the fragments are projected on to aspects of the ambience of the job situation which are then consciously and honestly, but mistakenly, experienced as the problem about which something needs to be done, usually by someone else. Responsibility has also been fragmented and often projected into unknown others— 'Them', the authorities. ... Such defensive reactions to institutional problems often mean the institution cannot really learn. The solutions tried before had failed, but they will work this time—as though there is a kind of magic about them. Effective resolution can only come when the institution, with or without the help of a consultant, can address itself to the heart of the matter and not only to its ambience, and introduce relevant changes there (p. 30).

All the elements in this account—the presence of a focus of deep anxiety and distress accompanied by feelings (conscious or unconscious) of despair; fragmentation of the problem so that it cannot be reflectively held; projection of these fragments as it were across the psychic field of the organisation; personalisation in terms of an establishment (the authorities) accompanied by a splitting of aspects of one's mental apparatus (responsibility)—are strikingly congruent with Steiner's description of the patient's internal organisation.

At the same time, I think Steiner's work adds something to this picture. For example, his rooting of the internal problem in the issue of dealing with primitive destructiveness, draws attention to and helps make sense of the strong undertow of hostility, punitiveness, resentment, and grievance that often accompany defensive states in organisations and which may be simultaneously and collusively mobilised in a way that makes it difficult to disentangle victim and oppressor. His concept of the illusory container draws attention to the underlying fear of and attack on meaning and helps to account for the difficulty consultants can face in working in this field, as Isabel Menzies Lyth was to experience herself in her original nursing study. Indeed this difficulty is compounded in working with actual organisations since the defensive system, spread across the whole structure of roles and relations, can be very hard to bring into focus. (In my own view, this is somewhat less true where the immediate client is a senior executive post holder, or at least where one has access to such a post holder, although I am not sure colleagues in the field would necessarily agree.)

In what follows I shall use the term 'inner world organisation' to refer to Steiner's formulation and 'organisation-in-the-mind' to refer to what we encounter in real life organisations.

The consonance between Steiner's inner world organisation and organisation-in-the-mind raises some intriguing and ticklish questions. Is what is happening in external organisations an enactment of an internal state, or is it rather that external organisations, if I may coin a handy neologism, in-act, or make active, an internal repertoire of response to anxiety? Another question that arises—and could probably only be answered by practising analysts with experience in both domains—is what happens in a person's internal world if he or she is also a participant in a collusively structured external organisation.

Leaving these questions aside, I want to propose the following:

1. Every organisation contains a pathological version of itself (a shadow side).
2. This pathological version is collectively and unconsciously constructed in a way that parallels the construction of pathological organisations in the internal world.
3. The function of the pathological version is to serve as a 'psychic retreat' when the internal or external situation of the organisation threatens the limits of its capacity—as a voluntary assembly

cooperating in relation to a 'real' task—to contain the psychic challenges of the work.

4. This pathological version is potentially built in to the organisation from the outset, not only in relation to what Menzies Lyth refers to as the organisation's 'ambience', but also including conventional structural arrangements (hierarchies, procedures and explicit or implicit sets of rules). I am not suggesting that such arrangements are inherently pathological, but rather that they can readily lend themselves to this purpose. Bion's descriptions of a group's attempt to establish procedures in the early phases of its existence illustrate this neatly (Bion, 1961). More recently Larry Hirschhorn (1997) has persuasively argued that hierarchies may function equally as 'illusory containers' (my phrase rather than his).

5. Recourse to or mobilisation of the pathological version, as a latent system within the organisation, may be temporary or longer lasting or, at the extreme, chronic. It does not necessarily prevent work from being done, but it interferes with it through robbing it of vitality and meaning. As a consequence, there is a preoccupation with the political world of the organisation: who's in, who's out; the undertow of competitive struggles, gossip, manoeuvring for position, and intrusive personal relations; repetitive and self-sustaining fights over the distribution of resources and/or rewards; or an obsessional search for illusory measurements of performance, which short-circuit the need for human judgement, that is necessarily provisional, qualitative, and subject to error.

6. It is important, nonetheless, not to assume that mobilisation of the pathological organisation is wholly destructive, although it risks being so. As Steiner illustrates continually in describing his patients, the movement into and out of a psychic retreat may be the only means through which the individual can gradually come to terms with and acknowledge the pain of development. The difficulty is that, as he puts it, 'the patient [can] become accustomed and even addicted to the state of affairs in the retreat and gain a kind of perverse gratification from it'. This observation, again, seems to me to echo an important aspect of the worlds in which as organisational consultants we currently work.

Over the past two or three years, a number of practitioners in the field have challenged or questioned the so called 'Tavistock paradigm' in organisational consultancy (Palmer, 2000, 2002). I say 'so called', because I do not think there is one such paradigm, but rather a variety of rather loosely linked conceptual approaches: psychoanalytic, socio-technical, open systems, systemic or psycho-systemic, socio-analytic, and so on. It is suggested that the emphasis on defensive processes and their mode of operation limits the atten-tion paid to the particular challenges which organisations are cur-rently facing, which increasingly concern questions of re-defining the nature and consequently the 'requisite structure' of the enterprise (to borrow Elliott Jaques' (1989) phrase), under conditions of radical technological and environmental change. Larry Hirschhorn's (1999) introduction of the concept of 'primary risk', and his recent venture into the worlds of Lacanian analysis and the links between 'desire' and mental 'flow' (Hirschhorn, 1998), are among a number of exam-ples. And certainly it is true that increasingly we ourselves, in the Tavistock Consultancy Service, are being asked to work with clients on more strategic themes of 're-visioning' the business or working on 'core values', or bringing about 'transformational change'.

Yet, paradoxically, Steiner's concept of the 'psychic retreat' would suggest that it is precisely in such circumstances that the pull towards pathology and the tendency to mobilise latent defensive constella-tions of response are most likely to be in evidence. Moreover, in so far as one consequence of technological and environmental change has been to challenge our tacit assumptions about boundaries (of task, technology, territory, and time), it is not only our 'rational', paradigms of organisation that are challenged, but also, as it were, the unconscious investments which those paradigms can elicit: the shadow side of conventional wisdom.

This is well illustrated by Larry Hirschhorn himself in his recent book on *Reworking Authority: Leading and Following in the Post-Mod-ern Organisation*. Hirschhorn's central concern is with what might be termed the 'psychic costs' of the evolution of what he describes as a 'culture of openness', characterised by the apparent suspension or relaxation of organisational boundaries, the attenuation of hierarchy and the search for more flexible and potentially creative patterns of relationship between role holders. 'The post-modern organisation requires that individuals at all levels make themselves more open to one another—how else can it draw on the individual creativity of all its members?—but faces the stark reality that people don't wish to look incompetent or feel ashamed' (Hirschhorn, 1997, p. 18). Much of the book consists of examples of the various stratagems through which members of the organisation unconsciously seek to ward off these psychic costs of development.

One such stratagem, for example, familiar enough in other organisational settings, turns on the ritualisation of meetings:

> In the past, management meetings ... were organized as performances. Individuals prepared for a meeting so that it could go off without a hitch, so that no real learning or discovery took place. This paradigm for meetings certainly helped all the members contain their anxiety—there would be no surprises; individuals who had performed badly could read the "signal" of the bosses' displeasure without being shamed in public; and the leader, fully in control, could protect his self-image as highly competent, if not invulnerable. The downside of this paradigm is that managers could not meet to do creative work together. Feeling suppressed by the format but also understanding the larger risks the organisation faced, people rushed out of the meeting at breaks to gossip about who was on top and on bottom today, who was scoring points, and who was losing credibility. The gossip relieved their anxiety and returned to them a sense of participating, at least in the "dirt" of the organisation. at the cost of failing to contribute to substantive discussions and decisions (ibid., p. 18).

I would see this example as an instance of the mobilisation of an available form of 'psychic retreat' built in to the unconscious structuring of the organisation. The retreat offers 'containment', but in an illusory form that forecloses rather than releases development.

Later in the book Hirschhorn suggests how the 'modern organisation', when 'it functioned well', could contain potentially destabilising feelings (aroused by real or phantasied dependence) by *depersonalising* them. Individuals experienced dominance and submission as artifacts of their role relationships. They might, consequently, take a 'political' view of their situation, e.g., that they were participating in the drama of 'labour versus capital', or they might develop a moral or normative stance, e.g., 'one should obey one's superiors'.

Similarly, factory supervisors who disciplined workers could protect themselves from feelings of guilt and anxiety by ascribing their harshness to the roles they occupied. While never completely resolving the tension between person and role, the modern organisation, by favoring the role, created a paradoxically helpful climate of depersonalization (ibid., p. 33).

Elsewhere, Hirschhorn describes what can happen to such unconscious stratagems where and when, for whatever reason, the gradient of risk increases beyond the capacity of what a particular management finds tolerable. Instead of relying on the role structure to delegate authority, management comes to

> rely on "technical" fixes and disorganizing politics. They try to use technically developed procedures or rules as substitutes for roles, and they employ the political principle of checks and balances to orchestrate inter-divisional relationships. Checks and balances replace unity of command, rules replace roles, and politics ultimately drives out teamwork. We create a bureaucracy. This suggests that bureaucracy (particularly in high-risk settings) is usefully interpreted not as a rational form of work organisation but as a *regressed form of hierarchy* (ibid., p. 66–67; italics in original).

To my mind this is a most persuasive description both of how, under developmental anxiety, what I am terming a 'psychic retreat' can be mobilised within the organisation, and of how the form of this retreat, as it were, borrows from but simultaneously parodies and perverts the very organisational forms that hitherto have served to sustain 'good enough' work.

Every element of organisational life, I suggest, is subject to this kind of unconscious manoeuvre, or perhaps it would be more accurate to say that this kind of manoeuvre is a latent potential in the repertoire of all organisational behaviour. There is something about the organisational (or indeed the societal) domain that elicits it. I think this 'something' links to Steiner's account of the function of the organisation in the internal world which, under the pressure of uncertainty—the not known—real life organisations collectively cathect.

This is still, for me, the territory in which psychoanalytically informed consultancy has a distinctive contribution to make. I am not wholly convinced that we have much to offer in contributing *directly* to the creative challenges that organisations are facing. If we did then surely that would be where we would choose to work. But I think we have a great deal to offer in helping, with patience and with sympathy, organisations that are facing such challenges to avoid the misrepresentations and illusory investments which such challenges inevitably evoke.

Postscript

As a postscript to this paper I want, tentatively, to describe a rather different version of a 'psychic retreat' faced currently by organisations. It is a form of retreat that has some links to the constellation which Gordon Lawrence and his co-authors have identified as basic assumption Me-ness (baM). This they describe as a 'temporary cultural phenomenon, salient at this time in history' (Lawrence, Bain, & Gould, 1996, p. 35).

> In particular we are putting forward the idea that as living in contemporary, turbulent societies becomes more risky so the individual is pressed more and more into his or her own inner reality in order to exclude and deny the perceived disturbing realities that are of the outer environment. The inner world becomes thus a comforting one offering succour. ... Our working hypothesis is that baM occurs when people—... meeting to do something in a group—work on the tacit, unconscious assumption that the group is to be a non-group. Only the people present are there to be related to because their shared construct in the mind of 'group' is of an undifferentiated mass. They therefore act as if the group had no existence, because if it did exist it would be the source of persecuting experiences (pp. 33 & 36).

Later in the paper, the authors suggest that this assumption, although serving a defensive purpose can have its 'temporary uses': 'There is a sense in which baM can be viewed as a dependency on oneself and one's own resources in order to have a basis of dependability to participate in and hearken to the realities of the environment.' (p. 50.) In my view, however, this 'sophisticated' use, as with the other basic assumptions, is at best precarious. One can compare this with what Steiner has to say about Donald Winnicott's work on transitional objects and transitional spaces:

> There are many similarities between transitional spaces and psychic retreats but also some central differences. In particular is the value given by Winnicott to the transitional area which he sees as a place of cultural and personal development. In my approach, I emphasize them as areas of retreat from reality where no realistic development can take place. In my view, the retreat often serves as a resting place and provides relief from anxiety and pain but it is only as the patient emerges from the retreat that real progress can occur (Steiner, 1993, p. 41).

The experience which prompted the line of thought I want to describe happened to occur around the time that I first began reading Steiner's book. It took place in the context of a five-day programme entitled 'Understanding and Working with Groups', which was one of a series designed and led by the Tavistock Consultancy Service for a number of years and sponsored by a large multi-national IT organisation. Members attending these programmes came from the sponsoring company and a variety of other organisations including large consultancy firms. What stimulated the establishment of the series was the sponsoring company's felt need to develop a more consultancy-based approach to the development and delivery of IT services to client organisations.

The aim of the programme was twofold: to develop skills of facilitation in working with groups and teams and to explore the dynamics of groups and teams in an organisational setting. The method of work owed something to Harold Bridger's conception of the 'double task' in working conferences (Bridger, 2001). Thus the core event of the programme was a Study Group that had the task, firstly, of designing a programme of sessions in which each member would have an opportunity to work as a 'facilitator' to the group; secondly of taking 'time out', usually towards the end of each session, to review and comment on the group 'process' as different members were experiencing this. Each group met with a consultant present, whose primary focus was on this second task. In addition to these Study Groups there were Consultancy Syndicates where members gave and received individual consultancy to and from each other, in the presence of observers. There were also, on this occasion, large group meetings which all members and staff attended. These were referred to as Whole System Meetings, with the task of 'studying the current dynamics of the whole workshop through an exploration of one's actual experience in the here and now'. Staff worked in these meetings as consultants to this task, which was seen as opening up a more organisational dimension that might illuminate and suggest links to the external organisational worlds members brought in with them.

For some time the Tavistock staff working on these programmes had been aware of a number of recurring experiences. These included the tendency of members to invest emotional energy in the Study Groups, while apparently appearing quite listless, fractious and sceptical in any larger group setting (plenaries, whole system meetings). More significantly, it had become apparent that much of the learning which members felt and said they derived from the programmes was 'personalised'. That is, they felt they had learned important things about themselves as persons, rather than, for example, as role holders, members of groups or organisations, and so on. Over time this had led to a covert 'institutionalising' of an unplanned event towards the end of each cycle of Study Groups, where members 'gave feedback' to each other on how they perceived them. These sessions were often extraordinarily intense, almost cathartic, as if they were the culmination of something that had a flavour of personal exposure, of opening up and inviting feelings of vulnerability in oneself and others. They became part of the 'myth' surrounding the programmes, passed on in elusive hints to intending future applicants. Within the staff group involved in the programmes there was considerable, sometimes conflictual, discussion about this development and its legitimacy.

The occasion which set me puzzling was the penultimate session of a Study Group I had been working with and that had followed much the same pattern I described above. Members were reviewing what they felt they had each gained from their experience. The youngest member of the group, who held a position of considerable responsibility in his company, began talking about how the course had raised for him the question of what was his 'true self'. (This was not a term that had been used hitherto, nor was there any evidence of familiarity on the part of any member with its more technical origins and use.) He said that it was as if he were in a room which had a glass floor. Beneath this floor was his true self. He felt that there had been a thick carpet on the floor which prevented him seeing and having access to his true self. During the Workshop he said, this carpet had begun to be partly rolled back. The other members of the group, including myself, seemed intensely moved by this image. It set the tone for everything the others said, which had to do with their experience of coming to acknowledge feelings and emotions they had not hitherto allowed themselves fully to recognise or use in the presence of others. These included positive feelings of warmth, concern, generosity, and negative feelings of anger, hostility, and shame.

But these feelings, made public to each other now, were seen as an essentially private matter, that had little or nothing to say about members engagement in the public and organisational worlds they lived in. There was no sense of members feeling they could take this discovery back into the working world, but only into the world of more intimate relations, within the family or with partners. It was as if, it seemed to me, nothing was to be allowed to disturb or mitigate the very negative, persecutory construction of the organisational world which had emerged in much of the material elsewhere in the Workshop. This was presented as a world driven by a survivalist mentality, a world of political manoeuvring, disregard of the human costs of change, which spoke the language of development but was unable truly to act on it.

It then occurred to me that what one might be experiencing, indeed participating in, was a kind of splitting of the personal and the organisational, which, however important in recovering a fuller sense of self, itself represented a strategy of survival rather than development: a kind of psychic retreat in reverse, that is a privileging of the self which leaves the self-in-the-organisation exactly where it is.

In his book, *The Claustrum*, Donald Meltzer, in the course of a rather doleful account of the part played by group mentality in mental life, nonetheless makes the point that we would be deceiving ourselves if we thought it possible to carry on an activity with others without participating in the communal aspect, for 'there is always a community. And since there is a community, there are problems of organisation and communication where the borderland between friendly and hostile, communication and action, governing and ruling, opposing and sabotaging becomes obscure' (Meltzer, 1992). We can perhaps retreat psychically from this borderland, but only at the cost of organisational or communal health.

References

Bion, W.R. (1957). Differentiation of the psychotic from the non-psychotic personalities. *International Journal of Psychoanalysis*, 38:266–275.

Bion, W.R. (1961). *Experiences in Groups and Other Papers*. London: Tavistock. [Reprinted London: Routledge, 1989; Brunner-Routledge, 2001].

Bion, W.R. (1962). *Learning from Experience*. London: Heinemann Medical Books. [Reprinted London: Karnac Books, 1984].

Bion, W.R. (1963). *Elements of Psychoanalysis*. London: Heinemann Medical Books. [Reprinted London: Karnac Books, 1984].

Bridger, H. (2001). The working conference design. In: G. Amado & A. Ambrose (Eds.), *The Transitional Approach to Change* (pp. 137–160). London: Karnac Books.

Hirschhorn, L. (1997). *Reworking Authority: Leading and Following in the Post-Modern Organization*. Cambridge, MA: MIT Press.

Hirschhorn, L. (1998). Beyond anxiety: Passion and the psychodynamics of work—learnings from Lacan. Philadelphia, PA: Center for Applied Research.

Hirschhorn, L. (1999). The primary risk. *Human Relations*, 52:5–23.

Jaques, E. (1989). *Requisite Organization*. Arlington, VA: Cason Hall & Co.

Klein, M. (1946). Notes on some schizoid mechanisms. *International Journal of Psychoanalysis*, 27:99–110.

Lawrence, W.G., Bain, A. & Gould. L.J. (1996). The fifth basic assumption. *Free Associations*, 6, No. 37:28–55.

Meltzer, D. (1968). Terror, persecution and dread. *International Journal of Psycho-Analysis*, 49:396–401. [Reprinted Perthshire: Clunie Press, 1973, pp. 99–106].

Meltzer, D. (1992). *The Claustrum: An Investigation of Claustrophobic Phenomena*. Strathclyde, Perthshire: Clunie Press.

Menzies Lyth, I. (1989). A psychoanalytic perspective on social institutions. In: I. Menzies Lyth, *The Dynamics of the Social. Selected Essays, Volume 2* (pp. 43–85). London: Free Association Books.

Palmer, B. (2000). In which the Tavistock paradigm is considered as a discursive practice. *Organisational and Social Dynamics*, 1:8–20.

Palmer, B. (2002). The Tavistock paradigm: Inside, outside and beyond. In: R.D. Hinshelwood & M. Chiesa (Eds.), *Organisations, Anxieties and Defences: Towards a Psychoanalytic Social Psychology* (pp. 158–182). London: Whurr.

Rosenfeld, H.A. (1971). A clinical approach to the psychoanalytic theory of the life and death instincts: An investigation into the aggressive aspects of narcissism. *International Journal of Psycho-Analysis*, 52:169–178.

Steiner, J. (1993). *Psychic Retreats: Pathological Organizations in Psychotic, Neurotic and Borderline Patients*. London: Routledge.

'Negative capability': A contribution to the understanding of creative leadership

Robert French and Peter Simpson
Bristol Business School, University of the West of England

Charles Harvey
Newcastle University Business School

Our aim in this chapter is to suggest how the idea of 'negative capability' may contribute to an understanding of the creative leader. We begin by exploring the origins of the term negative capability and its meaning in the creative arts and in psychoanalysis. We then assess its value as a concept in relation to leadership. Creative leadership is called for at the edge between certainty and uncertainty, both a necessary and a difficult place to work in the current context of organizational life. Whereas, positive capabilities direct leaders and followers toward particular forms of action rooted in knowing, negative capability is the ability to resist dispersing into inappropriate knowing and action. We suggest that appropriate combinations of positive capabilities and negative capability can generate and sustain a 'working space' or 'capacity' for creative thought at this edge between knowing and not knowing. Creative leaders are characterised by their ability to generate such spaces not merely for themselves but also for others within the organization. Some of the problems for organizational leaders in working with negative capability are raised and explored.

Introduction

The aim of this article is to propose a way of conceptualising the qualities required for creative leadership by drawing attention to the tantalising yet elusive notion of 'negative capability.'

A leader's 'positive capabilities' are those which are generally described as the skills, competencies, knowledge and technologies of leadership. The underpinning image of leadership is based on knowing and is manifested through activity, work and achievement. There is, however, a quite other dimension of leadership, based on not knowing, on not doing, on being-done-to, and on being no longer in control of one's own situation. It is the capacity to work creatively with this dimension of human experience that the poet John Keats called *'Negative Capability.'*

In leadership studies, and in leadership training, the overwhelming emphasis is on *positive* capabilities, and for this reason our focus is on understanding the relevance to creative leadership of *negative* capability. Our proposition is that at the edge between certainty and uncertainty a capacity for creative thought is formed by the appropriate combination of negative capability and positive capabilities.

'Negative capability': The origins and meaning of the term

Keats described negative capability as a state in which a person

> 'is capable of being in uncertainties, Mysteries, doubts, without any irritable reaching after fact & reason.' (Keats, 1970: 43)

Since Keats' first—and only—use of the term 'negative capability', in a letter to his brothers in 1817, 'one of the most puzzling of all his letters' (Bate, 1964: 236–7), it has had a rich life of its own. Mainly focussed on its original context, the exploration of the nature and origins of artistic creativity, it has also been applied to religious experience (Scott, 1969; Toynbee, 1973), to the role of the psychoanalyst (see, for example, Bion, 1978: 8–9; 1984a: 124–5; 1990: 45–6; 1991: 207; Eisold, 2000; Ghent, 1990; Green, 1973; Hutter, 1982; Leavy, 1970; Rosen, 1960), and, most recently, in the fields of management and organization studies (Bennis, 1998: 148, 2000; Handy, 1989: 54, 183).

Keats was only twenty-two years old when, in a period of intense exploration and speculation, he coined the phrase in a sequence of attempts to describe the 'prime essential' of a poet (Muir, 1958: 107). Following such experiments as 'scepticism', 'pessimism', 'Wordsworthian humanitarianism', 'disinterestedness' and—closest to our theme—'humility and the capability of submission', 'negative capability' was the final 'dovetailing' of concepts in Keats' emerging understanding of the poetic imagination (Bate, 1964, chapter x; Caldwell, 1972: 5).

Negative capability suggests a peculiarly human capacity for 'containment': that is, the capacity to live with and to tolerate ambiguity and paradox, and to 'remain content with half knowledge' (Ward, 1963, p. 161), 'to tolerate anxiety and fear, to stay in the place of uncertainty in order to allow for the emergence of new thoughts or perceptions' (Eisold, 2000: 65). It implies the capacity to engage in a non-defensive way with change, without being overwhelmed by the ever-present pressure merely to react. It also indicates empathy and even a certain flexibility of character, the ability 'to tolerate a loss of self and a loss of rationality by trusting in the capacity to recreate oneself in another character or another environment' (Hutter, 1982: 305). Bridgwater focuses explicitly on this openness and capacity for identification with the 'other':

1. By 'negative capability' Keats meant the lack of personal identity, of preconceived certainty, which he believed to mark all great poets. It was necessary, Keats believed, for the poet to be, above all, open to impressions, sensations or whatever, which means that the 'camelion' (chameleon) poet is forever changing his/her ideas (1999: xv).

At first sight, it may seem ridiculous to think of a leader as a chameleon or as lacking personal identity: 'forever changing his/her ideas.' The current cult of leader-as-personality or -hero, 'turning companies around', stresses the very opposite of such chameleon-like colour changes; that is, the need to nail one's colours to the mast, to embody the organization's vision, and to be proactive, creating environments not just responding to them. However, as with many organizational paradoxes, 'the truth is not in the middle, and not in one extreme, but in both extremes' (Charles Simeon, 1847).

At one extreme, the articulation and constant re-presentation of the vision—giving a lead and sticking to it—may indeed be a key element in the success of any organizational venture. At the other extreme, however, effective leadership can involve seeing moment by moment, day by day, what is *actually going on*, in contrast with what was planned for, expected or intended. In order to assess the impact of events in this way, and to adapt, shift and adjust as necessary, 'chameleon' leaders might indeed be thought of as putting their *self* to one side, in order to allow their minds be changed by 'truth-in-the-moment' (French and Simpson, 1999; Simpson and French, 2006). The heart of the paradox is that it may only be by changing and re-visioning the organization's reality as it evolves that a leader can preserve the focus on the task.

For example, in 1982 Jim Burke, CEO of Johnson and Johnson, took charge of the 'Tylenol crisis' when several people died after poison had been inserted into Tylenol capsules. Burke removed the product from the shelves, against the wishes of the U.S. Food and Drug Administration and the FBI, who were concerned that this action would alarm the public—and at a cost of $125 million. Burke explained, "we put the public first. We never hid anything from them and were as honest as we knew how to be." This included appearing on the *Donahue* television programme and on *60 Minutes*. The corporation had not worked in this manner before—nor had it faced such a crisis. "Only one person here supported what I was doing" recalled Burke, "when I decided to go on *60 Minutes* the head of public relations told me it was the worst decision anyone in this corporation had ever made, and anyone who would risk the corporation that way was totally irresponsible, and he walked out and slammed the door."

In his honesty and openness, refusing to try to avoid the problem through politically expedient actions or explanations, Burke made himself and the corporation vulnerable. This did indeed represent a genuine risk, and may have opened up a route for escalating blame and recrimination.

In terms of the framework we are offering, we would say that Burke was able to mobilise both his positive capabilities and his negative capability in a way that, in the event, turned out to be appropriate. He describes the importance of his training in market research and consumer marketing, his contacts in the media, and being guided by a "philosophy of life" that was sorely tested. This combination of positive capabilities and negative capability, in this particular situation, generated a space within which the corporation, the media and the public at large were able to find and create a new way to think about the problem. In addition, nine weeks after the first headlines new tamper-resistant packaging was in production. Burke suggests that they managed to design the new packaging "overnight practically, when it would have normally taken two years." Within a year Tylenol was back as the top over-the-counter analgesic in the U.S. The organization could continue its task, and Burke appeared on the front cover of *Fortune* magazine, lauded as an innovator. (Bennis, 1998: 151–4)

The fact that this case is cited as a model example of corporate responsibility and crisis management has led to a number of 'formulaic' responses to crises, largely based on sending the company CEO out to deal with public and media. However, the imprisoning in India of Union Carbide's CEO, Warren Anderson, following the Bhopal poisonings is just one example that illustrates the danger of a one-dimensional understanding of Burke's achievement. The danger arises from treating the essentially creative, dynamic and contingent relationship between positive capabilities and negative capability as though it were simply a skill or a technique. Burke was not applying a learned formula. What he knew was indeed important in the Tylenol crisis, but it was the integrity with which he accepted and addressed what he did *not* know, as well as what he did, that generated a capacity within which everyone involved could engage creatively with the problem.

It appears paradoxical, but positive capabilities provide the basis for mobilising negative capability. For example, it is the knowledge that I do not know that allows me to do nothing. It is my confidence in my own judgement that allows me to accept that, for the moment, my judgement is failing me.

Allowing oneself to be influenced, as Burke did, by the experience of the reality of the moment was indeed Keats' practice as a poet: 'His own personality seemed to him to matter hardly more than the strings of the lyre; without which, indeed, there would be no music audible, but which changed no single note of the music already existing in an expectant silence' (Symons, 1901: 1626–7). While the *form* of a poet's intervention is very different to that of an organizational leader, their effectiveness may be based on a remarkable similarity of intention and desire: 'to be a voice, a vision; to pass on a message, translating it, flawlessly, into another, more easily apprehended tongue' (ibid.). Through the exercise of negative capability the leader becomes, like the strings of a lyre, an instrument—not for music or poetry, but for organizational inquiry, learning and creativity: 'what is deepest in the human mystery gives way only before a *Negative Capability*.' (Scott, 1969: xii–xiii)

Following Wittgenstein's method of 'family resemblances', we would argue that the pursuit of creative imaginings and insights links a distinct 'family' of roles, that includes poet, psychoanalyst, theologian or philosopher—*and leader*. Whilst these roles may have 'no one thing in common which makes us use the same word for all', Wittgenstein's method suggests that 'they are *related* to one another in many different ways.' (Wittgenstein, 1963, paras 65; his italics.) Our suggestion is that the key link is negative capability: *all of these roles depend for their effectiveness on developing and mobilising negative capability.*

However, insights into resemblances between roles can only be of practical value if differences are identified with equal clarity. A leader may, after all, be a poet, a philosopher, a theologian or even a psychoanalyst, but this does not mean that the reverse is also true. Without highlighting differences, it is all too easy to draw interesting but contestable conclusions about the 'leader-as-poet' or about 'philosopher-kings.' (Plato, *The Republic*: 473d)

Organizational leaders must be oriented towards the unknown, creative insight of the moment and hence towards 'the edges' of their ignorance. However, unlike poet or analyst, the 'insight' sought by leaders is much more obviously conditional, contingent as it is on *the task of the organization*. When leaders search out those new thoughts which can only arise at the edge of uncertainty and not-knowing, they do so in order to establish or to maintain their competitive advantage and to ensure that their organization can thrive in the face of competition and of market forces, or to make sure that the needs of clients are met. For the most part, they are not in search of creativity *per se*. They do not follow the insight wherever it may take them. Rather, they must search for the idea relevant to the organization in its context. As a result of insights gained, the leader may, of course, come to redefine this task, even quite radically, but that would be a by-product.

Leadership 'at the edge' between certainty and uncertainty

An analogy with the visual arts may illuminate the relationship between negative capability and positive capabilities. It also explains why it is that the overwhelmingly 'positive' and practical notion of 'capability' is amplified rather than contradicted by being described as 'negative', and why developing one's negative capability involves 'not a negation of self but an affirmation of self.' (Hutter, 1982: 305)

In the visual arts potent use is made of the idea of 'negative space.' In looking at an object or a scene, our tendency is to notice and to observe its features—whether it be a vase, a tree or a chair. However, every object—or 'positive form'—also has 'negative spaces' around or within it. An artist's 'awareness of shapes and relationships' can be enhanced by focussing on these negative spaces, 'switching attention from the meaningful objects to the shapes they leave empty against the background' (Gombrich, 1977: 258): 'In teaching people to draw, one of the most difficult things is to convince them that objects are not all-important—that the spaces around the objects are of at least equal importance.' (Edwards, 1987: 152; her italics.) It is indeed 'counter-intuitive' to think that one's ability to draw an object can be improved by focusing on the spaces around it. (Edwards, 2000: 123).

Many visual 'puns' or illusions depend on this relationship between positive and negative images. For instance, in a well-known brainteaser (reproduced in Figure 1), a focus on the object , reveals the silhouette of a vase. When one concentrates on the negative image, however, it 'turns into' two faces in profile looking at each other. In this case, either image could, in truth, be negative or positive, depending on which image the eye selects. No value judgement is implied; it is not better to focus on the 'empty shape' than on the 'meaningful object': 'The concept most difficult to grasp, perhaps, is that the spaces unify the objects. Or better said, the spaces and the objects link together to form a unified image.' (Edwards, 1987: 152; her italics)

In a similar way, it may be counter-intuitive to argue that it is the 'negative' attributes of leadership—not knowing or not acting, for instance—which unify the leader's positive capabilities of knowing and acting. Or, to echo Edwards' phrase, a leader's negative capability and positive capabilities link together to form a unified whole.

Figure 1. Positive form/negative space.

Here too, one is not *better* than the other. Nor are they *opposites*: the opposite of one is incompetence, and of the other, dispersal. 'Dispersal'—into *explanations, physical activity* or *emotions*—is Needleman' s term (1990: 167) for the way we behave when our negative capability is not adequate to the demands of a situation. Unable to hold the tensions and anxieties and to live with problems that may be intractable, accepting paradoxes and dilemmas for what they are—unable, that is, to gather or conserve our energies—we 'disperse' them. For example, we rush too quickly into action, or without adequate consideration we break problems down into apparently manageable 'bits' in an effort to make them *seem* manageable after all. (See French, 2001)

Most importantly, the unified whole created by the linking of positive and negative is not solid: negative capability brings to it a holey-ness. Not knowing and not acting leave spaces that are essential for establishing a creative capacity. A cup made of clay, paint and glaze (the positive capabilities) designed to form an appropriate space (negative capability) has the capacity to contain liquid. In a similar sense, an appropriate combination of positive capabilities and negative capability can create a capacity to work at the edge between certainty and uncertainty, containing the thoughts and feelings of the individual in a manner that allows the pressures towards dispersal to be resisted. In this place, new thoughts may be received or conceived and then worked with or allowed to 'take', to settle and mature. This work is far from 'easy', however, because it can bring the individual in his or her role face to face with the very uncertainties, mysteries and doubts that we prefer to avoid: 'When those mysteries begin to touch a man directly, when they become, as Keats would call them a "burden," the mind grows increasingly less capable of ignoring them.' (Ryan, 1976: 157)

The establishing of a creative capacity might be seen as stepping beyond the 'formulation and articulation of a vision', in order to open up potential spaces for new visions. It amounts to taking up illusory spaces or 'intermediate' positions between what *is* and what *could be*. The '*entrepreneur*', for example, exploits creative gaps by 'taking up' the 'space between'—*entre*, between; *prendre*, to take. In psychoanalytic terms, this is the intermediate space identified by Winnicott as the space of *play*. (Winnicott, 1971)

The capacity to work at the edge, in the intermediate space, enables a leader to move back and forth between a state of knowing and one of not-knowing, *to continue to think* in the 'limbo' state between certainty and uncertainty, or to seek out and cross the edge into the unknown, in order to return with new insight. In Martin Buber's phrase, this is the capacity to stand on 'the narrow ridge', which Friedman describes as the central metaphor of Buber's life. On this 'narrow rocky ridge', leaders can no longer rely on 'the sureness of expressible knowledge.' Instead, they face the possibility of 'meeting what remains undisclosed' (Buber, in Friedman, 1993: 10). One thing is certain, and it may be this that makes the margin both a frightening and an exciting place to be: by standing on the edge of their knowledge and facing their ignorance, leaders always face the prospect of *learning something new*.

However, the actual *experience* of 'being at an edge' is seldom considered in all its emotional ambiguity. Paul Tillich, for example, described the edge ('boundary') as the best place for acquiring knowledge. However, he was in no doubt about the inherent ambiguities and tensions of living and working in that space:

> Since thinking presupposes receptiveness to new possibilities, this position [at the boundary between alternative possibilities

for existence] is fruitful for thought; but it is difficult and
dangerous in life, which again and again demands decisions
and thus the exclusion of alternatives. This disposition and
its tension have determined both my destiny and my work.
(Tillich, 1967: 13)

Everyday language suggests that the edge is powerfully present as
a metaphor in organizations. It can represent many things, such as
danger ('*dead*-lines'), exclusion (the 'glass ceiling'), power relations
('toe the line'), or success in relation to others ('leading', 'cutting' or
'competitive' edge). For Buber and Tillich, by contrast, living on the
edge was a way of life, a way of being. It seems they *had to* seek out
the boundary, in order to engage with the world with integrity.

Something similar is true of leaders. In some way they too *need* to
live on the edge. Why else would someone put themselves through
such an experience? Those theories that emphasise a leader's 'character traits' or 'style' may have identified the 'internal' component,
as it were, of leadership: unsettling though the experience may be,
some people *enjoy* getting to the edge of uncertainty and discovering new insights as a result. In a similar way, some people enjoy
rock-climbing: it gives them a sense of being fulfilled rather than
'edgy', and of pushing the limits, alive through being in danger.
Contingency theory, on the other hand, recognises that in certain
cases the circumstances themselves can create the leader. Certain
conditions may demand people with the ability to work in this
intermediate space where new thoughts may arise, people who
have, to use Tillich's word, the necessary 'disposition' to cope, even
if only for a moment, with the tension inherent in not knowing and
not acting.

Creative thought at the edge

It is unfashionable to talk about 'the search for truth.' The post-mod-
ern deconstruction of 'grand narratives' problematised all essential-
ist notions of 'Truth': 'men are ...', 'women are ...', 'organizations
are ...', 'leadership is ....' In one sense, however, 'truth' has always
been an 'essentially contested concept' (Gallie, 1955/6). What may
have been lost, in the deconstruction of oppressive or controlling
notions of 'truth', is the creativity and energy that can be mobilised

by the search, the broadening of imagination that can occur when one is somehow in touch with or touched by the truth of *this* moment and context, limited and provisional though it inevitably is.

> 'Negative capability' then would be a capacity to give free rein to the imagination. The disparate, absurd, inchoate, illogical, impossible would not represent stop-signs. It can be taken for granted that equipped with this gift any person might attain hitherto unrecorded—because personally unique—imaginings. All that prevents that from happening is the restraint ordinarily imposed in the face of 'uncertainties, Mysteries, doubts' and a need for the security of 'fact and reason'; it is these that balk the flight of fancy. They induce sobriety, make for order, propriety, punctuality, accomplishment, but—this is what counts—they block the way to truth.' (Leavy, 1970: 177)

'Imagination' and 'the way to truth', these are the very stuff of the revival inspired in and by the Romantic movement: 'To live by the Imagination is Blake's secret of life' (Raine, 1991: 5); 'I am certain of nothing but the holiness of the heart's affections and the truth of imagination—what the imagination seizes as beauty must be truth—whether it existed before or not.' (Keats, 1970: 36–7; letter to Benjamin Bailey 22 Nov, 1817) From his work as a psychoanalyst, Victor Rosen identified some common factors underlying 'disturbances in the capacity for imagination' in a variety of clinical conditions. They read like the conditions which lead to stagnation in organizations:

> a relative inability to relinquish images and concepts once formed, an inability to retain the elements of a decomposed image through a series of transformations, a disturbance of the synthetic function, an incapacity for 'controlled illusion' or 'make believe' with difficulties in coping with perceptual ambiguity. (Rosen, 1960: 230)

The great ability and contribution of the leader is to represent or embody a thought, whether for good, as with Nelson Mandela or Ghandi, or for evil, as with Hitler or Pol Pot. Some leaders also have the ability to create, discover or develop the thought itself, but this is in no way a prerequisite for effective leadership. Indeed, the modern idealisation of originality—in the arts and sciences, in academia and in business—may in some ways be a societal side-track. To have claimed originality in many other societies would have been to exclude oneself voluntarily from being taken seriously (Illich, 1993: 8–13; Lewis, 1967: 210–11), or even to endanger oneself: '[they] were guilty of "innovation", a term virtually synonymous with heresy' (Giakalis, 1994: 22). In an organizational context, it does not matter whether leaders conceive a thought themselves, or copy, borrow, buy or steal it—although there may be an organizational equivalent of Eliot's contention that 'immature poets imitate; mature poets steal.' (Eliot, 1920: 125)

However, this notion of 'thoughts' depends on a definition that is wider than that of thought as a rational product of the human capacity for thinking, as expressed in language. Thoughts can be unconsciously held as well as consciously expressed. A dream is a 'thought'—whether a dream at night-time, a daydream or a vision: "I have a dream!". 'Thoughts' can also transcend the individual as manifestations of 'social' thinking, as myths, for example, or 'social' dreams (Lawrence, 1998), or as the kind of group, organizational or social dynamics that Bion called 'assumptions.' (Bion, 1961)

In organizational contexts, a vision statement is a thought, as is an organization's culture, which is a collective thought, expressed in ways of behaving, relating—and thinking. Willmott's penetrating analysis highlights the way in which the idea of organizational culture can be used as a 'thought' which will infiltrate and control from within the thinking of employees 'by managing what they think and feel, not just how they behave' (1993: 516). A product too is a thought 'produced'; an organizational structure is the 'realisation' of a thought; a strategic plan is an evolved or 'emergent' thought; the physical lay-out of offices or the shop floor, the hierarchy of roles and responsibilities, the headings on note paper and the signs at the entrance: all of these are thoughts made manifest. One might even say that the leader too and the organization as a whole exist as thoughts in the minds of stakeholders. It is for this reason that we are sometimes unable to understand the remains of ancient civilisations: what we dig up are the physical representations of embodied thoughts, and we have lost the thought.

In this sense, organizations are thoughts made visible. They can also become a 'forum' ('market place' and 'political arena') for thoughts that are 'in the air', waiting to be found. Bion has argued that 'thinking has to be called into existence to cope with thoughts' (1984b: 111). If this is true, then the way to find new thoughts in organizations is continually to develop new mechanisms for thinking that are adequate for discovering the as yet un-thought thoughts of the moment. The reason that teams, focus groups, departments, roles, 'away days', partnerships—and leaders—*can* achieve such remarkable things is that at times they provide precisely the 'mechanism for thinking' that is necessary to crystallise a new idea. Such moments may arise when leaders and followers know that they do not know, so that the risk of thinking new thoughts—or the urgent need to do so—is shared by all. Within a context of sufficient self-belief, the shared and acknowledged ignorance of all is sufficient basis for the shared endeavour. The combination of leaders' and followers' positive capabilities and negative capability may then create a capacity, a space, to contain anxiety well enough for new thoughts to arise.

However, if the necessary negative capability is lacking, as a consequence of past failures but also perhaps of past success, these same groupings or mechanisms may not only become unproductive but might also have an entirely deadening effect on thinking. A new thought would be experienced as a dangerous thought that could not be contained. What on the surface might appear to be functioning successfully, in practice becomes what Bion called a 'basic assumption group', whose 'complex forms of interpersonal defences' prevent them from working 'in an objective and consistent manner.' (Hopper, 1997: 443; Bion, 1961)

In his paper on leadership in the prison service, Abbott emphasises the benefits to be gained from the Prison Governor walking the landings of the prison and meeting people 'where they actually work.' In effect, he outlines the negative capability of the Prison Governor and its potential for creating a space where 'old thoughts' can become 'new thoughts.' Although his description does include some active verbs—for example, 'the opportunity *to do* casual management casework' (italics added)—the overwhelming sense is of passivity and receptivity leading to transformation. He talks, for example, of 'the opportunity *to be seen*', 'the opportunity *to listen*', and 'the opportunity *to observe.'* Most explicitly, he writes: 'Above all else it [walking the landings] provides the opportunity *to feel* the institution and having felt it *to work with and on the feeling.* The task is *to absorb* the emotion and thus allow people to take up their role free of negative emotion, which detracts from their performance. Often *just being there* will remove the emotion. Often *just listening* to the anger will move it.' (Abbott, 2000: 4; all italics added)

As Armstrong has written: 'it seems to me that emotion in organisations, including all the strategies of defense, denial, projection, withdrawal, yield intelligence. And it is because they yield intelligence in this way that they may be worth our and our clients' close attention.' (Armstrong, 2000: 3) Abbott's description makes it clear that the value to be gained from exercising negative capability in this way—that is, from paying close attention to emotions in the organization—is not only to be measured in terms of practical outcomes. There may indeed be immediate work to be done and important information to be gained that will translate into new strategies or practices. However, 'just being there' and 'just listening'—in other words, just offering containment—may be enough. This is a much broader view of the importance of working with emotion than that generally portrayed, for example, in the literature on 'emotional intelligence' in relation to leadership, which tends to take a more cognitive-behavioural approach and to talk in terms of the 'repair' of negative emotions and of 'using' emotions 'in functional ways.' (George, 2000: 1036)

The problem of status

The hypothesis about leadership that this article explores is based on the view that the conditions of organizational life demand the capacity to seek out and work at the edge of uncertainty in a new way. Because of their role, leaders today are powerfully caught between competing societal forces. On the one hand, there are the pressures imposed by the principle of *performativity*, which dominates our culture at all levels and 'serves to subordinate knowledge and truth to the production of efficiency' (Fournier and Grey, 2000: 17). On the other hand, we are faced by the gap left by the disappearance of the certainties on which a personal and a work identity could once be constructed, as a result of the loss of institutional containment—from family to community, from work-place to church: 'These days patterns and configurations are no longer "given", let alone "self-evident"; there are just too many of them, clashing with one another and contradicting one another's commandments.' (Baumann, 2000: 7)

On top of these pressures, leaders face one central imperative: in order to meet the demands of key stakeholders, especially share-holders, management boards and politicians, they must ensure that their organizations achieve increasing wealth through competitive advantage. Indeed, changing political and economic pressures mean that what might once have been demanded primarily of business enterprises is now required too of public sector and even voluntary organizations. Although the language used in the different sectors varies, the impulse and the pressures are similar. As a result, it seems inevitable that capacities such as negative capability, which are intrinsically un-measurable, will tend to atrophy by being excluded from dominant organizational discourses.

Among the discourses competing for space and legitimacy in organizations, the active and the technical dominate over the passive and the humane. Thus, leaders or theorists may argue strongly the case for 'putting people first', or for raising the status of training and development, introducing teamwork and encouraging a culture of openness, collaboration and involvement. Again and again, however, when the pressure is on, the 'default' position proves to be: control. Where performativity rules—that is, 'efficiency measured according to an input/output ratio' (Lyotard, 1984: 88)—'league tables' come to measure the relative success even of schools and universities, of hospitals and health authorities, and of police forces and local authorities.

In such an environment, how is one to attribute value to low status aspects of behaviours such as waiting, patience, passivity, observing, illusion, imagination, detachment, disinterest, desire, trust, withdrawing, tempering, adapting, indifference, humility, copying? For example, at a time when leaders are encouraged to 'communicate, communicate, communicate', it may be hard to hear that they should also 'ignore, ignore, ignore.' Similarly, 'teamworking' may appear to be given high status, but the 'rules' of dialogue, on which effective teamwork may depend, do not command the same automatic respect: 'slow down', 'hold up assumptions for scrutiny', 'listen intently' to others and to the 'language' of one's own feelings.

(Isaacs, 1993; Senge, 1990) In a particular context, however, any one of these low status behaviours might trigger a combination of positive capabilities and negative capability in a way that facilitates the space—or capacity (French, 1999)—for a creative breakthrough. It is the breakthrough that will be recognised and rewarded.

Over half a century ago, Chester Barnard, President of the Rockefeller Foundation and previously President of the New Jersey Telephone Company, clearly reflected the low status of such language, when he wrote:

> many things a leader tells others to do were suggested to him by the very people he leads ... this sometimes gives the impression that he is a rather stupid fellow ... In a measure this is correct. He has to be stupid enough to listen a great deal, he certainly must arbitrate to maintain order, and he has at times to be a mere centre of communication. (1948: 93)

Not only does the language of negative capability have low status, the experiences it describes may in themselves be difficult and also lack the immediate appeal that attaches to the skills and competences of management and leadership. The *capacity for waiting*, for example, is central to creative activity, and yet, 'Waiting can be the most intense and poignant of all human experiences—the experience which, above all others, strips us of affectation and self-deception and reveals to us the reality of our needs, our values and ourselves.' (Vanstone, 1982: 83)

Conclusion

In this paper, we have drawn attention to the relationship between the somewhat elusive notion of negative capability and the more accessible positive capabilities of leadership. In practice the two are dynamically related. Creative leadership is called into being at the point where negative and positive meet, or the space created by the tension between them. The leadership capacity created by the appropriate combination of positive capabilities and negative capability allows a transformation to occur from the unknown into the realm of the knowable. Once this transformation, or act of creation, has occurred the thought can be worked on and developed by the full range of positive capabilities, 'enlarging inhibited reason in the realm of praxis' (Rose, 1999: 32). In a situation where negative capability is well embedded in an organization, particularly in leadership at all levels—that is, not only in the person of 'the leader', but as an intrinsic function of *all* roles and a characteristic of systems and procedures at all levels—a climate can be created which stimulates learning and the development of new or expanded positive capabilities.

If the relationship between the negative capability and positive capabilities of leadership is, therefore, dynamic and fluctuating, then achieving the 'right combination' is bound always to be a provisional achievement, demanding constant, ongoing work and attention. Negative capability may indeed be a 'gift', as Kathleen Raine suggests (Raine, 1986: 322), a 'native virtue of [the] mind' (Caldwell, 1972: 7), or 'an intrapsychic inheritance' (Leavy, 1970: 187). However, like the capacity for language, it is a gift that is received by all, if unevenly, as an aspect of our humanity, and then developed equally unevenly over the course of our lives. If negative capability can be taken sufficiently seriously as a leadership capacity, then thought can be given to ways in which it can be developed both in leaders and in systems, in order to stimulate creative leadership throughout organizations.

References

Abbott, W.A. (2000). Prison management. Paper given in the Tavistock Institute Series, 'Programme of Dialogues: Worlds of Leadership 2000', 6 July.

Armstrong, D. (2000). Emotions in organisations: Disturbance or intelligence?. Paper presented to the Annual ISPSO Symposium, London, June 22–4. Published in Armstrong, D. (2005). *Organization in the mind*, ed. R. French. London: Karnac, pp. 90–110. Available on the ISPSO website at: http://www.sba.oakland.edu/ispso/html/2000 symposium/schedule.htm

Barnard, C. (1948). The nature of leadership. In C. Barnard, *Organization and Management*, Cambridge, Massachusetts: Harvard University Press, reprinted in K. Grint (1997) (ed.), *Leadership: Classical, contemporary, and critical approaches*. Oxford: Oxford University Press, 89–111.

Bate, W.J. (1964). *John Keats*. Cambridge, Massachusetts: The Belknap Press of Harvard University Press.

Baumann, Z. (2000). *Liquid modernity*. Cambridge: Polity Press.

Bennis, W. (1998). *On becoming a leader*. London: Arrow (1st publ. 1989).

Bennis, W. (2000). An angle on leadership in a 24/7 world. Paper presented to the Leaders in Management Seminar, Association of MBAs, London, July 14.

Bion, W.R. (1961). *Experiences in groups*. London: Tavistock Publications.

Bion, W.R. (1978). *Four discussions with W.R. Bion*. Strath Tay, Perthshire: Clunie Press.

Bion, W.R. (1984a). *Attention and interpretation*. London: Karnac Books. (Tavistock Publications, London, 1970.)

Bion, W.R. (1984b). *Second thoughts*. London: Karnac Books. (London: William Heineman Medical Books, 1967.)

Bion, W.R. (1990). *Brazilian lectures: 1973 São Paulo; 1974 Rio de Janeiro/ São Paulo*. London: Karnac Books.

Bion, W.R. (1991). *A memoir of the future*. London: Karnac Books.

Bridgwater, P. (1999). Introduction. In R.M. Rilke, *Duino elegies*, tr. P. Bridgwater. London: The Menard Press.

Caldwell, J.R. (1972). *John Keats' fancy: The effect on Keats of the psychology of his day*. New York: Octagon Books.

Edwards, B. (1987). *Drawing on the artist within*. London: Collins.

Edwards, B. (2000). *The new drawing on the artist within*. London: Souvenir Press.

Eisold, K. (2000). The rediscovery of the unknown: an inquiry into psychoanalytic praxis. *Contemporary Psychoanalysis*, 36(1): 57–75.

Eliot, T.S. (1920). *The sacred wood: Essays on poetry and criticism*. London: Methuen.

Fournier, V. & Grey, C. (2000). At the critical moment: Conditions and prospects for critical management studies. *Human Relations*, 53(1):7–32.

French, R. (1999). The importance of *capacities* in psychoanalysis and the language of human development. *International Journal of Psycho-Analysis*, 80(6):1215–1226.

French, R. (2001). *Negative Capability*: Managing the confusing uncertainties of change. *Journal of Organizational Change Management* 14(5):480–92.

French, R. & Simpson, P. (1999). Our best work happens when we don't know what we're doing. *Socio-Analysis*, 1(2):216–30.

Friedman, M. (1993). *Encounter on the narrow ridge: A life of Martin Buber*. New York: Paragon House.

Gallie, W.B. (1955/56). Essentially contested concepts. *Proceedings of the Aristotelian Society*, 167–98.

George, J.M. (2000). Emotions and leadership: The role of emotional intelligence. *Human Relations*, 53(8):1027–55.

Ghent, E. (1990). Masochism, submission, surrender: Masochism as a perversion of surrender. *Contemporary Psychoanalysis*, 26(1):108–36,

Giakalis, A. (1994). *Images of the divine: The theology of icons at the seventh Ecumenical Council*. Leiden: E.J. Brill.

Gombrich, E.H. (1977). *Art and illusion: A study in the psychology of pictorial representation*. Oxford: Phaidon: 5th Edition.

Green, A. (1973). On negative capability. *International Journal of Psycho-Analysis*, 54, 115–9.

Handy, C. (1989). *The age of unreason*. London: Business Books Ltd.

Hopper, E. (1997). Traumatic experience in the unconscious life of groups: A fourth basic assumption. *Group Analysis*, 30:439–70.

Hutter, A.D. (1982). Poetry in psychoanalysis: Hopkins, Rosetti, Winnicott. *International Review of Psycho-Analysis*, 9:303–16.

Illich, I. (1993). *In the vineyard of the text: A commentary to Hugh's 'Didascalicon'*. Chicago: University of Chicago Press.

Isaacs, W.N. (1993). Taking flight: Dialogue, collective thinking, and organizational dynamics, *Organizational Dynamics*, 22(2):24–39.

Keats, J. (1970). *The letters of John Keats: A selection*. ed. Gittings, R., Oxford: Oxford University Press.

Lawrence, W.G. (1998). *Social dreaming @ work*. London: Karnac Books.

Leavy, S.A. (1970). John Keats' psychology of creative imagination. *The Psychoanalytic Quarterly*, 39:173–97.

Lewis, C.S. (1967). *The discarded image: An introduction to medieval and renaissance literature*. Cambridge: Cambridge University Press.

Lyotard, J.-F. (1984). *The postmodern condition*. Manchester: Manchester University Press.

Muir, K. (1958). The meaning of 'Hyperion', in Muir, K. (ed.), *John Keats: A reassessment*, Liverpool: Liverpool University Press, pp. 102–22.

Needleman, J. (1990). *Lost Christianity: A journey of rediscovery to the centre of Christian experience*. Shaftesbury, Dorset: Element Books.

Plato (1992). *Republic*, tr. G.M.A. Grube, revised by C.D.C. Reeve. Indianapolis: Hackett.

Raine, K. (1986). Magic mirrors and grass roots, *Temenos*, 7:321–325.

Raine, K. (1991). *Golgonooza, city of the imagination: Last studies in William Blake*. Ipswich: Golgonooza Press.

Rose, G. (1999). *Paradiso*. London: The Menard Press.

Rosen, V.H. (1960). Imagination in the analytic process. *Journal of the American Analytic Association*, 8:229–51.

Ryan, R.M. (1976). *Keats: The religious sense*. Princeton, New Jersey: Princeton University Press.

Scott, N.A., Jr. (1969). *Negative Capability: Studies in the new literature and the religious situation*. New Haven: Yale University Press.

Senge, P.M. (1990). *The fifth discipline: The art and practice of the learning organization*. London: Random House.

Simeon, C. (1847). *Memoirs of the life of the Rev. Charles Simeon, M.A., with a selection from his writings and correspondence*. New York: Robert Carter.

Simpson, P. and French, R. (2006). Negative capability and the capacity to think in the present moment: some implications for leadership practice. *Leadership*, 2(2):245–55.

Symons, A. (1901). John Keats. *Monthly Review*, 5, reprinted in C. Franklin (ed.) (1998) *British romantic poets—the Wellesley series, Vol. IV*. London: Routledge/Thoemmes Press, pp. 1621–31.

Tillich, P. (1967). *On the boundary: An autobiographical sketch*. London: Collins.

Toynbee, P. (1973). *Towards the holy spirit: A tract for the times*. London: SCM Press.

Vanstone, W.H. (1982). *The stature of waiting*. London: Darton, Longman and Todd.

Ward, A. (1963). *John Keats: The making of a poet*. London: Secker and Warburg.

Willmott, H. (1993). Strength is ignorance; slavery is freedom: Managing culture in modern organizations. *Journal of Management Studies*, 30(4):515–52.

Winnicott, D.W. (1971). *Playing and reality*. London: Tavistock Publications.

Wittgenstein, L. (1963). *Philosophical investigations*. (trans. G.E.M. Anscombe), Oxford: Basil Blackwell.

Against all reason: Trusting in trust

Burkard Sievers

"Trust is a double-edged sword. It can open opportunities of mutual productive work and at the same time, can be a sophisticated trap, in which the partners of trust are captured."

Amitzi and Schonberg, 2000

"Trust is a peculiar quality. It can't be bought. It can't be downloaded. It can't be instant … . It can only accumulate very slowly, over multiple interactions. But it can disappear in a blink."

Kelly, 1999

"A crisis of trust cannot be overcome by a blind rush to place more trust."

O'Neill, 2002

"On September 11, 2001 … Americans realized the fragility of trust. … Our trust was shaken again only a couple of months later with the stunning collapse of Enron."

Kramer, 2002

The importance of trust is heavily emphasized in contemporary organization theory and management practice. Although I am convinced that trust is a good thing and a necessary constituent of the social fabric, I am interested in understanding the social (and political) thinking underlying the current academic and non-academic view of trust. My working hypothesis is that management attempts to engineer trust reflect an underlying denial of the loss of hope regarding both the relatedness between organizational members and the value and meaning of organizations. The experience of non-relatedness and lack of trust cannot be acknowledged by management, therefore the loss of hope has to be hidden behind the propagation of the importance of trust (and relatedness). The denial of the loss of hope is an expression of psychotic thinking concomitant with the inability to see reality and to mourn loss. The engineered propagation of trust thus becomes a substitute for trust itself.

Introduction

This paper emanates from my fascination with the fact that the virtues of trust are frequently praised and often emphasized in contemporary organizational literature and management practice. Though it is the case that both individuals and organizations would not be able to face or survive to the next day without a high amount of trust, the excessively important role given to trust in the literature (e.g. Bachmann, 1998, 2001; Bachmann et al., 2001; Gambetta, 1988; Gebert and Boerner, 1999; Hardy et al., 1998; Kramer et al., 1996; Lane and Bachmann, 1998; Sitkin et al., 1998; Sprenger, 2002) is, to a major extent, not in accord with my own experience of contemporary organizational life. What seems to be almost totally neglected is, in fact, the lack of trust in today's organizations, the inflation of its necessity, and even its occasional bankruptcy. The absence of trust is broadly denied by the emphasis on 'the substantial and varied benefits, both individual and collective, that accrue when trust is in place' (Kramer, 2003, p. 342). Instead of acknowledging the lack of trust as a significant reality and contemporary problem, trust is propagated as an external entity and a needed solution. All we need is more trust!!

I certainly do not doubt the relevance of trust both in everyday life and in organizations and society at large. How could anyone be against trust per se? It is like motherhood and apple pie—a good thing and a necessary constituent of the social fabric. As Elliot Jaques (1996, p. 15) put it: 'People do not have to love each other, or even to like each other, to work together effectively. But they do have to be able to trust each other in order to do so'. There is no doubt that trust is an important source of social capital within social systems (Fukuyama, 1995; Kramer, 2003; O'Neill, 2002). 'It may [even] be said that ... trust forms such an important part of the basis of the current social structure that without trust and trustworthiness we could not have our form of society' (Isaacs et al., 1963, p. 462).

My reservations about the present use of trust concern its fashionable character and the 'lightness' (not to say 'naivety') with which it is often treated. For example: 'Leadership is a relationship, founded on trust and confidence. Without trust and confidence, people don't take risks. Without risks, there is no change. Without change, organization movements die' (Kouzes and Posner, 1995; quoted in Dando-Collins, 1998, p. 26). This is an extreme example of what is widely propagated as business wisdom.

The ongoing dominant concern for trust also reflects ambiguity on the part of organizational theorists. While on the one hand, they increasingly regard trust as an appropriate concept for a better understanding and management of organizational reality, they seem, on the other hand, to lack the courage to face and acknowledge the 'heart of darkness' (Joseph Conrad) of organizational life. Predominantly guided by the 'politics of salvation' (Lawrence, 2000b), organizational theorists tend to suggest solutions to the dilemmas of roleholders in organizations based on the assumption that they are lacking both the competence and the authority to alter their own situation.

As the latest in an almost endless series of managerial panaceas, trust is often seen as the current 'saving grace' of organizations. Though the present emphasis on trust may to some extent be interpreted as a kind of reverberation from the debate on organizational culture and its rhetoric (e.g. Graf, 2000), it can also be seen as a defence against the underlying anxieties experienced by management in its attempts to cope with the ongoing chaos inside its organizations and in the respective external environment. Like whistling in a dark forest—it obscures the common contemporary experience of disorientation and the resulting fear and despair. The predominant 'trust in trust' defends both social scientists and managers alike against the idea that traditional modes of organization and the organization of work in particular may no longer be adequate to meet the more difficult and chaotic challenges facing today's organizations. The regressive use of trust functions as a means of re-establishing 'order and organization' in order to cope with the 'disorder and disorganization' (Cooper, 1986; cf. Knights et al., 2001). The emphasis on trust and the tendency to engineer it in familiar ways can, therefore, be interpreted as an expression of a longing for more creative and innovative developments both in the field of study and its object.

Despite these tendencies, there are also a number of authors who go beyond such a naive, fashionable, and glib representation of trust. Some of them express a remarkable concern for trust as a collective dimension as it is related to broader organizational contexts both in and between organizations (cf. Sievers, 2003b).

The engineering of trust

As trust is necessary for organizations to function—global and virtual enterprises in particular (cf. Kelly, 1999, p. 133ff.)—it is often assumed that it has to be enforced and engineered, despite the common experience that organizations and their top-management are often not at all trustworthy. Enterprises and their management thus are confronted with the dilemma of 'enforcing' trust.

This tendency toward engineering is reminiscent of the debate on the lack of organizational heroes nearly two decades ago. An example is the following almost cynical suggestion of Deal and Kennedy (1982; cf. Jewett, 2003; Lawrence and Jewett, 2002): 'Heroes are required for an enterprise in order to be successful. If you don't have them, create them!' Not unlike these 'situational heroes', much of what is taken for trust in contemporary enterprises is 'situational', in the sense that it just meets the needs required to survive the next battle; it is but 'hope for a season', as the poet Thomas Campbell put it.

In addition to its short-term value, others see trust as necessary for long-term survival. This can well be illustrated by the following quote from one of the mainstream texts on trust:

"Recent discussions by both scholars and the business press suggest that trust is a central factor in organisational behaviour and organisational survival for both public and private organisations, even in non-crisis contexts. Several scholars have recently proposed that trust is a central factor enhancing organisations' long-term success and survival, especially because environments have become more uncertain and competitive." (Mishra, 1996, p. 282)

There is a common view in much of the scientific literature that trust is one of the few white spots left on the organizational map, and that the improvement of work efficiency relies to a major extent upon the effectiveness with which trust can be engineered and/or exploited. For example:

"Both practitioners and scholars have even proposed that a new paradigm of management and organisation must be developed with trust as a core component if organisations, both profit and not-for-profit, are to survive into the 21st century." (Sculley, 1987, p. 125, quoted in Mishra, 1996, p. 283; cf. Tyler and Kramer, 1996, p. 129; cf. Hardy et al., 1998; Knights et al., 2001; Sydow, 1998)

Though trust cannot be produced in the same way as soap or metal (Zucker, 1986, p. 65), the ever-growing 'market' for trust and the hope it represents seem to be driving the increasing amount of research and publications on the topic (ibid., p. 54). Following Gabriel's (2002) provocative critique that organizational theories committed to the realm of managerial practice increasingly have become paragrammatic insofar as programmatic and pragmatic intentions have merged into one single model, theories of trust have degenerated into commodities and have become subject to a deterioration process.

Ancient notions of trust

There can be no doubt that most people in general and organizations in particular no longer subscribe to the slogan, 'In God we trust!', which was taken for granted by previous generations—and which still appears on the American dollar bill. Trust—to an enormous extent—has lost the certainty which faith previously provided. Even if this seems somewhat romantic, the notion of trust originates from and refers to a quality of 'man's' (and woman's) relatedness to their various 'objects'—fellows, 'nature', the world and God or Gods alike—and may be regarded as a human 'trait' as old as humankind.

Both existentially and etymologically, trust is related to and is an expression of reliability, fidelity, confidence, help, support, consolation; the word 'trust' is based on *tru- (true, trow)*, which is also the root of the noun 'truth' (Hoad, 1986, pp. 507–508). Its middle English version, *trist* (compare the French *triste* or the Latin *tristis*), indicates the relatedness of trust to the feeling or expression of sorrow or sadness (Brown, 1993, p. 3399). We may also be reminded that trust, in its 'ancient' notion, was embedded in faith and was, as such, an expression of *Eros*, the will for life. Contemporary social science puts the main emphasis on risk, in that the problem of trust is a problem of 'risky precommitment' (Luhmann, 1968, p. 21). Notions of truth, faith, sorrow or even love are strikingly absent in the organizational discourse on trust. The debate on trust could certainly find further depth by addressing these 'ancient' dimensions of organizational reality—even though they may, at first sight, appear antiquated.

Organizational theorists have lost sight of the tragic dimensions, which inevitably characterize life and work in organizations as well as our private and personal worlds. Theories about human nature, work, and life, which mainly underlie the notion of trust in the present debate, are restricted to an emphasis on Eros, the will for life and survival. They do not sufficiently take into account the destructive and deadening dynamics of organizational reality—expressions of *Thanatos*—which are at the core of destruction, annihilation, and ultimately death. The predominant emphasis on trust and its virtues fosters a perspective of work and life in organizations in which social experiences and dynamics like anger, rage, shame, contempt, denial, envy, greed, humiliation, suffering or despair are either deliberately neglected or deemed non-existent. The debate on trust mainly produces monochromatic images of organizational reality instead of making full use of the palette of colours.

Psychotic dynamics of trust in organizations

The organizational perspective in this paper is based upon the metaphoric frame provided by the 'psychotic organization', further elaborated since my presentation at the 1998 ISPSO Symposium in Jerusalem (Sievers, 1999a, 2003a). I still feel a certain uneasiness with this concept, particularly in relation to social phenomena, due to the clinical pathological implications of psychosis. It is, however, the notion of psychotic anxiety as the in-between-state between the paranoid-schizoid and the depressive position that challenges me to use the notion of the psychotic organization. I am especially encouraged in this choice by Fornari (1975), the Italian psychoanalyst, who in *The Psychoanalysis of War* anticipated most of the major insights of what some time later was conceptualized as the theory of the 'pathological organization' by authors like Steiner (1979, 1982, 1987, 1990, 1993) and O'Shaughnessy (1981; cf. Hinshelwood, 1991, p. 381ff.).

Like Bion and the early Jaques (1953, 1955; cf. Menzies Lyth, 1988), Fornari chooses as his point of departure the defence against psychotic anxieties in the formation of society and its institutions. He identifies the inability to mourn, i.e. the paranoid elaboration of mourning, as the critical characteristic of war as a psychotic kind of social organization. His theory of war is implicitly based on pathological fixation and stagnation in the paranoid-schizoid position and its defences.

My *working hypothesis* is that the attempt to engineer trust by management is an expression of an underlying denial of the loss of hope both with regard to the relatedness between organizational members (co-managers and 'workers' alike) and to the value and meaning of organizations. To the extent that the experience of non-relatedness and non-meaning (not to mention the lack of trust) cannot be acknowledged by management, the resulting loss of hope has to be hidden behind the propagation of the importance of trust (and relatedness). This denial is an expression of psychotic thinking that is characterized by the inability to see reality and to mourn loss. Relatedness and trust are at the core of containment. As management increasingly lacks the ability to provide containment for its organizational members, the engineered propagation of trust becomes a substitute for trust itself. Therefore the engineering of trust can be seen as a psychotic substitute for trust and containment.

Contemporary organizations and their cultures are to a varying extent characterized by psychotic dynamics that find their expression in aggression, sadism, and destructivity, a reaction to the apparent threat and persecution emanating from the outer world of markets and competitors. In defending against these perceived and actual threats, the inner world of organizations is caught in a behaviour and way of thinking that reflects social psychosis

(Bion, 1957; Sievers, 1999a). The emergence of these dynamics has largely been ignored and has, in fact, generally been regarded as normal.

In order not to be misunderstood, I would like to emphasize that these dynamics are not regarded as an expression of individual psychopathology. I perceive psychotic dynamics in organizations as being socially induced. The thinking (or non-thinking) in organizations induces members to mobilize the psychotic rather than the non-psychotic parts of their personalities. They are thus made to react in less mature ways than they would in other circumstances (Lawrence, 1995).

Commoditization of enterprises, money and people

As the lack of hope has to be denied, organizations are still conceptualized as if they were based on social relatedness both amongst individual actors and of management and the 'workforce' in particular. In the contemporary business world, enterprises themselves are commodities on international (capital) markets and thus the target of takeovers and mergers; they often undergo turbulent restructuring with a focus on reduced costs, increased accountability, and decreased security for management and workforce alike. Even in non-profit organizations 'financial issues outweigh human ones', and there is increasing evidence 'that market mentality, which bases transactions on price and return, has entered into the fabric of organizational life' (Astrachan and Astrachan, 2000, p. 46). People in organizations have subsequently become commodities themselves and can easily be fired, if no longer required, or replaced if 'outworn'. As a consequence, they are in danger of abandoning all hope. And as they are no longer able to 'calculate' the risk of trust, trust tends to be replaced by illusions, whose self-deceiving character is hidden in order to escape the underlying despair.

Money—commoditized money in particular—makes the world go round, through the increasing predominance of shareholder value optimization propagated and buoyed by the financial services industry. This commodization has increasingly determined the reality of contemporary organizational life. As commoditized money becomes the ultimate value and turns every other value into a commodity (Wolfenstein, 1993, p. 296), money no longer can be regarded as a symbol of meaning and represents nothing else but mere meaninglessness.

By propagating and engineering trust, management hides both from itself and from organizational members that both are but commodities of the corporation's and the world's markets. From this perspective, the propagation of trust can be perceived as a romantic attempt to socially enrich an organizational reality whose predominant or exclusive economic character must permanently be denied. By ignoring the fact that enterprises and, above all, global corporations have become economic and even exclusively monetary 'arrangements', with no further aim or primary task than to beget commoditized money, the illusion is nurtured that the actors in the global money game are still human beings—or at least human resources (Sievers, 2003a).

The inherent meaninglessness ultimately resembles hell where all that people share is eternal damnation. To the extent that management can no longer trust itself and others no longer appear trustworthy, the psychotic dynamic in organizations, on a metaphoric level, resembles Jean-Paul Sartre's (1947) 'hell': 'L'enfer c'est les autres, hell are the others'. Whom would you dare trust in hell?—As it has increasingly become difficult, if not impossible, to acknowledge that we have lost hope, we permanently have to convince each other that we trust—even when this trust is based on nothingness or meaninglessness. Since, unlike God, the 'devil' cannot be an 'object' into which trust can be invested, the engineering of trust—in the metaphoric context chosen here—is a futile attempt to baptize the devil—or as Herman Melville (1967) put it in Moby Dick (Chapter 113, The Forge): 'Ego non baptizo te in nomine patris, sed in nomine diaboli' (I do not baptize you in the name of the Father but in the name of the Devil).

Reservations about the present view of trust

In order to elaborate my reservations about the present view of trust in theory and practice a bit further, I would like to sketch the following:

1. *As an expression of the denial of hopelessness, the debate on trust is broadly biased and lacks a meta-debate on the assumptive framework*

of both trust itself and the 'nature' of 'people', of organization, and the relatedness between people and their organizations.

The way we conceptualize and frame the notion of trust influences not only the problems we anticipate but also—in very profound and consequential ways—how we intervene in organizations in the attempt to create or foster trust (cf. Kramer et al., 1996, p. 382). The rhetoric on trust often resembles the Guinness advertisement. Like 'Guinness is good for you!' trust must be too (cf. Nieder, 1997; Landau et al., 1998; Marshall, 1999; Newstrom and Scannell, 1998; Ryan and Oestreich, 1998; Shurtleff, 1998). Just as Guinness is predominantly driven by an increase in market share (and profit) through the consumption of its product, while neglecting its influence in fostering alcoholism, it often seems that the propagators of more trust are not concerned with the consequences of an 'overconsumption' or 'watering down' of trust. The implicit assumptions of the underlying 'image of man' or the assumptive frameworks of trust's relevance for the meaning of work in organizations are seldom made explicit. The debate on trust too often mirrors the wisdom found in 'Heathrow organization theory' (Burrell, 1997, p. 27).

2. *Though the role and function of trust is analysed in various contexts— individual, dyadic, groups, intra-, inter-organization, networks, and (on few occasions) society—an integrative, systemic perspective is broadly missing.*

The conceptualization of trust, in American publications in particular, is dominated by the social-psychological perspective that trust is primarily an individual, dyadic or group phenomenon. Whereas, on the one side, researchers tend to regard trust as almost exclusively a trait of the individual in relationship with other individuals, others support Luhmann's (1968, 1979, 1988) point that trust, as an object of research for the social sciences and for sociology in particular, is to be regarded as a mechanism for reduction of complexity in social systems. It appears that the polarization of trust as either an *intersubjective* or a *systemic* phenomenon is an expression of a more general deficit in social theory—especially the theory of social systems, which broadly lacks a common frame for relating the individual and the organization.

What is missing is Bion's (1961, p. 8; cf. Sandler, 2002) perspective of 'binocular vision'. Referring to the Oedipus myth as a metaphoric frame, he emphasized that—contrary to Freud's exclusive interest in the triadic relationship between Oedipus and his parents, Laius and Jocasta—a more adequate fulfilment of the myth includes an equally deep concern for its other part, the project of the Sphinx. The Sphinx is related to the broad question of the nature of humankind and the political constituency of knowledge. As opposed to monocular vision, which views trust either as an individual or an organizational phenomenon, Bion's binocular vision—as recently reemphasized by Lawrence (1997, 2000a)—provides a way of understanding how the social and psychic dynamics of trust are interrelated. Seen from the project of the Sphinx, trust can be understood as socially induced by the organization. An organization's ability to provide containment has a major impact on whether organizational role holders will experience and activate trust or regress into a kind of social retreat, in which they reduce their contributions to the minimum demanded from them in their roles. As the underlying power relationship requires trust in management, the subordinate all too often retreats into a cynical position: ' "We've got to trust them" means in fact: "We don't trust them but feel constrained to submit to their discretion" ' (Fox, 1974, p. 95; quoted in Hardy et al., 1998, p. 67).

3. *As the main emphasis lies on management's responsibility to generate trust, broader organizational and societal issues are neglected as is the reality of non-relatedness and non-meaning for management and workers alike.*

Although there is repeated reference to the increasing impediments to trust in contemporary organizations in some of the literature, a deeper analysis and understanding of the dynamics and factors that enhance the difficulty and improbability of this trust are missing. The extent to which these impediments are primarily indicated but not further investigated is exemplified by the suggested tools for the improvement of trust, e.g. management by objectives, quality circles, self-managing work teams, team building, and training (Newstrom and Scannell, 1998; Ryan and Oestreich, 1998; Steinle et al., 2000, p. 12). They are the standard repertoire of organization development and human resources management, which no longer appear innovative or appropriate. These and similar devices often not only fail to reverse the lack of trust but reinforce it. 'Indeed, those companies that try hardest to eliminate negative or ambivalent feelings may instead stimulate the most resentment, mistrust and suspicion' (Miller and Stein, 1993, p. 36; quoted in Miller, 1998, p. 15).

As the source of trust in organizations is mainly seen as coming from management, the main or often exclusive 'social' variable taken into account is the respective 'management philosophy' of the managers supporting trust.

"In organizations ... the predisposition to trust or distrust is embedded in managers' philosophies and has been displayed throughout time in the different organizational structures and mechanisms that their philosophies prescribe and/or accommodate." (Creed and Miles, 1996, p. 23)

One aspect of this management philosophy is the idea that trust would be appropriate for those employees whose 'trustworthiness' could somehow be measured and thus guaranteed. One is, however, left pondering how this management thinking can be implemented at a point in time when top-management, in its continual pursuit of shareholder value optimization, is increasingly dependent on investment and pension fund organizations whose representatives they cannot trust (Sievers, 1999a, 2003a). As a journalist recently commented regarding corporate restructuring: 'Self-conscious business leaders are mutating into henchmen of the capital markets; the shrill bustle does not even give employees and customers the time to reflect upon their feelings of insecurity' (Student, 2000, p. 124).

The following example from the literature on trust demonstrates that the guiding metaphors about trust often are contradictory. Whereas the authors (Creed and Miles, 1996, p. 32) emphasize on the one side what one easily could agree with, i.e. that, 'building trust depends in part on the emerging knowledge of mutual interest ... and a genuine concern for the well-being of organizational participants', on the other side they refer to 'good generals' as 'the managerial mirror image of the employee as a good soldier' (ibid., p. 34). Though one may assume that the metaphor mainly refers to times of peace, I wonder if it also applies to times of war.

From my own study of a German corporation—Volkswagen—I have concluded that the notion of competition, both in organization theory and in the business world, may be a euphemism for actual war and hides the underlying dynamic of destruction or even annihilation (Sievers, 2000; Stein, 1995, 1997, 1999). Despite the apparent absence of bloodshed or casualties in enterprises, big corporations, in particular, tend to projectively ascribe their failures and losses to their competitors, who are then regarded as enemies. As a consequence they are mobilized to defeat them either by grasping bigger market shares or by incorporating them through acquisition or merger. The incorporation of a former competitor often enough results in rationalizations, downsizing, and the cannibalization of unprofitable units.

To the extent that competition among big corporations actually is war, the creation and maintenance of trust becomes highly problematic, if not impossible. This competition involves major unconscious dynamics and has a critical impact on inter-company relationships, the inner world of role holders, and the internal dynamic of these corporations. There is, for example, a high probability that war itself, inside the corporation and towards its competitors, is dealt with as an 'unthought known', a term which has been offered by Christopher Bollas (1987, 1989). It refers to what, 'is known at some level but has never been thought or put into words, and so is not available for further thinking' (Lawrence, 2000a, pp. 11–12). This knowledge cannot be grasped, because it cannot be phrased in language or metaphor. As it cannot be thought, named or put into an idea, it is acted out primarily in situations of high anxiety and chaos, which foster the exportation of the threat of internal terror. In a paradoxical sense, it seems that the increasing use of war metaphors in the business world is primarily intended to keep the known truth unthought—i.e. that in many corporations and major sectors of the global economy, the world is in a state of ongoing and ever intensifying war.

4. *The debate on trust in organizations is based on theories and methodologies that emphasize rational and behavioural dimensions of organizational reality. As a result, unconscious dimensions and dynamics of organizations and their relevance to trust are ignored.*

Both people in organizations and organizational theorists have broadly come to accept the 'rational madness' (Lawrence, 1998, p. 126; Sievers, 1999b) in organizations as normal. They have lost sight of the actual irrationality, madness, and suffering (Dejours, 1998) that is part of the daily experience of organizational members. Similar to the way in which patients with severe personality disturbances often do not appear psychotic, but rather give the impression that they have fixed their disorder on a certain level, social organizations—and profit-oriented organizations in particular—often seem to cover their internal anxiety level with a somehow curious, but nevertheless normal appearance.

Psychoanalysis and trust

Having sketched my reservations about the present view of trust in organizational theory and practice, I have asked myself what contribution psychoanalysis might make to better understand this issue. From first sight there appear to be few psychoanalytic contributions to the understanding of trust in the general psychoanalytic literature, much less in organizational theory. The term does not appear frequently in the titles of psychoanalytic books or articles. While it appears in Rycroft's (1995) *Critical Dictionary of Psychoanalysis*, it is usually not listed in related (or similar) dictionaries. Though Erikson (1958; cf. Conzen, 2002) explores the difference between 'trust' and 'basic trust' and Searles (1965/1986) writes of the lack of parental trust, the need for trust in acceptance of death's inevitability, and the significance of trust for the therapeutic relationship (cf. Ellman, 1991, 1998a,b), Isaacs, Alexander and Haggard (1963) seem to be the only authors who provide a more extended psychoanalytic elaboration of the meaning and functions of trust. As Amitzi and Schonberg (2000, p. 5) stated on the occasion of the 2000 ISPSO Symposium in London: 'A well-developed psychoanalytic theory of trust does not yet seem to exist, although the main elements for it are quite ready ... to use'.

It would, however, be misleading to assume that psychoanalysis cannot contribute further insight into trust. In questioning the praise of trust in the face of the prevailing organizational vision shared by most top-management—permanent growth, shareholder value optimization, and/or maximization of profits—a psychoanalytic perspective sees the apparent amount of mistrust, anxiety, pain, hopelessness, and despair as a kind of undercurrent to (or dark shadow of) these megalomaniac goals. That they are commonly taken for granted may well be explained by the fact that, as members of organizations, we permanently lie to one another and pretend to believe those lies in order not to face our experience of confusion, impotence, and despair in our attempts to cope with the unrelenting pressure to meet top-management's targets. Once visions are stated, they are no longer to be questioned openly, despite apparent doubts. As a consequence, contempt (Aktouf, 1996, p. 506; Hoepfl, 1995; Pelzer, 2002; Sievers, 1994, pp. 74–82) for top-management gradually replaces a sense of trust in its reliability and in the belief that one's job is relatively safe and that the enterprise will survive, even if targets are not met.

Many authors rightly emphasize that trust not only manages risk, uncertainty, and expectations but also requires 'one party's willingness to be vulnerable to another party' (Mishra, 1996, p. 265; cf. Miettinen, 2000; Rousseau et al., 1998, p. 395). Though the acceptance of vulnerability is 'based upon positive expectations of the intentions or behaviour of another' (Rousseau et al., 1998, p. 395), it further requires the capacity to deal with injury, humiliation, and loss, if one's trust is disappointed or ultimately fails. The greater the risk trust has to 'absorb', the greater the capacity required to cope with the loss when one's trust is violated.

Aside from more institutionalized mechanisms, which allow for certain legal procedures of investigation and reparation, there are at least two contrary ways in which an organization and/or its members cope with the loss caused by disappointed or failed trust: mourning and avenging. Psychoanalytically, they can be differentiated as non-psychotic (mourning) and psychotic (avenging). The non-psychotic reaction demands more, because it means acknowledging the loss as bereavement and undertaking the labour of mourning in order to ultimately accept it. The psychotic reaction is based on the assumption that the loss cannot be accepted; it is a wrong, which, as it has been caused by others, has to be avenged.

Whether organizations react to failed trust by mourning or by revenge (Bies and Tripp, 1996) is to a high degree dependent on the extent to which their internal non-psychotic or psychotic dynamic predominates. There is convincing evidence that organizations and enterprises in particular—driven by greed, omnipotence, megalomania, tyranny, and contempt—tend to cope with disappointment and loss mainly in a psychotic way. This is partly due to the fact that projecting wrong onto others, who can then be sued or attacked, defends one against the acknowledgement that one's strategies and actions have failed. The psychotic dynamic nurtures control and power, because it cannot bear the inherent uncertainty, vulnerability, and risk that trust implies. In a similar way, the psychotic parts of an organization may be activated when previously reliable structures come under increasing threat (cf. Grey and Garsten, 2001; Heisig and Littek, 1995). The present ongoing economic threat, for example, to health care institutions and universities in most of the Western world is as serious in its own way as the impact of the many mergers and acquisitions in the private sphere.

Conclusion

As I conclude this argument, I must leave it up to you, the reader, to consider whether 'psychotic organizations' and their inherent states of mind are found exclusively in fairy tales, fiction, and/or science fiction, or in our contemporary business world as well. If my assumption is shared, then the exploration of trust in organizational theory would need to be extended and reframed.

I am quite aware that the thoughts I have presented so far are just a sketch. What I am arguing for and what I would like to express with the title I have chosen for this article 'Against all Reason: Trusting in Trust' is not only that we cannot work and live in organizations without trust, but that a serious concern for trust in contemporary organizations cannot be restricted to a claim for the necessity of more trust. Instead it has to seriously take into account the reservations, difficulties, and despair which people experience again and again in their attempts to trust their organizations and give their leaders their trust. Instead of further managing or engineering trust 'through the institution of relevant procedures (Zucker, 1986), ... the display of the appropriate symbolic representation (Lewis and Weigert, 1985)' (Hardy et al., 1998, p. 67) or audits designed to increase accountability (Power, 1994; O'Neill, 2002, p. 43ff.), we must acknowledge that, 'no two people will see the same event in the same way or have the same feelings about it' (Weber, 1993, p. 41). The challenge is to learn new ways of creating trust between partners who do not necessarily share the same goals and values.

The paradoxical and tragic understanding of trust which such a venture requires is expressed in St Paul's notion of *spes contra spem* (*hope against hope*) (Romans, 4, 18), i.e. any serious attempt to trust will inevitably trigger the impossibility of trust—or to trust against all reason.

Acknowledgement

I am very grateful to Rose Redding Mersky for her enormous effort in editing this paper.

References

Aktouf, O. (1996). Traditional Management and Beyond: A Matter of Renewal. Montreal: Morin.

Amitzi, V & Schonberg, A. (2000). "I don't know why, but I trust you". Trusting the Consultants in a Paranoid Environment: A Case Study'. Paper presented at the 2000 Symposium of the International Society for the Psychoanalytic Study of Organizations, London. Available at: http://www.sba.oakland.edu/ispso/html/2000Symposium/schonberg2000.htm

Astrachan, B.M & Astrachan, J.H. (2000). 'The changing psychological contract in the workplace", in E.B. Klein, F. Gabelnick and P. Herr (eds), Dynamic Consultation in a Changing Workplace. Madison, CT: Psychosocial Press, pp. 33–50.

Bachmann, R. (1998). 'Conclusion. Trust: conceptual aspects of a complex phenomenon", in C. Lane and R. Bachmann (eds), Trust Within and Between Organizations: Conceptual Issues and Empirical Applications. Oxford: Oxford University Press, pp. 298–322.

Bachmann, R. (2001). 'Trust, power and control in trans-organizational relations", Organization Studies, 22:337–365.

Bachmann, R., Knights, D & Sydow, J. (eds) (2001). 'Trust and control in organizational relations", Organization Studies (special issue), 22(2).

Bies, R.J & Tripp, T.M. (1996). 'Beyond distrust: "getting even" and the need for revenge", in R.M. Kramer and T.R. Tyler (eds), Trust in Organization: Frontiers of Theory and Research. Thousand Oaks, CA: Sage, pp. 246–260.

Bion, W.R. (1957). "Differentiation of the psychotic from the non-psychotic personalities, International Journal of Psychoanalysis, 38:266–275.

Bion, W.R. (1961). Experiences in Groups, and other Papers. London: Tavistock.

Bollas, C. (1987). The Shadow of the Object: Psychoanalysis of the Unthought Known. London: Free Association Books.

Bollas, C. (1989). Forces of Destiny. London: Free Association Books.

Brown, L. (ed.) (1993). The New Shorter Oxford English Dictionary on Historical Principles II. Oxford: Clarendon Press.

Burrell, G. (1997). Pandemonium: Towards a Retro-organization Theory. London: Sage.

Conzen, P. (2002). "Urvertrauen". In: W. Mertens and B. Waldvogel (eds), Handbuch Psychoanalytischer Grundbegriffe. Stuttgart: Kohlhammer, pp. 778–780.

Cooper, R. (1986). "Organization/disorganization", Social Science Information, 25(2): 299–335.

Creed, W., Douglas E. & Miles R.E. (1996). "A conceptual framework linking organizational forms, managerial philosophies, and the opportunity costs of control", in R.M. Kramer and T.R. Tyler (eds), Trust in Organizations: Frontiers of Theory and Research. Thousand Oaks, CA: Sage, pp. 16–38.

Dando-Collins, St. (1998). The Penguin Book of Business Wisdom. Ringwood, Victoria: Penguin.

Deal, T.E & Kennedy A.A. (1982). Corporate Cultures: The Rites and Rituals of Corporate Life. Reading, MA: Addison-Wesley.

Dejours, C. (1998). Souffrance en France: la Banalization de l'Injustice Sociale. Paris: Seuil.

Ellman, S. (1991). Freud's Technique Papers: A Contemporary Perspective. Northvale, NJ: Jason Aronson.

Ellman, S. (1998a) "The unique contribution of the contemporary Freudian position", in: C. Ellman, S. Grand, M. Silvan and S. Ellman (eds), The Modern Freudians: Contemporary Psychoanalytic Technique. Northvale, NJ: Jason Aronson, pp. 237–268.

Ellman, S. (1998b) "Enactment, transference, and analytic trust", in: S. Ellman and M. Moskowitz (eds), Enactment. Northvale, NJ: Jason Aronson, pp. 183–204.

Erikson, E.H. (1958). Childhood and Society. New York: Norton.

Fornari, F. (1975). The Psychoanalysis of War. Bloomington: Indiana University Press.

Fox, A. (1974). Beyond Contract: Work, Power and Trust Relations. London: Faber.

Fukuyama, F. (1995). Trust: The Social Virtues and the Creation of Prosperity. New York and London: Free Press.

Gabriel; Y. (2002). "Essai: on paragrammatic uses of organizational theory—a provocation'. Organization Studies, 23:133–151

Gambetta, D. (ed.) (1988). Trust: Making and Breaking Cooperative Relations. New York: Blackwell.

Gebert, D & Boerner S. (1999). "Krisenmanagement durch Vertrauen? Zur Problematik betrieblicher Öffnungsprozesse in ökonomisch schwierigen Situationen", in J. Freimuth (ed.), Die Angst der Manager. Göttingen: Verlag für Angewandte Psychologie, pp. 137–161.

Graf, A. (2000). "Vertrauen und Unternehmenskultur im Führungsprozess", zfwu, 1:339–356.

Grey, C & Garsten C. (2001). "Trust, control and post-bureaucracy", Organization Studies, 22:229–250.

Hardy, C., Phillips, N & Lawrence, T. (1998). "Distinguishing trust and power in interorganizational relations: forms and facades of trust", in C. Lane and R. Bachmann (eds), Trust Within and Between Organizations: Conceptual Issues and Empirical Applications. Oxford: Oxford University Press, pp. 64–87.

Heisig, U & Littek, W. (1995). "Wandel von Vertrauensbeziehungen im Arbeitsprozess", Soziale Welt, 46:282–304.

Hinshelwood, R.D. (1991). A Dictionary of Kleinian Thought. London: Free Association Books.

Hoad, T.F. (ed.) (1986). The Concise Oxford Dictionary of English Etymology. Oxford: Clarendon Press.

Hoepfl, H. (1995). "Performance and customer service: the cultivation of contempt", Studies in Cultures, Organizations and Societies, 1:47–62.

Isaacs, K.S., Alexander, J.M & Haggard, E.A. (1963). "Faith, trust and gullibility", International Journal of Psychoanalysis, 44:461–469.

Jaques, E. (1953). "On the dynamics of social structure", Human Relations, 6:3–24.

Jaques, E. (1955). "Social systems as a defence against persecutory and depressive anxiety", in M. Klein, P. Heimann and R.D. Money-Kyrle (eds), New Directions in Psycho-Analysis. The Significance of Infant Conflicts in the Patterns of Adult Behaviour. London: Tavistock, pp. 478–498.

Jaques, E. (1996). Requisite Organization: A Total System for Effective Managerial Organization and Managerial Leadership for the Twenty-first Century. Arlington, VA: Cason Hall.

Jewett, R. (2003). "Captain America and the crusade against evil", in The Dilemma of Zealous Nationalism. Grand Rapids: Wm. B. Eerdmans.

Kelly, K. (1999). New Rules for the New Economy. Radical Strategies for a Connected World. New York: Penguin Books.

Knights, D., Noble F., Vurdubakis, T & Willmott, H. (2001). "Chasing shadows: control, virtuality and the production of trust", Organization Studies, 22:311–336.

Kouzes, J.M & Posner, B.Z. (1995). The Leadership Challenge. San Francisco: Jossey-Bass.

Kramer, R.M. (2002). "When paranoia makes sense", Harvard Business Review, July: 62–69.

Kramer, R.M. (2003). "The virtues of prudent trust'. (Chapter 12a) in R. Westwood and St. Clegg (eds), Debating Organization: Point-Counterpoint in Organization Studies. Oxford: Blackwell, pp. 341–356.

Kramer, R.M., Brewer, M.B & Hanna, B.A. (1996). "Collective trust and collective action: the decision to trust as a social decision", in R.M. Kramer and T.R. Tyler (eds), Trust in Organizations: Frontiers of Theory and Research. Thousand Oaks: CA: Sage, pp. 357–389.

Landau, R.J., Krueger, J & Krueger, J.E. (1998). Corporate Trust Administration and Management. New York: Columbia University Press.

Lane, C & Bachmann R. (eds) (1998). Trust Within and Between Organizations: Conceptual Issues and Empirical Applications. Oxford: Oxford University Press.

Lawrence, J.S & Jewett, R. (2002). The Myth of the American Superhero. Grand Rapids: Wm. B. Eerdmans.

Lawrence, W.G. (1995). "The seductiveness of totalitarian states of mind", Journal of Health Care Chaplancy, 7:11–22.

Lawrence, W.G. (1997). "Centering of the sphinx for the psychoanalytic study of organizations'. Paper presented at the 1997 Symposium of the International Society for the Psychoanalytic Study of Organizations, Philadelphia. Available at: http://www.sba.oakland.edu/ispso/html/1997 Lawr.htm

Lawrence, W.G. (1998). "Social dreaming as a tool of consultancy and action research", in W.G. Lawrence (ed.), Social Dreaming at Work. London: Karnac, pp. 123–140.

Lawrence, W.G. (2000a) "Thinking refracted", in W.G. Lawrence (ed.), Tongued with Fire: Groups in Experience. London: Karnac, pp. 1–30.

Lawrence, W.G. (2000b) "The politics of salvation and revelation in the practice of consultancy", in W.G. Lawrence (ed.), Tongued with Fire: Groups in Experience. London: Karnac, pp. 165–179.

Lewis, J.D & Weigert, A. (1985). "Trust as a social reality", Social Forces, 43:967–985.

Luhmann, N. (1968). Vertrauen. Ein Mechanismus der Reduktion sozialer Komplexität. Stuttgart: Enke.

Luhmann, N. (1979). Trust and Power. Chichester: Wiley.

Luhmann, N. (1988). "Familiarity, confidence, trust: problems and alternatives", in D. Gambetta (ed.), Trust: Making and Breaking Cooperative Relations. New York: Blackwell, pp. 94–107.

Marshall, E.M. (1999). Building Trust at the Speed of Change: The Power of the Relationship-based Corporation. New York: AMACOM.

Melville, H. (1967). Moby-Dick. An Authoritative Text, in H. Hayford and H. Parker (eds), Reviews and Letters by Melville, Analogues and Sources, Criticism. New York: W.W. Norton.

Menzies Lyth, I.E.P. (1988). "The functioning of social systems as a defence against anxiety", in I.E.P. Menzies Lyth (ed.), Containing Anxiety in Institutions. Selected Essay, Vol. I. London: Free Association Books, pp. 43–85.

Miettinen, A. (2000). "Virtuality and swift trust as a management challenge", in H.-J. Pleitner and W. Weber (eds), Die KMU im 21. Jahrhundert. Impulse, Ansichten, Konzepte, Beiträge zu den "Rencontres de Saint-Gall. St Gallen: KMU/HSG, pp. 81–89.

Miller, E.J. (1998). "The leader with the vision. Is time running out?", in E.B. Klein, F. Gabelnick and P. Herr (eds), The Psychodynamics of Leadership. Madison, CT: Psychosocial Press, pp. 3–25.

Miller, E.J & Stein, M. (1993). "Individual and organization in the 1990 s: Time for a rethink?", The Tavistock Institute Review, 1992–1993: 35–37.

Mishra, A.I.K. (1996). "Organizational responses to crisis: the centrality of trust", in R.M. Kramer and T.R. Tyler (eds), Trust in

Organizations: Frontiers of Theory and Research. Thousand Oaks, CA: Sage, pp. 261–287.

Newstrom, J & Scannell, E. (1998). The Big Book of Team-building Games: Trust-building Activities, Team Spirit Exercises, and other Fun Things to Do. New York: McGraw-Hill.

Nieder, P. (1997). Erfolg durch Vertrauen. Abschied vom Management des Misstrauens. Wiesbaden: Gabler.

O'Neill, O. (2002). A Question of Trust. Cambridge: Cambridge University Press.

O'Shaughnessy, E. (1981). "A clinical study of a defensive organiza-tion", International Journal of Psycho-Analysis, 62:359–369 [also in E. Bott Spillius (ed.) (1988). Melanie Klein Today. Vol. I: Mainly Theory. London: Routledge, pp. 292–310].

Pelzer, P. (2002). "The contemptuous manager: an introduction into an (almost) non-existent but ubiquitous topic'. Paper presented at The European Academy of Management, 2nd Annual Conference on "Innovative Research in Management", May 9–11, Stockholm, Sweden.

Power, M. (1994). The Audit Explosion. London: Demos.

Rousseau, D.M., Sitkin, S.B., Burt, R.S & Camerer, C. (1998). "Not so different after all: a cross-discipline view of trust", Academy of Management Review, 23:93–404.

Ryan, K & Oestreich, D.K. (1998). Driving Fear out of the Workplace: Creating the High-trust, High-performance Organization. San Francisco: Jossey-Bass.

Rycroft, C. (1995). A Critical Dictionary of Psychoanalysis. London: Penguin.

Sandler, P.C. (2002). "Binocular vision and the practice of psy-choanalysis'. Available at: http://psychematters.com/papers/psandler.htm

Sartre, J.-P. (1947). Huis Clos. Paris: Libraire Gallimard.

Sculley, J. (1987). Odyssey. New York: Harper & Row.

Searles, H.F. (1965/1986) Collected Papers on Schizophrenia and Related Subjects. London: Maresfield Library [reprinted London: Karnac Books].

Shurtleff, M. (1998). Building Trust: A Manager's Guide for Business Success. Menlo Park, CA: Crisp Publications.

Sievers, B. (1994). Work, Death and Life Itself. Essays on Management and Organization. Berlin: de Gruyter.

Sievers, B. (1999a) "Psychotic organization as a metaphoric frame for the socio-analysis of organizational and interorganizational dynamics", Administration and Society, 31:588–615.

Sievers, B. (1999b) "Accounting for the caprices of madness: narrative fiction as a means of organizational transcendence", in R.A. Goodman (ed.), Modern Organizations and Emerging Conundrums: Exploring the Postindustrial Subculture of the Third Millennium. Lanham, MD: Lexington Books, pp. 126–142.

Sievers, B. (2000). "Competition as war: towards a socio-analysis of war in and among corporations", Socio-Analysis, 2:1–27.

Sievers, B. (2003a) "Your money or your life? Psychotic implications of the pension fund system: towards a socio-analysis of the financial services revolution", Human Relations, 56:187–210.

Sievers, B. (2003b) " "Fool'd with hope, men favour the deceit", or, Can we trust in trust?' (Chapter 12b), in R. Westwood and St. Clegg (eds), Debating Organization: Point-Counterpoint in Organization Studies. Oxford: Blackwell, pp. 356–367.

Sitkin, S.B., Rousseau, D.M., Burt, R.S & Camerer C. (eds) (1998). Special topic forum "Trust in and between Organizations", Academy of Management Review, 23(3).

Sprenger, R. (2002). Vertrauen führt. Worauf es im Unternehmen wirklich ankommt. Frankfurt: Campus.

Stein, H.F. (1995). "Domestic wars and the militarization of American biomedicine", Journal of Psychohistory, 22:406–415.

Stein, H.F. (1997). "Euphemism in the language of managed care", Journal of the Oklahoma State Medical Association, 90:243–247.

Stein, H.F. (1999). "The case of the missing author: from parapraxis to poetry and insight in organizational studies'. Paper presented at the 1999 symposium of the International Society of the Psychoanalytic Study of Organizations, Toronto. Available at: http://www.sba.oakland.edu/ispso/html/1999Symposium/schedule.htm

Steiner, J. (1979). "The border between the paranoid-schizoid and the depressive position in the borderline patient", British Journal of Medical Psychology, 52:385–391.

Steiner, J. (1982). "Perverse relationships between parts of the self: a clinical illustration", International Journal of Psycho-Analysis, 62:241–252.

Steiner, J. (1987). "Interplay between pathological organization and the paranoid-schizoid and the depressive position", International

Journal of Psycho-Analysis, 68:69–80 [also in E. Bott Spillius (ed.) (1988). Melanie Klein Today. Vol. 1: Mainly Theory. London: Routledge, pp. 324–342].

Steiner, J. (1990). "Pathological organizations as obstacles to mourning", International Journal of Psycho-Analysis, 71:87–94.

Steiner, J. (1993). Psychic Retreats. Pathological Organization in Psychotic, Neurotic and Borderline Patients. London: Routledge.

Steinle, C., Ahlers, F. & Gradtke, B. (2000). "Vertrauensorientiertes Management", Zeitschrift Führung und Organisation, 4:208–217.

Student, D. (2000). "Es wogt hin, und es wogt her. Corporate restructuring", Manager Magazin, 8:122–129.

Sydow, J. (1998). "Understanding the constitution of interorganizational trust", in C. Lane and R. Bachmann (eds), Trust Within and Between Organizations: Conceptual Issues and Empirical Applications. Oxford: Oxford University Press, pp. 31–63.

Tyler, T.R & Kramer, R.M. (1996). "Whither trust?' in R.M. Kramer and T.R. Tyler (eds), Trust in Organizations: Frontiers of Theory and Research. Thousand Oaks, CA: Sage, pp. 1–15.

Weber, A. (1993). "What's so new about the new economy?", Harvard Business Review, January/February, 24–42.

Wolfenstein, E.V. (1993). Psychoanalytic-Marxism. Groundwork. London: Free Association Books.

Zucker, L.G. (1986). "Production of trust: institutional sources of economic structure, 1840–1920", in B.M. Staw and L.L. Cummings (eds), Research in Organizational Behavior. Greenwich: CT: JAI Press, pp. 53–111.

Sad, mad or bad: What approaches should we take to organisational states-of-mind?

Susan Long

The book and subsequent film 'The Corporation' (Bakan 2005) took as its theme 1) the idea of the corporation created as a legal entity similar to an individual in the Law and 2) following this, the evaluation of the behaviour of corporations against descriptions of psychopathic syndromes in the DSM IV. The conclusion was: many corporations are psychopathic. Not surprisingly, organisational theorists and consultants are interested nowadays in the emotional and irrational aspects of organisational life. Increasingly, it seems the discourse surrounding organisations includes the idea of madness as well as badness.

But the distinctions between mad and bad have long been problematic for those attempting to deal with extreme or abnormal behaviour; such as the institutions of psychiatry and prisons (nowadays, corrections). Despite the controversies surrounding the work of French social historian Michel Foucault,[1] he did offer many compelling arguments about the historical development of the shifting boundary between medicine, psychiatry and the law (Foucault 2003; 1963). That this boundary is problematic is not in doubt. The modern psychiatric diagnosis of 'personality disorder' encompasses its difficulties. With issues of behavioral disturbance, narcissism and anti-social behaviour taking center stage, many of those falling within this diagnosis populate the world's prison systems and might be described as suffering from symptoms like 'a lack of remorse'.[2] One might ask about the line between symptoms and character; suffering and accountability. Moreover, with the advent of new-styled therapeutic courts on the one hand and cognitive-behaviour modification on the other, it seems we have judges as social workers and psychiatrists as behavioural custodians; the boundaries between aspects of their roles become ever more complex and interdependent.

With respect to the social institutions concerned, it is not simply a boundary of compassion on one side and punishment on the other: both psychiatry and prisons have histories of cruelty and compassion. Yet, this problematic boundary disappears when it comes to what we actually do with the mad or the bad. Throughout history they have been treated similarly-locked away from society questionably for their own good or the good of others, often neglected.

But now it seems that the boundary between the institutions of medical psychiatry and the law has entered a new phase of development through its involvement with business. If our organisations are new psychological (not simply legal) entities within the law, can we think of them as sad, mad or bad and do the problematic boundaries between these states-of-mind also come into the picture here?

Can organisations really be thought of as having a state-of-mind?

A first response to the question as to whether an organisation can have a state-of-mind is the simple one that individuals have minds, albeit, emergent from brains, while organisations do not. After all, it is the individual who thinks, feels, acts, makes decisions and uses language and communication. It is the individual who is the agent within the organisation. To impute an organisation with a mind seems to be dubious beyond even such childish anthropomorphisms that impute reasoning to animals or toys.

But I want to take a step back and approach this issue from another direction. Let us take a view through a systems perspective. Rather than making the differences between living systems a focus, take a look at the similarities and at the idea of emergent properties. A system is basically a set of interacting parts such that change in one part affects the others. Living systems are complex. While we can isolate and study single celled animals and plants, or even parts of them, they do not exist separately as individual parts or even as individual organisms, but as eco-systems encompassing the interactions between groupings of animals, plants and inorganic matter. In the twenty-first century humans are becoming increasingly aware of the nature of eco-systems and the inter-dependencies within them. The threat of global climate change has provided a focus.

Human culture is one part of the broader eco-system in which it operates. Rather than see culture as opposed to nature, a systems perspective regards culture as part of nature. Culture is basically what we collectively do and how we do it. It involves the ways we communicate and interact together. It can be understood as patterned behaviour within the group and among group members. Importantly, culture is a property of the whole not of any particular individual. Language, for example, is shared throughout a culture and grows through interactions between people. Stories, myths, ceremonies, rituals and events belong to the group. Individuals may take them up, enact, think and live them but such cultural products have their meaning between as well as within individuals. Similarly, individuals may experience an emotion, but in its fullness, this is also a cultural product. Love is for someone, anger against someone, triumph over someone. Moreover, emotion is not a simple individual sensation but a complex of thought, feeling and impetus to action, all influenced by culture and learning within culture.

By seeing culture as a property of the whole, it is understood as an emergent property. The substrata of human society and interaction are its basis. However, in ecological terms, it is more accurate to view society and culture as co-evolving phenomena. In co-evolution, the emergence is two-way, each affecting the development of the other. This can be said also for the relation between body and mind. While it is accepted that the mind is an emergent property of the brain, there is evidence that the brain and body are affected and develop as a result of mind and its expression in culture (Begley 2007). One very simple instance is that we (our minds) have developed a science of the brain and can intervene surgically and pharmacologically to bring about intended effects.

Taking the argument further, the idea of cultural systems, and hence organisations, permits a collective state-of-mind. It resides not so much in a place—the brain or a physically locatable consciousness—but is an emergent property of a culture. To apprehend the collective state-of-mind, the idea of mind requires rethinking. Traditionally thought of as 'something' inside a person, a systems psychoanalytic perspective (socio-analysis) regards mind as emergent from culture. It is a social infinite because emergent thoughts are infinite just as the number of possible sentences and paragraphs emergent from a language are infinite, or as compositions from musical notes are infinite; most yet to be expressed. The innumerable potential thoughts that make up the infinite social mind are the unthought implications of our culture. They may be entertained, perhaps temporarily by individuals, but many are not yet able to be thought of or about because the time is not right.[3] Some thoughts may be unbearable until we have the right context to hold them. Without that context, these thoughts are unable to be contained by either the culture or the individual (Bion 1970). They may be implications yet to be unraveled from the implicate order (Bohm 1980). Such implications, intrinsic to the cultural order or even to the physical world not yet apprehended, may press upon us for recognition. But they go unrecognised because there is no structure within which they can be held. No container for the potential contained.[4] Mind is emergent from culture and culture is emergent from mind. This is a reciprocal co-evolving process.

The collective state-of-mind is basic. What then, does it look like if the organisation rather than the individuals within it is sad, bad or mad? What if these states belong to the collective, even if experienced or entertained at different times by different individuals?

Each organisational state-of-mind has a different appearance. These appearances can be understood with reference to the neurotic, psychotic and perverse states-of-mind for individuals, but there are differences.

Neurotic, psychotic and perverse states-of-mind

The neurotic/normal position primarily employs repression, that is, active forgetting and removal from conscious thought. Reality becomes distorted because parts of it are unbearable. But repressed thoughts return and when they threaten to become conscious, defensive mechanisms are employed. These act to distort reality. For Freud, the neurotic position emanates from the oedipal conflict and its resolution at least in the recognition of the incest taboo, the threat of castration and the need to find one's own love objects outside the family. The relation to reality is adjustive and when the neurotic achieves normality (that is, when the neurotic is more able to *think his or her thoughts* rather than turn unwanted thoughts into symbolic symptoms) then the relation to reality can be based non-defensively on experience. The neurotic position might simplistically be seen as the sad position.

The psychotic position involves a severe splitting of both reality and the ego because much of reality is hated and rejected. Attention and focus turn inward and thinking is out of touch with reality and dominated by phantasy. In this position destructivity is aimed at the relation with reality and hence thinking and linking are destroyed because thinking is a transformation of experience within a real but frustrating environment.[5] The psychotic position is narcissistic and the relatedness to others is detached and split off. It is easily seen as the mad state of mind.

How then can we define the perverse? As with the psychotic position, the ego is split. However, the relation to reality is more ambivalent. It is dominated by denial. Like repression, the major neurotic defence, denial implies some acceptance of reality prior to its rejection. However, unlike repression, recognition of reality sits ambiguously side by side with its denial, even in conscious fantasy. This describes a certain psychological position or state-of-mind; the purely perverse, if you like. Apart from the perverse psychic position or state-of-mind, perverse sexuality and behaviour may be found within patients diagnosed as neurotic, psychotic, borderline or narcissistic according to modern psychoanalytic and psychiatric descriptions and classifications (Kernberg 2006).

In attempting a definition, it is not easy to locate the perverse as a mental illness in the same way as the neuroses and psychoses. Although the psycho-social ideas of developmental arrest and psychoneurotic defence are seen as central to most theories, so too are the socio-legal ideas of corruption, aggression and illegality in terms of social boundaries. This difficulty of definition shows itself most strongly in the way that societies handle perversity. The defining line tends to stand more with the law than through ideas of intrinsic health or illness. Whereas the anxious neurotic and deluded psychotic are accepted as ill, debates still rage about the etiology and treatment of sex offenders, for instance. Although modern psychiatry locates perversion within the character disorders or as symptoms of psychosis, a clear distinctive definition is unavailable. It is perhaps, the bad state of mind. But sad and mad are also in the mix because twentieth century psychology has made it hard to understand badness without sadness and madness. Hence, the remarks by the psychologist on the ABC mentioned earlier.

It is perhaps sufficient to say here that if we are to understand the perverse state of mind as a social system property (rather than as individually characterological or symptomatic), its essential system dynamics are more pertinent than its place in current popular or psychiatric classifications of individuals. What are these?[6]

1. The perverse state of mind is not simply a deviation from normative morality. It has to do with individual pleasure at the expense of a more general good, often to the extent of not recognising the existence of others or their rights. It reflects a state of primary narcissism.
2. The perverse state of mind acknowledges reality, but at the same time, denies it. This leads to a state of fixed ideation and phantasy to protect against the pain of seeing and not seeing at the same time.
3. The perverse state of mind engages others as accomplices in the perversion.
4. The perverse state of mind may flourish where instrumental relations have dominance in the society. This is because instrumentality ignores the rights of others to have an independent existence. This in itself is abusive. The perverse state-of-mind turns a blind eye.
5. Perversion begets perversion. Abusive cycles are hard to break. Corruption breeds corruption because of the complicity of the accomplices and their subsequent denial and self-deception (Long 2008).

Translating these indicators into social and organisational terms means that perversion is exemplified by:

*   Individual pleasure at the expense of mutuality (or, in broad social terms, at the expense of a more general good);
*   The paradoxical dynamic of denial of reality, where what is known is at the same time not known, (or, as an example in

corporate terms, disparate and contradictory public and private images exist in parallel);

• The use of accomplices in an instrumental social relation; and,
• The self perpetuation or closedness of the perverse dynamic (Long 2008).

The case of One.Tel

One.Tel was an Australian grown telecommunications company primarily focused on the youth market in mobile phones and internet connections.[7] First established in 1995, it was disbanded in 2001 and investigated by the Australian Securities and Investments Commission (ASIC) for trading while insolvent. This has become one of Australia's longest running civil investigations and the liquidation of One.Tel's assets has not yet been completed, as of 2007.

Between the years 1995 and 2000 One.Tel grew into a business 'that spanned seven countries, employed 3,000 staff and had annual sales close to $1 billion' (Barry 2002, 185). There were several factors that contributed to this growth. First were the entrepreneurial efforts of its founders Jodie Rich and Brad Keeling, who convinced others to invest in their ideas. The dynamics of their relations with investors and major stakeholders read as a series of deals brought about through family and old-boy school connections, together with Rich's capacity to charm—a capacity that apparently could be put on or taken away at will (Barry 2002).

Second was the business and market context of the times. Dot. com companies and Telco's along with them were the new hope of the late 90's. Belief in communications and the internet had reached a high. These technologies seemed to offer vast possibilities for the future, and investors were chasing them despite the reality that many showed no evidence of creating profits and were little more than business plans. All eyes were on the future and the promise of profits to come.

Thirdly, One.Tel had initially managed to contract with a major telecommunications provider, Optus, to on-sell its services in the form of mobile phones. At this time mobile phones were the next big thing in telecommunications. Optus, itself a fairly new player in Australia, had laid out a network and as well as providing services directly—at first aimed at long distance telecommunications—was contracting several mobile phone companies to on-sell. As part of One.Tel's contract, Rich was able to secure a deal whereby Optus paid a $120 bonus every time One.Tel signed up a new customer. This turned out to be a significant deal for One.Tel in its first two years (and one that angered other Optus on-sellers when they eventually discovered that One.Tel had an advantage that they did not). Maybe Optus executives did not foresee the implications. For instance, by not writing in that these had to be long-term customers, One.Tel staff created many ways in which new customers were gained, even those who turned out to be short-term, non-paying or even non-existent. For example, all they had to do was to sell a SIM card and link it up to the network. Some One.Tel dealers even paid 'new customers' $10 for buying a SIM card. Others posted new SIM cards out to existing customers and linked them to the network. This way they registered new customers, even if the new cards and numbers were never used. All this meant a loss for Optus, which was not rectified in those first two years.

Later, Rich, together with board member Rodney Adler, was able to convince James Packer and Lachlan Murdoch, sons of the media Moguls Kerry Packer and Rupert Murdoch, to invest millions in the company. This gave One.Tel profile in the eyes of smaller investors and to sections of the media. This all occurred despite misgivings voiced in some quarters about Rich's ability to successfully run the business, given his previous failure the decade before with a company called Imagineering, which also had grown immensely before crashing. Such is the nature of gambling for high stakes. Risks are minimised and hype takes over. But, of course, this is easily said in hindsight.

One.Tel grew to be considered a great success. In November 1999, it was estimated to be worth more than five billion dollars. But, this was in the inflated dot.com market at the close of the twentieth century and, despite its market value, in June 2000 One.Tel reported a loss of $291 million. Spending had been high in overseas extensions to the company and in expensive attempts to get into the local calls market. Packer and Murdoch continued to believe in the company and injected more funds. However, the company's value was eventually found to be an empty bubble in the wind, and these two investors finally withdrew a last ditch rescue bid in 2001. Share prices had been grossly overblown, and by 2001 the dot.com bubble burst. As share prices fell, the real losses of the company could no longer be denied beneath a gloss of imagined profits to come and hidden and delayed debts and other dubious accounting practices. Eyes could no longer be focused on the future, as the real present situation had to be examined. The accounting practices of held-over debts were revealed. What looked like profits were losses. Mismanagement became evident and board members later claimed that they were misled as to the state of the company finances. Eventually Rich and Keeling were dismissed by the board. The ASIC investigation looked at possible charges of misguiding the public given massive losses to investors.

The story of One.Tel is a familiar one to those who followed, for example, the stories of HIH in Australia and Enron in the US. There is a picture of leaders who misjudged investments, who seemed to be greedy in accumulating their own personal fortunes, who failed to listen to warning signs when they were given and who seemed hell-bent on growth at the expense of sustainability. 'Hubris' is the word given to the blinding pride and misjudged belief self evident in many such cases. On top of these failings comes the gradual dawning knowledge of the likely collapse of the company, the 'clever' accounting practices to disguise this, practised in the hope that future believed-in profits would rectify the situation. Eventually, come the desperate attempts to gain further capital to patch over the inevitable and the pitfall of continuing to trade while actually insolvent.

Most of the players in the One.Tel story have accepted the judgements made throughout the ASIC case, including the allegations of mismanagement and misleading the board. Jodie Rich, however, continues to maintain that the company could have remained solvent with the planned capital raising of $132 million. This belief is contrary to the judgment of the enquiry (Elisabeth Sexton, Sydney Morning Herald, August 23, 2007).

Is this simply a story of a handful of players? How does this story fit with the indicators of organisational perversity, revealing a systemic process rather than simply the story of the failure of a few avaricious and all too clever men? That individual pride, greed and self-deception play a role is evident. But, for us to consider it a case of corporate perversity, systemic social processes must be seen to interweave with the personal ambitions of the leaders. Argus-like, the eyes of many, must be closed, blinded or turned aside. This idea is to some degree now recognised in the law.

> One of the most interesting lessons that can be derived from recent events has profound implications for regulators. The lesson is that, when organisations go bad, it is rarely the result of just one or two "rotten eggs". Regulations are usually contravened in an organisational environment that fails to crack down on breaches and allows them to continue without proper remedial action.
>
> This is one of the reasons the Commonwealth *Criminal Code* incorporates the idea of "organisational blameworthiness" to determine when criminal responsibility can be attributed to a corporation. This was largely inspired by the work of prominent legal academic and lawyer Brent Fisse ... Organisational blameworthiness is reflected in a number of ways. For example, the *Code* attributes acts and omissions of employees, agents or officers of a corporation to the corporation itself, as long as the relevant person was acting within the actual or apparent scope of their employment or authority.
>
> Most interestingly for present purposes is the way in which the *Code* attributes the intention, knowledge or recklessness of a corporate agent to the corporation. The *Code* provides that this fault element of an offence must be attributed to a corporation that expressly, tacitly, or impliedly authorised or permitted the commission of the offence. The *Code* relies on traditional means of attribution to corporations such as showing that the corporation's board of directors or a high managerial agent intentionally, knowingly or recklessly carried out the relevant conduct (Williams 2003, 3).

This well describes important aspects of organisational perversity over and above individual corruption. Its implications are extensive. For instance, 'bad' individuals may cry that they were only following orders, that is, the tacit orders of the organisational culture. Regulating bodies and courts will have to assess such arguments requiring complex data in order to do so. The complexity of the investigation of One.Tel by ASIC, for example, has required an extensive amount of data in order to judge whether or not the company *might have* remained solvent had the plans of the managing directors gone through, had they not been sacked. Judgments about the realistic nature (or not) of organisational players intents as well as their actions thus become part of the data for investigation. Yet again, 'deluded' individuals may well believe that they are acting in company and shareholder interests, especially if their delusion is shared by a vast number of 'accomplices'.

The One.Tel case can now be examined in terms of the indicators of this organisational perverse state-of-mind.

First, I consider individual pleasure at the expense of the general good. This is demonstrated most strongly in the attitudes taken by One.Tel executives toward shareholders, employees and customers that became entrenched in the work culture. Barry (2002) describes how, despite company rhetoric, customers were exploited time and again. Apart from the early practice of sending out new SIM cards to existing customers who did not request or need them, senior executives held meetings that were internally know as 'milking the customer' meetings. In these meetings more and more additional charges were developed to gain revenue. In one instance, this involved sending the customer an unsolicited birthday greeting and then charging him for it. Increasing complaints from customers failed to be heard as poorly managed and under resourced call centers were unable to take them. Those complaints that did get through were often from frustrated and sometimes abusive customers resulting in high staff turnover in the call centers.

The culture of One.Tel, at first dynamic and creative with no hierarchy (except of course for the boss) and slogans such as 'give your opinions' and 'a happy team means happy players' (Barry 2002, 78), was hard to maintain once the company grew in numbers. Few systems were in place and management was haphazard and inexperienced. On the one hand there was exploitation of customers, on the other hand the billing system was woefully inept, so that many who should be paying were not.

But through all this, and despite senior management decisions that resulted in huge losses, the chief players gained massive wealth spent on expensive houses and lifestyles. Apart from their shares and high salaries, huge bonuses were taken by Rich and Keeling in 2000 on the basis of the One.Tel share price. These caught the attention of the media at the time and fuelled the anger of many shareholders who had not been told of the bonuses, especially in light of a massive $291 million loss for the company that year.

All this indicates a culture of individual greed, pride and narcissistic self-interest. This was the case with One.Tel, but was supported more broadly by the dot.com boom and leads to the second indicator, the use of denial as a major defense. Barry describes how, following the collapse of One.Tel, chief executive Jodie Rich continued to deny the problems, blamed others and believed his decisions were in the best interests of the company. He does this to this day and is pursuing litigation to receive monies that he believes are owed to him (Elisabeth Sexton, Sydney Morning Herald, August 23, 2007). But the dynamic went far beyond him. In the early years, cash flow was high. One.Tel was getting massive sales as it cashed in on the deal with Optus. The company rode high on this with no real thought for the consequences and the pull back of funds from Optus that would eventually come when the 'fake' customers failed to pay.

The boom in the dot.com and telco stock market was widespread. It bolstered the fantasies of people like Rich and Keeling, along with their board members such as John Greaves, Rodney Adler, James Packer and Lachlan Murdoch, the latter two ending up investing $950 million of their companies' monies in One.Tel. The hope for the new technology was high. It was believed that nearly everyone would want a mobile phone. Overseas businesses would take One. Tel even further. Many were taken in by the hype. And, One.Tel then did what Rich had said they would never do: they invested in fixed wire home-based calls believing that by giving cheap local prices to gain the predicted two million Australian customers, revenue would be balanced or grow from long-distance calls.

But, the dream was unraveling. The evidence is that despite out of control losses occurring, One.Tel's directors were blind to this. Or, more honestly, they both knew and did not know. Local call costs were not being balanced; it seems the company had no real reason to believe they would be. It was all guesswork. The billing system was a disaster; many overseas operations were not living up to their predicted successes. Financial reporting to the board was incomplete and sketchy. But the managing directors continued to convince the non-executive board members that One. Tel would reach its targets and bring in profits. It is unclear whether they were simply inept or whether their misrepresentations were part of massive denial and self-delusion.

> It seems quite extraordinary that a company the size of One.Tel did not actually know that one of its key businesses was losing money...Most of all, it seems extraordinary that the company's top managers could take so long to accept that their company was millions of dollars behind budget, and work out why. One of those involved believed Rich and Silbermann (CFO) were in 'denial' about the problem for three to four months: they knew cash was pouring out of the company, and should have investigated the fixed-wire business far earlier, "but they insisted on believing they were right and everybody else was wrong" (Barry 2002, 268).

They knew and they did not know. The fantasy that losses would be regained predominated over the reality for too long. Warning signals were denied. Staff members who had the information were not listened to or discouraged from speaking. An atmosphere of bullying pervaded senior management and a coterie of yes-men surrounded the boss. Those who did not toe the One.Tel line soon left. But if the eyes of the executives were blind, this was heightened by the searing light of greed and the promise of quick riches shining throughout the share market.

A company cannot grow to the size that One.Tel did in the time that it did, (and without good management and sustainable systems) simply through the efforts of a few individuals. Neither its growth, nor its failure, nor the blindness to its impossible fantasy could be sustained by just a few. Accomplices are needed. These were found in investors willing to believe in the possibilities of the company, who put trust in its managing directors and who failed to appreciate its risks. The sub-title of Paul Barry's book *Rich Kids* is 'How the Murdoch's and Packers lost $950 million in One.Tel'. There were rumours that the younger generation of Murdochs and Packers were simply throwing around their influence to show it off to their immensely powerful fathers or to flaunt them. One.Tel was perhaps a stage for oedipal rivalries and the setting was big and tickets costly. The young image of One.Tel, the future hopes for telcoms and friendships with Rich and Adler drew them. All of this was no real substitute for clear and careful examination of the company and its business plans, yet it carried the day. Moreover, the fact that News limited (Murdoch) and Publishing and Broadcasting Ltd. (PBL, Packer) were major investors led many other investors to have faith in One.Tel. Bankers Trust, for example, was one. A broad system of accomplices was involved despite the company never making any profits. No-one was carefully keeping a watch over what was going on.

The next indicator is a context of instrumentality. The attitudes towards employees, shareholders and customers described earlier sat within a context of general exploitation. One.Tel was aiming its mobile phone sales at single mothers, low-paid workers, teenagers and others on low-incomes. Despite the fact that some of their 'free time' offers, their poor billing and other customer systems meant that they lost revenue from non-payers (Yogi Bear, amongst others, was on their customer list still counted as income rather than as a bad debt), their aim was to take as much revenue as possible from wherever they could with as little cost to themselves as possible. This may seem a normal business strategy, but while other companies were increasingly looking toward customer satisfaction, One.Tel cared not a hoot.

This was mirrored in stories of Rich's and Keeling's legendary rudeness and abusive language when crossed or angered. They were 'kids' of an abusive, instrumental corporate culture. They learned the attitude but somehow missed any lessons on good business practices. It may be, as some thought, that they had initially intended to grow the business then sell-out when share prices were high—the ultimate form of corporate instrumentality. But either they were victims of their own fantasies, or they locked themselves into a position from which they couldn't back out.

Finally, we can say that a perverse culture breeds more perversity. Barry (2002) is at pains to point out that One.Tel was a bigger and more spectacular replay of Rich's earlier failure in Imagineering.

Whether or not criminal charges are laid and corruption is indicated through evidence about deliberately misleading the public, eventually the question of cause arises from such cases as Enron, HIH and One.Tel. Should we look upon these cases as the result of individual arrogance, greed and incompetence followed by denial, fear and cover-up? Certainly legal action must be taken when individuals clearly transgress the law. Should we look upon them as the result of narcissistic leaders who lose touch with the realities of their companies and refuse advice, whose belief in themselves turns to self-delusion as Barry (2002) reports may have been the case with Jodie Rich? In this case, should we bring in psychiatry as well as the law to fix corporate ailments?

Working with organisational perversity

This chapter suggests another perspective. While the law and psychiatry may be needed to deal with the fallout of a perverse dynamic, it is in understanding this dynamic that better solutions can be found. The perverse state-of-mind in organisations is accompanied by smoke and mirrors around agreements made in secret and within an abusive culture of objectifying the other for instrumental ends.

What is the language or discourse that can work with the organisational perverse state-of-mind? Psychiatric discourse traditionally deals with the sad and the mad, legal discourse with the bad. In both these discourses, the question of personal responsibility arises. But are these two ends of a continuum? What of the idea of *organisational blameworthiness*? As stated by the then Australian Attorney-General in 2003:

> Intention, knowledge or recklessness may be attributed to a corporation where it is established that, first, a corporate culture existed within the corporation that directed, encouraged, tolerated or led to non-compliance with the relevant provision; or, secondly, that the corporation failed to create and maintain a corporate culture that required compliance with the relevant provision (Williams 2003).

It seems that the law is moving toward an increased understanding of the role of culture in corruption. There seems to be in this an implicit continuum between bad and shall we say, 'troubled'? In Australia, *The Corporations Act* allows for ASIC, its corporate watchdog, to bring civil cases against corporations and their leaders. However, whether criminal or civil charges are laid, it is recognised that prosecution should be the apex of a pyramid of ways to deal with corporate bad behaviour, and these ways include education and regulation (Clough/Mulhern 2002). Regulatory bodies should include ways to help corporations meet their responsibilities rather than simply deal out punishments.[8]

In business and organisational consultancy the processes of therapy and correction are echoed by the solutions of consultation, change management and re-engineering. This leads straight back to the boundary between sad, mad and bad and the unconscious solutions that emanate from the institutions of psychiatry and law, because these are the only institutions currently available to work at this boundary. These solutions are: (i) it's sad or mad so heal it! (ii) it's bad, so punish it and put in watchdogs!

Several decades of organisational 'therapy' seem only to have helped pockets of well-motivated staff toward improved corporate life (Long 2006). A simple therapeutic understanding, as if all organisational problems were those of neurosis or psychosis, is limited in dealing with the issues outlined in this chapter. In the worst scenario, organisational consultants simply serve to acclimatise workers to a perverse culture. Yet, a move simply from understanding the 'mad', to clarifying what is 'bad' or perverse is not best served by a simple reversion to the law or legal process. A new space is needed.

Ideas in socio-analytic thinking

The major ideas currently available from systems psychodynamic thinkers seem to fall into a few main groups. Some of these groupings of ideas are combined, for example in the Group Relations literature (Gould/Stapley/Stein 2001). Briefly, they are:

(i) analysis of key individuals and their interpersonal relationships;
(ii) social defense theories that explore unconscious collusions against difficult emotional experiences and, linked to this,
(iii) systems theories (both open systems theory pioneered through Katz and Khan; Miller and Rice and closed systems theory expounded by Maturana and Varela) conceptualising the organization-as-a-whole with possible neurotic and psychotic type structures and dynamics.

These latter two approaches tend to theorise the system as working through the dynamics of co-dependent individuals.

(iv) systemic approaches that focus on whole system dynamics such as proposed through chaos theory, or the operation of a symbolic level of social functioning as understood in Lacanian (1970) approaches, or Lawrence's (2005; 2007) social dreaming. In these latter approaches, the individual or even the group is considered as epi-phenomena with the field of the unconscious or infinite, as Lawrence describes it, as the primary reality.

These ideas thus range through a major focus on the individual through to a major focus on the system. It is argued here that the study of organisational perversity demands a full systemic perspective. Psychoanalysis approaches thoughts and feelings primarily through (1) the study of mental disturbance and (2) the study of individuals. Mental disturbance is a good window into human minds, but leaves us with a heritage of the perspective (vertex) of the therapeutic. Here disturbance is an illness to be cured. The study of organizational life through the minds and psychology of individuals may lead us, through this heritage, to seeing organizations as having ills to be cured.

But mental disturbance is just one window. From an analysis of perverse dynamics, a focus on conscious and unconscious agreements is a more useful approach than a therapeutic perspective (Long 2002). Rather than seeing organizations as being 'sick' or in need of therapy, consultants can look to an understanding of the unconscious pacts, agreements and decision-making processes operating (Kaes 2002; Puget 2002). Of course the problems of individuals and the social defenses of groups will be at play, and will strongly influence the development of organizational structure and culture. But a shift in focus sees these as developed and supported through unconscious collusions and agreements (or disagreements) that have their own rituals.

Understanding organisations in this way may enable scrutiny to be placed on finding agreements for the general rather than individual good, finding processes to address and monitor risk realistically, understanding group dynamics and the role they play in supporting unconscious fantasy and denial and shifting a culture of instrumentality toward a culture of sustainability.

Understanding the human mind and the human organisation as complex systems, many aspects of which are unconscious, enables a different approach to their study. The organisation can be viewed as a set of role relations that require agreements between people. Disturbance is thus not seen as an illness, but as a problem in role relations, agreements, disagreements (many of which are unconscious) and communication. What is required is not so much therapy as the building of organisational community. In many ways this is the perspective available from Group Relations work.

Organisations are complex systems of agreements and contracts between people. Their multiple systems consist of tasks, social systems, socio-technical, emotional, political, economic, linguistic, cultural and symbolic systems. Because these systems meet in the internal world of the role-holders they become intimately connected. Socio-Analysis looks toward these psycho-socio-emotional systems and stresses their unconscious aspects (especially unconscious collusions) and the influence these have on other organisational systems. The Group Relations approach has deeply explored links between this and the task/ technical system. But, equally an examination of the political system and the agreements within it may lead to uncovering unconscious assumptions and collusions.

All this leads to the hypothesis that agreements and collusions are the fundamental dynamic of organisations. Some agreements are legitimized and authorized or endorsed. Some are unconscious and are lodged in assumptions and collusions or underlie misunderstandings and enmities. A process of projective identification (i.e., a subtle unconscious agreement in the transference of emotions), or a political alliance, in this sense, are each a form of agreement. And, the emotions may be considered a concomitant part of social relatedness: trust or mistrust, for example being contemporaneous with unconscious apprehensions and understandings about how the other engages us. The language of agreements takes us beyond interpersonal social/psychological /emotional systems into the task/political and socio-technical systems also present in organizations and in relations between organisations. How might trust be usurped, for instance, through the politics of acquisition or of deprivation, when individuals are caught in an unconscious collusive system at the institutional level? Can we understand betrayal in terms of the breaking of agreements sometimes at unconscious levels?

How this perspective might prevent re-occurrences of organisations such as One.Tel is only beginning to be explored. Analysis after the event is always easier. However, alongside the psychiatric perspective of therapy and the legal perspective of instituting checks, balances and deterrents, a socio-analytic perspective of creating and developing transparent systems of agreements and exploring the unconscious process around this is a start.

Notes

1. Michel Foucault has written extensively about historical changes in defining mental illness and abnormality. He emphasises the way that definitions have been torn between medicine and the law. It seems Foucault was unable to produce, when challenged, many of the primary sources he used to both support and exemplify his ideas. Nonetheless, his articulation of many ideas about the nature of our current institutions is enlightening.

2. This phrase was used by a psychologist on an Australian Broadcasting Commission (ABC) program 30.8.07 who described a convicted child murderer as not insane but possibly having a personality disorder with symptoms such as a lack of remorse.

3. We talk of 'entertaining' a thought and this colloquialism may be closer to the truth than is normally accepted.

4. The findings of science were not possible before scientific method and its technologies were available. But this is not a matter of one developing before the other. The evolution of science (or any cultural endeavor) occurs through the co-evolution of method, technology and ideas.

5. Wilfred Bion's work on thinking and psychosis examines attacks on linking.

6. Full details of the argument in support of these defining characteristics can be found in Long (2002) or Long (2007).

7. Most of my data about One.Tel comes from Paul Barry (2002) *Rich Kids: How the Murdochs and Packers lost $950 million in One.Tel* Bantum Books, Sydney. Other details come from reading newspaper clippings and discussions with Michael Long, who followed the story in the press at the time.

8. Many groups and publications are now available for improving corporate and organisational governance to protect against corruption. See for example, *Four Steps to Organisational Integrity* The Independent Commission Against Corruption (www.icac.nsw.gov.au).

References

Bakan, J. (2005). The Corporation—The pathological pursuit of profit and power. London: Constable.

Barry, P. (2002). Rich Kids—How the Murdochs and Packers lost $950 million in One.Tel. Sydney: Bantum Books.

Begley, S. (2007). How Thinking can Change the Brain. *The Wall Street Journal Science Journal.*

Bion, W.R. (1970). Attention and Interpretation. London: Tavistock.

Bohm, D. (1980). Wholeness and the Implicate Order. London: Routledge.

Clough, J./Mulhern, C. (2002). The Prosecution of Corporations. Oxford: Oxford University Press.

Foucault, M. (1963). Madness and Civilization—A history of insanity in the age of reason. NY: Random House.

Foucault, M. (2003). Abnormal—Lectures at the College de France 1974–75. London: Verso.

Gould, L., Stapley, L. & Stein, M. (Ed.) (2001). The Systems Psychodynamics of Organizations: Integrating the group relations approach, psychoanalytic and open systems perspectives. London: Karnac Books.

Kaes, R. (2002). Contributions from France—Psychoanalysis and institutions in France. In: Hinshelwood, R.D. & Chiesa, M. (Ed.), Organizations, Anxieties and Defences—Toward a psychoanalytic social psychology. London: Whurr Publishers.

Kernberg, O. (2006). Perversion, perversity and normality—diagnostic and therapeutic considerations. In: Nobus, D./Downing, L. (Ed.), Perversion—Psychoanalytic perspectives. London: Karnac Books. 19–38.

Lacan, J. (1970). Ecrits. London: Tavistock.

Lawrence, W.G. (2005). Introduction to Social Dreaming—Transforming Thinking. London: Karnac Books.

Lawrence, W.G. (2007). Infinite possibilities of Social Dreaming. London: Karnac Books.

Long, S.D. (2002). Organisational Destructivity and the Perverse State-of-Mind. *Organisational and Social Dynamics, 2,* 2:179–207.

Long, S.D. (2006). Organizational defenses against anxiety—what has happened since the 1955 Jacques paper? *International Journal of Applied Psychoanalytic Studies, 3,* 5:279–295.

Long, S.D. (2008). The Perverse Organisation and its deadly sins. London: Karnac Books.

Puget, J. (2002). Contributions from South America—From the group as jig-saw puzzle to the incomplete whole. In: Hinshelwood, R.D./ Chiesa, M. (Ed.), Organizations, Anxieties and Defences—Toward a psychoanalytic social psychology. London: Whurr Publishers.

Williams, D. (2003). Opening Address for Australian Compliance Institute, Regulators Compliance Conference: Protecting the Public—Techniques of Enforcement and nce: L'Aqua, Cockle Bay.

'Potential space': The threatened source of individual and collective creativity* **

Gilles Amado

Contrary to the transitional object, the notion of potential space, which is at the core of the transitional process described by D. W. Winnicott, has always been difficult to integrate within the psychoanalytic theory and practice because it is neither an object nor an agency.[1] Moreover, potential space does not appear as a completely stable and independent notion as it is named sometimes "transitional space", "intermediate area", "third area" for example. Still, potential space may be the most important idea in Winnicott's work. In the French version of his last book, *Playing and Reality*, "potential space" is even mentioned as the subtitle.

---

*I wish to thank Halina Brunning, Marlene Spero and Kenneth Eisold for their useful comments of this paper. A shorter version of this article has been presented at the ISPSO Annual Meeting *Potential Space—A source for creativity and terrifying anxiety. Exploring possibilities and limitations in organizational work.* June 25-July 1st, Stockholm.
**This talk is dedicated to the memory of Harold Bridger. In spite of the age difference between us, we shared during more than thirty years of friendship and cooperation a sort of "squiggling" relationship, very linked and inspired by Winnicott's spirit and work. The creation of the Institute for Human Relations in Zurich in the late 70's, later transformed in the Transitional Dynamics Network, illustrates in many ways our debt to Winnicott and the extension of his thinking to organisations and society.

It may seem somehow awkward that organisational clinicians pay attention to such a notion because it is originally intended to explore the first period of psychic life and mother-infant relationship. Still, if we do so, it is because we know today that such a space is at the source of true living and creativity and has, therefore, deep implications for people, organizations and societies.

In a first step, I'll try to specify it, remaining as close as possible to Winnicott. Then, I'll discuss the environmental conditions which facilitate or hinder the existence of the individual potential space. In a third part, I shall explore the applications of this notion to the social context, differentiating designed potential spaces from spontaneous ones through a series of examples and I shall end by pointing out the limitations and conditions of its use for democracy.

Winnicott and potential space

Potential space can be described as an intermediate area between subjectivity and objectivity, between fantasy and reality, an area of illusion and compromise.

Between 4 and 12 months, according to Winnicott (1971), the transition takes place from mother-infant unity to the state where there is mother-and-infant provided there is a potential space (never actual) between both of them. It is within the potential space that symbols originate. As Winnicott puts it, it is the loss of physical union and psychic fusion which leads to a satisfactory relationship with reality. Indeed, within the potential space, loss becomes a gain "because the symbol of union enriches more union experience than the union itself" (Winnicott, 1966).

As the Swedish psychoanalyst Arne Jemstedt (2000, p. 126) explains, "by giving her breast in the right place and at the right moment, the mother provides the infant with an illusion of having created the breast that it encounters. In this illusion, in the primary omnipotence where the infant creates the world (and in a sense is God), there resides the basis for a vital and creative interchange between the child and the environment". An important consequence of this assertion must be underlined: without such an early illusion, there may not be a later disillusionment. This also points to the quality of the holding environment provided by the mother and the consequences of an egocentric type of caring: "if this creative encounter between infant and breast does not come about, if the infant's impulses are not received but the mother's own activity dominates, then the child lets himself be fed, but his own vital strength and creativity do not partake. The child remains reactive and compliant, its spontaneity is kept hidden" (Jemstedt, op. cit.) and can be brought into a state of "unthinkable anxiety" (Winnicott, 1962), a kind of psychotic anxiety close to the "splitting anxiety"[2] described by Anzieu. The failure of a good-enough holding may also be the origin of the false self which is characterized by a premature self holding, "potentially leading to a rigid repudiation of contact with the environment" (Jemstedt, op. cit, p. 127), "a sense of futility, of not feeling real", or even a sort of alexythimia (Nemiah, 1977).

The necessity of a goodenough holding by the mother is linked to what Winnicott calls her capacity for *"rêverie"*, the capacity of paying attention to her child and at the same time to her own unconscious process without giving them predominance, a sort of sensitive and flexible relationship between containing and contained.

If potential space lies between the symbol and the symbolized, it requires threeness or an interpretive self (Diamond, 2007) to allow for creativity and what Ogden (1985) calls a "dialectic process". His psychopathology of potential space is especially interesting, building on the Winnicottian theory of the psychopathology of the symbolic function. He presents four forms of collapse of the capacity to maintain a psychic dialectical process:[3]

- The first form of failure happens when the reality pole (out of the realm of omnipotence) collapses. The subject then becomes "imprisoned in the realm of fantasy objects as things in themselves. The hallucination does not sound like a voice, it is a voice" (op.cit., p. 134). Without a distance, a differentiation between symbol and symbolized, there is no room to entertain ideas and feelings.
- The second form of failure is when reality is a defence against fantasy. Then imagination is foreclosed: "if a little girl is only a little girl, she is unable to play". This reminds me of a father's panic in front of his son's nightmares. In order to help him, he chose, before his son went to bed, each night to cut his dreams with scissors. One can imagine the psychic trouble of the son when nightmares appeared again. Trying to find meanings behind the apparent

scene with such handicapped people (here, the father) looks "like trying to get blood from a stone" (Ogden, op.cit., p. 135).

- The third case is where reality and fantasy poles are dissociated. This happens when there is a foreclosure of dialectic resonance that might generate meanings that one feels are dangerous. We'll come back to this process when we shall discuss the prohibition to think freely in some big organizations today.

- The last form of failure, the most extreme one, is the foreclosure of reality and fantasy. Here, perceptions remain raw sensory data. "Meanings are not denied, they simply are not created" (Ogden, op.cit., p. 136). It seems like a "state of non experience" and looks like "blank psychosis" (Green, 1975), similar to that of extreme cases of criminal coldness.

As Winnicott points out, it is within potential space that symbols originate and imagination can develop. Without it, there is only fantasy. We easily understand why empathy belongs to the potential space as it contains the paradox of being the other whilst remaining oneself, whereas projective identification is outside it. It is the negative of playing.

And playing is deeply linked to the potential space. It is the core of Winnicott's theory and practice. Let's remember his therapeutic "squiggle" among other features, and his assertion: "only in playing is communication possible"; and also "only in playing can the individual become creative and it's only by being creative that the individual discovers himself" (Winnicott, 1971, p. 76). By the way, at one stage, Winnicott thought of becoming a music-hall artist. Early deprivation can lead to the loss of the area of playing, to the loss of the symbolization capacity. It is also interesting to notice that illusion, which is at the source of primary psychic creativity, etymologically, from the latin *in-lusio*, means entering into playing.

As Ogden says (op.cit., p. 129), "... specific forms of potential space include the play space, the area of the transitional object and phenomena, the analytic space, the area of cultural experience and the area of creativity".

The capacity to use symbols, to be playing (even with psychosis) which is a sign of health and to refuse the sole principle of reality (that Winnicott considered as an "insult") allows the discovery of oneself, the access to a real freedom and an acceptance of reality (which in no way means an adaptation to it[4]). If it includes the negative capability (Keats, 1952) (mainly the capability to tolerate ambiguity and uncertainty) and destructiveness, potential space above all involves a psychic movement between the "created" object and the "found" object.

From this understanding of the origin and the nature of the potential space, one can easily understand that individuals differ from one another according to the way this early phase of psychic development has been experienced by each of them. We are not all equal in our present capacity to tolerate both our loneliness and our dependence, to contain ambiguity and paradoxes (and not try to solve or reduce them, as Winnicott insisted), to play with illusion whilst keeping a solid relationship with reality, a reality to which we should not be too much adapted in order to keep a healthy partial abnormality (Mac Dougall, 1978), to be able to express our emotions whatever they look like and be empathic.

Potential space and the new economic order

The danger

The present issue with such qualities, with creativity and potential space, is that the dominant feature of the economic and political order, at least within industrial societies, seems to run contrary to their development. Several critical thinkers are very clear about it. Maybe the most precise among them is the philosopher Axel Honneth, the Director of the Institute for Social Research, in Frankfurt, where he succeeded Jurgen Habermas. In his last book, Honneth (2005) shows how, for over twenty years, the neo liberal economic reforms have given birth to a sort of new individual whose relationship to himself would be deprived of reflexivity and of the capacity to have internal conflicts or internal dialogues. According to him, the neo liberal economy created what he calls "self reification" phenomena. These phenomena come from the economic pressure exerted on the individuals to produce themselves, to present themselves in a strategic way (like in recruitment interviews). This is what he calls the tendency toward "self objectivation", the tendency to consider oneself as somebody whose experience and personal thoughts can be *produced*. Such a tendency would be parallel and linked to a crisis within the psychoanalytic culture both in Germany and the U.S.A. and its replacement by a type of "biological" culture. Similarly, such phenomena have been pointed out in France where the norm of well being imposed by the media (Vigarello, 1999), the "managementisation" of the society (De Gaulejac, 2005), the increase of control systems, procedures type of management (Diet, 2005), speed in transactions leading to the "cult of emergency" (Aubert, 2003) in private and public organisations, have restricted the self-reflective capacity and psychic space. More widely and throughout the ages, top management (not to be confused with "the" organization) spends a lot of energy and money to make its employees identify with it, think about it, even dream about it, be good servants, idealize it and invest all their positive libido in it (Enriquez, 1972).

The symbolization function and the psychic dialectic process also seem to be especially threatened within today's organizations through a series of discourses and practices by leaders and top managers among which:

- Ideal presentations of the firm through beautiful external communication contrary in many ways to the inner experience of it by the employees, which creates an intrapsychic unadmittable conflict between pride and revolt.
- Creation of strong organizational cultures which requires normalized behaviours comparable to those of the sectarian groups' adepts (Amado, 1988).
- Use of pretexts, scapegoats or lures in order to prevent people from arguing: the globalization of the economy, and the omnipotence of the client are two dominant discourses daily used to quickly close discussions.
- Decrease of honest face to face confrontations, developments of one way evaluations.
- Use of "cool killers"[5] (Enriquez, 1997) to reduce costs and fire employees.
- Impossibility of mourning psychic and social spaces when mergers and acquisitions are undertaken (Brunning, 2003).

The fashion of emotional intelligence, boosted by many authors (Salovey & Mayer, 1990; Goleman, Boyatzis & Mc Kee, 2002; among many of them), seems to be mainly a new and naïve human technology whose first aim is to control and expel "negative" emotions. Employees get accustomed to keeping inside themselves feelings of shame, incompetence and loneliness, to attacking their own psychosoma integration (so crucial for Winnicott) to such an extent that they may commit suicide in the workplace: between one and three per day in France last year, according to research data...

In many ways, one could say that organizations hate potential spaces as they themselves tend to reject ambiguity, ambivalence, doubts, paradoxes, weaknesses, rêverie, unconscious meanings, and are afraid of the chaotic results of the free expression of fantasies and emotions, except when the latter can be instruments of their own power.

The limits of psychic control

Does this mean that organisations and societies are always able to control potential space, use it or destroy it? Hopefully not and for, at least, two reasons: first of all, under certain conditions, potential space of the first moments of life can be recaptured later on in adulthood through playing and action, as Ogden suggests (op. cit.) or, as I believe, with a support system and effective threeness. At the individual level, we may think of a person who decides to escape from a sectarian group, to take an extreme example. This is not an easy task but it can happen when the dialectics of the potential space have been re-established, which involves a threeness likely to draw the individual out of his alienated dependency. Second, at a collective level, something of the potential space can be recaptured through transitional spaces, i.e. spaces allowing for a transitional function. As Kaës (1979) puts it, "the transitional function is the restoration of the capacity to articulate symbols of union within a paradoxical playing space, beyond the constraining experience of separation-division or union-fusion". In order for interpretative or creative playing to take place, three elements are requested: the setting, the containing function and the transitional functions.

According to Winnicott, individual psychotherapy is typically a potential space between the therapist and the patient, even if its effects don't always demonstrate its transitional role.[6] As Susan Long (1992) summarises it, "this space neither belongs to the patient, nor to the therapist, but emerges between them. This space is not the internal world of the patient, i.e. his or her fantasies, wishes or dreams, nor is it the external world of shared and structural reality. It is a third space which overlaps the others. It is that place where play and illusion are possible".

Many psychoanalysts have developed this idea and I won't elaborate on it here. I shall focus on wider social potential spaces, most of them being constructed. But, surprisingly or not, life itself offers all sorts of potential spaces, spontaneous ones, which we may recognize, and sometimes "use".

Spontaneous potential spaces

I call spontaneous potential spaces those spaces which fulfil a transitional function without a planned purpose (Amado & Amato, 2001).

1. Here is a societal example which deals with **football and politics**. Iran, whose football team had not qualified for the World Cup since 1978, won its qualification for the 1998 World Cup after her victory in Australia in the fall of 1997. "Hysterical" reactions of happiness took place in the streets of Tehran, especially from thousands of young women who gathered in front of the Azadi Stadium, some of them taking off their veils. After short negotiations and under the control of the police, they were allowed for the first time to come into the stadium to celebrate the event. A first and deep breach had been made in the power of the conservative system, a system that Mohammed Khatami, the moderate recent President of Iran wanted to change. As Harold Bridger would say, the Iran victory and the invasion of the stadium by the women was the "right accident". Even more powerful than predicted if we remember that, for the World Cup itself, Iran was drawn to play against United States, considered to be "the" enemy by conservatives, especially since the hostage crisis of April 1980. Khatami from one side, who had been elected by a majority of women and young people, and Madeleine Albright, on the American side, who wanted to renew normal relationships, started deep diplomatic exchanges. President Clinton himself videotaped a message to the Iranian people that was showed

on T.V. during the half time of the game (Fathers Day in America) in which he hoped the match "can be another step toward ending the estrangement" between their nations. The International Federation of Football gave also (voluntarily or not) some help in making June 21 st the fair-play day of the World Cup, precisely the day of the Iran-US encounter. Observers of the match indeed noticed several symbolic gestures: exchanges of gifts and flowers before the game and the longest hand-shaking of the World Cup between the two captains of the teams. Even, instead of keeping apart, as is customary, the two teams mixed for the photograph and stood arm in arm. I have described in detail elsewhere (Amado & Amato, op. cit.) what happened afterwards. This is just an illustration to exemplify the role of unpredictable events which open potential spaces for change and creation, using a transitional object both found and created (here the football game) as a "cover" for dealing with underlying difficult issues. One could say that a spontaneous potential space occurred which was afterwards used in a more programmatic and instrumental way.

2. Another example can help illustrate spontaneous potential processes. It happened in a **nuclear plant**. Two technicians in charge of the maintenance were discovered by the foreman as they were playing scrabble "instead of" doing their job. A major aspect of this job consisted in paying attention to any abnormal noise which could signal a possible failure in the technical system. In fact, the discussion with the technicians demonstrated that, in order to defend themselves against the passive and boring aspect of their task, they had chosen to play a game which proved in reality to be the safer device to fulfil their job: indeed, the mental concentration required to play scrabble may be the best means to hear any abnormal noise. Here the transgression of the prescribed rules of the work opened the space for finding and inventing both the playful and adaptive mode to cope with reality. Because top management is generally focused on macro-management, it has no understanding of this. Henry Mintzberg (2005) insists: "Everyone is against micromanagement but I think macro-management is far worse: it means you are working at the big picture but you don't know the details. CEO who adopt this approach are incapable of coming up with interesting strategies or fresh approaches because they don't know what's going on in the business at the ground level".

As ergonomists and work clinical psychologists have shown, there is always a gap between the prescribed and the real. In a provocative mode, one could say that if all employees would strictly follow the rules prescribed by the management, no organisation could ever function. In fact, the effective functioning of organisations is linked to the capacity of their employees to invent the best ways to cope with management prescriptions. This is where potential space is so important. But it can be experienced as the enemy by centralized and authoritarian hierarchies because potential space is also the secret garden of the employees within their working activities.

Should an advanced type of management try to capture such secret gardens? Surely not, as "understanding" does not mean necessary "using". Such an attitude would be on the side of controlling, not on the side of creating.

Designed potential spaces

Of course, training sessions can be considered as transitional spaces in many ways. Larry Hirschhorn and Tom Gilmore (1993) have specified it. According to them, training is a transitional space, "one that lies between learning and action and provides the "appreciative" insights and "here and now" experiences that can help people redesign their work world upon their return. Like transitional objects, the training space lies between the reality of the work world and the enacted reality of the training encounter itself, in which commingled thoughts and feelings can emerge safely in a setting where the stakes, though limited, are palpable" (p. 139). And they add very rightly that training must protect the participants from the "operative norms of the ongoing business" (op. cit. p. 141).

In the same spirit, we shall focus on the work of clinically oriented action-researchers who have recreated collective potential spaces, starting from the above diagnosis about the unavoidable gap between "prescription" and "realization".

1. *Two clinical approaches to work and activity*, sociopsychoanalysis and self-crossed confrontation, may exemplify designed potential spaces. Both of these methodologies have in common

- to aim at empowering workers, which means increasing their power not on others but on their own acts
- to be based on homogeneous groups of workers (without any hierarchy)
- to use analytical settings exclusively focused on work.

The *sociopsychoanalytic approach* starts from the premise that one part of our personality—the "psychosocial" part—can only be understood and developed through our acts and the increase of power upon these acts, whereas the "psychofamily" part of our personality (the part which is the product of early childhood experiences) is better explored through psychoanalysis. It is this psychosocial aspect of our personality that organisations may not like very much. They would even tend to have their employees regress towards the psychofamily part of themselves, i.e. psychological interpretations of organisational and social issues.

Gérard Mendel, who published the French version of Winnicott's work in the early 70's, has identified the "will to create as a force which comes from the deepest part of oneself, from the period before the unconscious and consciousness and which intervenes within and upon reality to modify it. The object of the world upon which the subject acts in his own act becomes, in this situation, the very early successor of the transitional object. It is both oneself and not oneself, both found and created" (Mendel, 1999, p. 126).

In order to develop the psychosocial aspect of the personality, Mendel proposes homogeneous groups built according to the technical division of labour whose objective is to exchange only about their "act" of work and to communicate questions and proposals to other homogeneous groups working in parallel. The total organisation is involved with an obligation from each group to respond. Communications are only by writing. This setting is considered as a third channel within the organisation (looking like the third area of cultural experience?), a channel which is parallel to the managerial (or hierarchical) channel and the union channel. The peer group acts as a containing space where responsible questions and proposals can be elaborated and answers from the other groups worked through in a safe environment.

An intervention using this approach has been undertaken for more than twenty years now in a bus company in the centre of France and hundreds of modifications proposed and implemented about the day to day work through discussions across all levels of the organization.

Mendel's transitional thinking applied to work is, in many ways, close to Yves Clot's *self-crossed confrontation method* (2001). This is a sort of action-research method aimed at developing the workers to observe their own activity so that they can discover not only what they are really doing but also what they are not doing, what they are preventing to do, and what they could be doing. This method is based upon a subtle use of video recording of an activity within a peer group of professionals. The outside researcher films a series of activity sequences of each member of the group; then he films the worker's own comment when he/she watches the images of his/her own activity (simple self-confrontation). The self crossed confrontation happens afterwards when the researcher gathers the members of the group by pairs in order to film the comments that one of the two workers gives to his colleague when confronted to the recording of his colleague's work. Such a setting opens the way to what Yves Clot calls "professional disputes" about the style of action of each of them. Through the reflective activity of the peer group about its own work, this object (which is a psychic object) is recreated in a new context and thus appears differently. This type of methodology has been used with very interesting results in a hospital in Burundi (Lhuilier, 2005) in order to identify the obstacles and critical conditions for the development of preventive practices, especially in front of the HIV AIDS epidemy.

Both of the approaches above described can be answers to the diagnosis made at the very end of the 20th century by Peter Drucker (1999): "Amazingly few people know how they get things done. Indeed, most of us do not even know that different people work and perform differently".

2. *Increasing autonomy and creativity within a football team*. Coming back to the football game, I would like to present now a constructed transitional design likely to increase autonomy and creativity within a team.

The command from the coach of a football team was the following: our next match is so important that I would like the players to feel more responsible when they are playing, not only to depend on my orders but also being able to eventually modify slightly their organization if they discover that any prediction about the opponent team's strategy is not correct. Group discussions, he added, are not effective because football players are accustomed to wait for my analysis and decisions. After some discussion with him, I proposed the setting below. We would select through a video a match that had already taken place between their future opposing team (B) and a team (C) which was very like their own one (A). They would watch the game between teams B and C in their two periods. For the first half of the game, they would be divided "horizontally" between back line, middle line and front line and watch the same first half time in three different rooms.

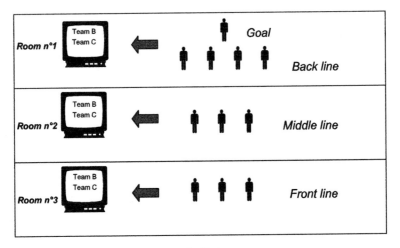

First half time

During these first 45 minutes and after (30 minutes), they were asked to observe how players of team B were playing, their skills, handicaps, tactics, what kind of tactics team C had been inventing and what they could suggest by themselves in order to win their future game against team B. After their observations and discussions within each room, they gathered in a plenary meeting to report their analysis and possible proposals. The coach was anxious about his role (what about my authority?) but I, as a consultant, reassured him, explaining that listening to them didn't mean necessarily arguing with them. Because illusion, omnipotence, fantasies are possible, thanks to the design and his knowledge of the capacities and psychology of each player, he would be able to contain and evaluate their proposals in a more effective and realistic way.

The idea was the following: the players would interact more easily with their colleagues from the same "line" without the presence of the coach. Playing with illusions, new ways of acting would be expressed more freely. Simultaneously, solidarity would be increased. The coach himself would discover unexpected proposals or analysis. During the second half of the same game, the whole team would stay together in the same format (45 + 30 minutes) without the intervention of the coach. The team would develop solidarity and test out some of the ideas exposed during the first plenary meeting. The final decision about the organisation of the team A and its strategy would be proposed by the coach the day after so that he did not feel pressured and had time to reflect.

The fact that the team won its next game was not as important a result as the spirit which thus was created and led to increase both the responsibility of the players in the future confrontations and the pleasure of the coach to share his views with them in a more cooperative mode.

3. *Playing with metaphors in an IT board.* The next example is drawn from one of my interventions in an IT firm and illustrates the use of playing which is so important in potential space. The CEO asked me to help his team which was not cohesive enough, had interpersonal conflicts and was not really capable of defining a clear vision of its objectives. He was a highly educated man, a direct product of the French elite system with a diploma from Ecole Polytechnique[7] and had just come back from the United States where he was impressed by the group dynamics method inspired by Gestalt therapy: every member of the group alternatively sits in the middle of the group and the others around him tell him what they think of him. He proposed that we do the same with his team. I politely refused, explaining that I didn't like the games of the truth and that the inequality of power would make this game less risky for him than for his colleagues. He was

disappointed and asked about my proposal. After some reflection and several interviews with his colleagues, I proposed to try and explore the image of his organisation within his team through a childish game known as "If it were". I suggested that they decide individually how they would see their organisation: if it were a flower, a movie, a dish, a car, what would it look like? By his astonishment, I realized that, if I had not been a Professor of Management in a respected business school, I would probably have been fired with contempt. Fortunately, the perceived paradox (a childish game proposed by a Doctor in Psychology belonging to a famous business school) was in my favour and we started playing with the metaphors. After discussions around the images chosen by each of them, which were frequently similar in their meaning, they reached a group consensus: the flower was a rose with too many thorns, the movie was "Let's catch the young British girls",[8] the dish was the rijstafel, a Thai speciality composed of separated small vegetables dishes, and the car a splendid American one without any motor in it. In spite of the compulsive desire of the CEO to come quickly to rational, simple meaning, down to earth reality, we went on discussing metaphorically for several hours. It was not very difficult to understand the underlying meanings of the choices made: the external image of the firm was masking both internal tensions, the lack of a clear strategy and the scarceness of resources; the desire to conquer part of the British market was somehow omnipotent and illusory, and the absence of understanding and communication between the departments of the firm a real handicap. To give short examples of the nature of the ongoing metaphoric discussion, they rejected the replacement of rijstafel by simple porridge or a tasty orange marmalade but preferred a North African couscous or a Spanish paella where differentiation and integration could take place at the same time. And about the car, they preferred a Honda, not only because it was "civic" (the chosen brand) but because the internal solidity of the firm was considered as the priority.

Communication is through playing, Winnicott insists, as if direct communication maybe dangerous. In the case of this IT firm, undoubtedly it opened the space for a more relaxed way of handling difficult issues and the pleasure taken in the game helped reconcile fantasy and reality, the unconscious, the preconscious and the conscious and decrease the repression of all sorts of negative feelings and thoughts. Of course, the containing function and the threeness play a part in this kind of intervention and the risks of failure must not be underestimated.

Among the various examples of the social use of transitional objects, one may read Lisl Klein's story (2001) about a fictitious patient called the poor old Henry, and an imaginary day in a ward. This was an attempt to integrate work in a London hospital. Rafael Ramirez (2005), as well, using scenarios of the future, explains how he implemented this process in Shell Company. This is a method where the work between illusion and reality helps find and create organisational strategies.

A last word about playing. Harold Bridger, who was in command of 24 military units around the Orkneys islands during the second world war, discovered that his soldiers didn't read the written orders he sent them everyday, which was of course very dangerous. As he had a cartoonist in the regiment, he asked him to draw cartoons, without words, not to illustrate orders but to illustrate disorders. These cartoons about disorders were so funny that everyone watched them carefully. But the key aspect of the setting was that, in order to make sense of the cartoons, you needed to read the orders written besides. Even if Harold Bridger had not read Winnicott at that time, he intuitively knew something about transitional objects and their possible use in the day to day life. Of course, one could say that such an invention had a narrow and controlling objective: obedience, contrary to the open ended objective of potential spaces. Nevertheless, why avoiding such settings when they aim at protecting individuals against themselves?

4. In order to complete this series of examples about designed potential spaces, I would like to mention those which deal with *cultural and political problem solving attempts*. I wish to pay a tribute to the Israeli psychologist Dan Bar-On, for his repeated efforts to create potential spaces between young Germans and young Israelis (1989) and with the children and members of the family of Nazis executioners (2005) to facilitate symbolization and a working through of the holocaust tragedy. It is interesting to notice that, according to him, if Dan Bar-On was able to conduct such

sensitive and deep interviews in a context so difficult for him, it was because he had been able to recognize within himself the capacity to do harm. In other words, we may say that his extraordinary empathy in his work was made possible only thanks to the recreation of a potential space.

And it is such a space which seems to be stimulated or reactivated in some situations of political negotiation. I have described elsewhere how the conflicts between the two main communities (the Caldoches and the Canaks) in New Caledonia in 1988 had been reduced as a result of the "Mission of the Dialogue" and the 10 hours meeting with the main stakeholders of the conflict (Amado & Amato, op. cit.). The implementation of a secret physical (and mental) intermediary area in Norway between Arafat and Rabin in 1993 was another attempt to find peace between Israelis and Palestinians.

And the same spirit and design took place between Mandela and President de Klerk in South Africa in order to abolish apartheid (Legum, 2001). In all these instances, and of course many others throughout history, one may find the same qualities of the design and the mood of the partners-enemies: a desire to find a good enough solution, containing space through both time and space boundaries, threeness with the help of facilitators (Amado, 2006) able to implement what Harold Bridger called "the capacity to stay lost" and "active quietness" (Gold & Klein, 2004), two qualities likely to be diffused by the negotiating partners and facilitating both the containing and the transitional functions.

Potential space and democracy

Still, reality necessitates carefulness: in spite of the immediate success of the above encounters, the first two resulted in murders: both partners (Djibaou the Canak, Rabin the Israeli) were killed a short time later by extremists; which suggests that the specifics of such encounters, their emotional and intellectual intensity is so strong that people outside the process are not likely to either understand or easily accept the outcome, and not just because these people may be fanatical. This is a difficult lesson to be drawn from this form of in residence or intimate closed experiences. They somehow belong to the realm of illusion and need to be carefully tested out in reality, i.e. in the outside world. In order to extend the learning produced within such transitional spaces, one does not only need courage, as Harold Bridger (1990) suggested when closing his transitional working conferences: it is necessary to invent the proper design for the wider context to allow people to work through the issues at stake.

On a more general level, and reflecting on democracy, I would like to propose the following thought: a proper and innovative democracy should be the product of a good enough balance between potential spaces and legal translations of their meanings. In other words, free and spontaneous social movements (and events) all contain messages which, if understood and worked through by the governing institutions, could be partly translated into laws, services, new devices for collective well being or generate appropriate forms of resistance. Thus, the (more or less) anarchistic and chaotic expression, stimulated by and taking place within potential spaces, could be contained by adequate analytic settings, possible legal conclusions and new practices implemented. Fortunately, this is what happens in "authentic" democratic nations. But aren't they a minority?

Individual potential space and collective transitional spaces have always been the worst enemies of authoritarian leaders and totalitarian regimes. This is clear. What is less clear in the world of today's organisations is the variety of the means, softer ones, used to reduce potential spaces in the name of the "necessary" cohesiveness, expected transparency and adaptation to so-called reality. Therefore, it may well be a good time to focus on the best ways to resist new forms of economic and behavioural normalization if we want to keep alive the core of human beings and healthily conflictualized organisations. My personal hope is that these new forms of resistance be inspired by a transitional spirit, i.e. a spirit which encourages the open search for meanings together with collective ethical creation.

Notes

1. Agency: translation of the French word « instance » which refers for example to the three instances id, ego, superego.

2. Free translation for « angoisse de morcellement ».
3. "A dialectic process is a process in which two opposing concepts each creates, informs, preserves and negates the other, each standing in a dynamic (ever changing) relationship with the other" (Ogden, op.cit., p. 130).
4. "It is a creative apperception more than anything else that makes the individual feel that life is worth living. Contrasted with this is a relationship to external reality which is one of compliance, the world and its details being recognized but only as something to be fitted in with or demanding adaptation" (Winnicott, 1971, p. 65).
5. This expression was invented by Enriquez to specify that category of managers who can harass, fire or destroy people without guilt.
6. Franck Summers (2005), a specialist of the "self" theory, even differentiates the purposes of the therapeutic settings by saying that, in "transference space", the purpose of the analytic relationship is "limited to understanding the existing patterns", whereas in potential space, such a relationship is used "to create new ways of being".
7. The highest status French school for engineers.
8. Free translation of « A nous les petites anglaises ».

References

Amado, G. (1988). "Cohésion organisationnelle et illusion collective", *Revue Française de Gestion*, juin-juillet-août, n°69, pp. 37–43.

Amado, G. & Ambrose, A. (Eds.) (2001). *The Transitional Approach to Change*, London & New York, Karnac Books.

Amado, G. (2006). "Harold Bridger, militant transitionnel", *Nouvelle Revue de Psychosociologie*, n°1, pp. 205–209.

Anzieu, D. (1984). *The group and the unconscious*, London, Routledge.

Aubert, N. (2003). *Le culte de l'urgence*, Paris, Flammarion.

Bar-On, D. (1989). "Holocaust perpetration and their children: a paradoxical morality", *Journal of Humanistic Psychology*, 29(4):424–443.

Bar-On, D. (2005). *L héritage du silence. Rencontre avec des enfants du IIIème Reich*, Paris, L'Harmattan.

Bridger, H. (1990). "Courses and working conferences as transitional learning institutions", in E. Trist & H. Murray (Eds.), *The Social Engagement of Social Sciences*, a Tavistock Anthology, Vol. 1, *The Socio-Psychological Perspective*, 221–245.

Brunning, H. (2003). "Organizational merger. A dance of constructive and destructive elements", *Organizations and People*, February, vol. 10, n°1, pp. 2–8.

Clot, Y., Faïta, D., Femandez, G., Scheller, L. (2001). "Entretiens en auto-confrontation croisée: une méthode en clinique de l'activité", *Education Permanente*, 146:17–25.

De Gaulejac, V. (2005). *La société malade de la gestion*, Paris, Le Seuil.

Diamond, M.A. (2007). "Organizational change and the analytic third: locating and attending to unconscious organizational dynamics", *Psychoanalysis, Culture and Society*, 12:142–164.

Diet, E. (2005). "Le thanatophore, travail de la mort et destructivité dans les institutions", in R. Kaës et coll., *Souffrance et psychopathologie des liens institutionnels*, Paris, Dunod, coll. « Inconscient et culture », pp. 121–189.

Drucker, P. (1999). "Managing oneself", *Harvard Business Review*, April-May, 65–74.

Enriquez, E. (1997). *Les jeux du pouvoir et du désir dans l'entreprise*, Paris, Desclée de Brouwer.

Gold, S. & Klein, L. (2004). "Harold Bridger. Conversations and recollections", *Organisational and Social Dynamics*, 4(1):1–25 & 4(2):173–190.

Goleman, D., Boyatzis, R. & Mc Kee, A. (2002). *Primal Leadership: Realizing the Power of Emotional Intelligence*, Harvard Business School Press.

Green, A. (1975). "The analyst, symbolization and absence in the analytic setting", *International Journal of Psychoanalysis*, 56:1–22.

Hirschhorn, L. & Gil more, T. (1993). "The psychodynamics of a cultural change: learning from a factory", in L. Hirschhorn & C.K. Barnett, *The psychodynamics of organizations*, Philadelphia, Temple University Press.

Honneth, A. (2005). *La réification*, Paris, Gallimard.

Jemstedt, A. (2000). "Potential Space. The Place of Encounter between Inner and Outer Reality", *International Forum Psychoanalysis*, 9:124–131.

Kaës, R. (1979). *Crise, rupture et dépassement*, Paris, Dunod.

Keats, J. (1952). *Letters*, London, Oxford University Press.

Klein, L. (2001). "Transitional intervention", in G. Amado & A. Ambrose, *The Transitional Approach to Change*, London & New York, Karnac Books.

Legum, C. (2001). "The role of facilitators as mediators in transitional process: a South-African case study", in G. Amado & A. Ambrose, *The Transitional Approach to Change*, London & New York, Karnac Books.

Lhuilier, D. (2005). "Action-research and transitional processes: risk prevention in a hospital in Burundi", in G. Amado & L. Vansina, *The transitional approach in action*, London & New York, Karnac Books, 175–194.

Long, S. (1992). "Working with Potential Space: Individuals, Groups and Organizations", *Australian Journal of Psychotherapy*, vol. 11, n°2.

Mc Dougall, J. (1980). *Plea for a measure of abnormality*, New York, International University Press.

Mendel, G. (1999). *Le vouloir de création*, Paris, Editions de l'Aube.

Mintzberg, R. (2005). *European Business Forum*, issue 23, Winter.

Nemiah, J.C. (1977). "Alexithymia: theoretical considerations", *Psychotherapy Psychosomatics*, 28:199–206.

Ogden, T. (1985). "On Potential Space", *The International Journal of Psychoanalysis*, 66:129–141.

Ramirez, R., Drevon, C. (2005). "The Tale and limits of methods in transitional change process", in G. Amado & L. Vansina (Eds.), *The transitional approach in action*, London & New York, Karnac Books.

Salovey, P. & Mayer, J. (1990). "Emotional intelligence", *Imagination, Cognition and Personality*, n°24, 9(3):185–211.

Summers, F. (2005). "The self and analytic technique", *Psychoanalytic Psychology*, Vol. 22, No. 3, 341–356.

Vigarello, G. (1999). *Histoire des pratiques de santé*, Paris, Le Seuil.

Winnicott, D.W. (1962). "Ego integration in child development", in Winnicott D.W., *The maturational processes and the facilitating environment*, London, Hogarth Press, 1975.

Winnicott, D.W. (1966). *The child and the family: first relationship*, London, Routledge, 2001.

Winnicott, D.W. (1971). *Playing and reality*, London, Tavistock/Routledge.

LIST OF ORIGINAL REFERENCES

The papers in this book have been (re-)published with permission of the authors (or their estates) and the previous publishers; they were first published as:

Amado, Gilles (2007): 'Potential Space': The Threatened Source of Individual and Collective Creativity. Unpublished manuscript.

Armstrong, David (2004): Psychic Retreats: The Organizational Relevance of a Psycho-Analytic Formulation. Free Associations, 11 A: 57–78; again in: David Armstrong (2005): Organization in the Mind: Psychoanalysis, Group Relations and Organizational Consultancy, edited by Robert French, London: Karnac, 69–89.

Bridger, Harold (1987): To Explore the Unconscious Dynamics of Transition as it Affects the Interdependence of Individual, Group and Organizational Aims in Paradigm Change. TIHR Doc. No. 2T 568. London: Tavistock Institute of Human Relations.

Diamond, Michael A. (1985): The Social Character of Bureaucracy: Anxiety and Ritualistic Defense. Political Psychology 6, 4, 663–679.

French Robert, Peter Simpson & Charles Harvey (2001): 'Negative Capability': The Key to Creative Leadership. Unpublished manuscript.

Gould, Laurence J. (1991): Using Psychoanalytic Frameworks for Organizational Analysis. In: Manfred F.R. Kets de Vries (Ed.), Organizations on the Couch. San Francisco: Jossey-Bass, 25–44.

Hirschhorn, Larry (1998): The Primary Risk. Human Relations 52, 5–23.

Isabel Menzies Lyth (1990): Institutional Consultancy as a Means of Bringing About Change in Individuals. Unpublished manuscript.

Krantz, James & Thomas N. Gilmore (1990): The Splitting of Leadership and Management as a Social Defense. Human Relations 43, 183–204.

Lawrence, W. Gordon (1998): Social Dreaming as a Tool of Consultancy and Action Research. In: Lawrence, W.G. (Ed.) Social Dreaming @ Work. London: Karnac Books, 123–140.

Long, Susan (2008): Sad, Mad or Bad: What New Approaches Should We Take to Study Organisational States-of-Mind? In: Arndt Ahlers-Niemann, Ullrich Beumer, Rose Redding Mersky & Burkard Sievers (Eds.), Organisationslandschaften. Sozioanalytische Gedanken und Interventionen zur normalen Verrücktheit in Organisationen/The normal madness in organizations: Socioanalytic thoughts and interventions. Bergisch-Gladbach: Verlag Andreas Kohlhage, 225–242.

Sievers, Burkard (2003): Against all Reason: Trusting in Trust. Organizational and Social Dynamics 3, 1, 19–39.

Stein, Howard F. (1997): Death Imagery and the Experience of Organizational Downsizing: Or, is Your Name on Schindler's List? Administration & Society 29, 2, 222–247.

INDEX